Clio's Foot Soldiers

Clio's Foot Soldiers

*Twentieth-Century U.S. Social Movements
and Collective Memory*

Lara Leigh Kelland

University of Massachusetts Press
Amherst and Boston

Copyright © 2018 by University of Massachusetts Press
All rights reserved
Printed in the United States of America

ISBN 978-1-62534-343-7 (paper); 342-0 (hardcover)

Designed by Sally Nichols
Set in Adobe Garamond Pro and Monotype Modern
Printed and bound by Maple Press, Inc.

Cover design by Rebecca Neimark, Twenty-Six Letters
Cover photo by Peter Pettus, *Participants, Some Carrying American Flags, Marching in the Civil Rights March from Selma to Montgomery, Alabama in 1965*.
Courtesy of Library of Congress.

Library of Congress Cataloging-in-Publication Data
Names: Kelland, Lara Leigh, author.
Title: Clio's foot soldiers : Twentieth-century U.S. social movements and collective memory / Lara Leigh Kelland.
Description: Amherst : University of Massachusetts Press, [2018] | Includes bibliographical references and index. |
Identifiers: LCCN 2017050252 (print) | LCCN 2018014779 (ebook) | ISBN 9781613765821 (e-book) | ISBN 9781613765838 (e-book) | ISBN 9781625343420 (hardcover) | ISBN 9781625343437 (pbk.)
Subjects: LCSH: Social movements—United States—History—20th century. | Collective memory—United States—History—20th century. | United States—Social conditions—20th century.
Classification: LCC HN57 (ebook) | LCC HN57 .K368 2018 (print) | DDC 303.48/4—dc23
LC record available at https://lccn.loc.gov/2017050252

British Library Cataloguing-in-Publication Data
A catalog record for this book is available from the British Library.

*For Jenrose and Jon, both of whom are
the very center of my chosen family*

Contents

Preface
IX

Acknowledgments
XI

INTRODUCTION
1

CHAPTER 1
In a Long Line of Protest
The Civil Rights Movement and a New Collective Memory
11

CHAPTER 2
Knowledge of Self
Liberation and Education through Black Separatist Collective Memory
39

CHAPTER 3
A History of One's Own
Feminist Collective Memory in the Second-Wave Women's Movement
71

CHAPTER 4
Scripted to Win
Collective Memory in the Gay Liberation Movement
101

CHAPTER 5
For the Sake of Cultural Survival
Red Power and Collective Memory
129

CONCLUSION
From Foot Soldiers to Citizen Historians
157

Notes
175

Index
199

Preface

Finding Clio's Foot Soldiers

I came to this project because my field of public history first told me an origin tale that centered on academics, not laypeople. This book offers an alternative narrative, demonstrating that grassroots movement activists shifted the terms of cultural and historical authority. Such a story matters because it is everyday acts, taken en masse, that change cultural forms and practices. It is comprised of the individuals and groups who don't have much visible power that make change in our world. And it matters because culture is political. History is a tool that informs who we are, where we came from, and where we might head.

This book traces activists' efforts during the 1960s, 1970s, and 1980s to use history for cultural and political aims. Many recognized the power of the past in forming new political identities, and deployed historical narratives toward several related goals. First, movement historians couched their contemporary activism in a long legacy of resistance and survival. Second, they understood the mobilizing power of the past, and developed narratives that served explicit movement goals. Third, they engaged the professional realm of history, training themselves as researchers; creating new historical knowledge; preserving the past through archives, interpretive projects, and the intergenerational transmission of heritage; and finding new means of transmitting historical education when liberal mainstream institutions failed them.

Clio's Foot Soldiers recognizes these efforts as fundamental to the genealogy of public history, a set of practices that has become an intellectual, creative, and professional meeting space for academics who are interested in the applied uses of the past and those employed in the cultural sectors of museums, historic preservation, heritage tourism, and the like. The field has traditionally narrated its origins as emerging in the 1970s from within the ivory tower. This book reframes that history, tracing how social movement activists played key roles in the cultural shift of identity-based groups claiming authority over their own pasts. Clio, the Greek muse of history, is often depicted as a young woman whispering in human ears, inspiring them toward curiosity about the past. As the authoritative voice of history shifted away from the communal sphere and toward academic scholarship in the nineteenth century, the figure of Clio became affiliated with academic organizations and professional history-making. In contrast, *Clio's Foot Soldiers* traces a more populist claiming of historical authority that took place in the latter half of the twentieth century. Inspired by stories of resistance and empowerment, social movement activists served as the transmitters of collective memory, effectively inspiring other social movement participants to look to the past for inspiration, contextualization, and identity-based pride.

As a result, historical authority looks very different in our contemporary moment than it did in the middle of the twentieth century. Instead of tweed-clad white men serving as the authoritative voice of the past, we now generally understand that traditionally marginalized voices must be heard as part of the historical record. The very question *Who can speak for whom?* in regard to the past is engaged, in part, because of the efforts of the activists contained in this book. By the late 1980s, museums and curriculum developers came under fire for the lack of and/or poor quality of representations of women, people of color, and sexual minorities in what became known as the culture wars. This moment has profoundly impacted a wide array of cultural and educational professions, and as such, must be accounted for in the lineage of historical authority—and it is this task that this book seeks to engage.

Acknowledgments

It is both humbling and a bit alarming to think about the collective energy that has fueled this project since 2006, and along the way it has sprawled and roamed and been reined in by countless folk. Still, I shall try to inventory the major players here as an entirely insufficient expression of gratitude.

This book has been improved by the hands of so many brilliant people. My colleagues Tracy K'Meyer and Cate Fosl both read the manuscript in its entirety and encouraged me along the way. I have been profoundly blessed to work with series editor Marla Miller at the University of Massachusetts Press, and her generous comments and years of encouragement are absolutely central to any success it enjoys. Likewise, Matt Becker has been a wonderful executive editor, making the ins and outs of publication less mysterious and entirely manageable. Comments from Reader A and Reader B also helped immeasurably by correcting factual errors and guiding the shape of my argument.

Funding for my research came from multiple sources at the University of Illinois at Chicago and the History Department at the University of Louisville, as well as a teaching release and a year of camaraderie with the Commonwealth Center for the Humanities Faculty Fellowship Program. I am also profoundly grateful for research assistance at the following archives and departments of special collections: Avery Research Center, Center for Southwest Research at University of New Mexico, Chicago History Museum, Cline Library at Northern Arizona University, Denver Museum of Nature and Science, GLBT Historical Society, Gerber/Hart Library, Highlander Research and Education Center, Lesbian Herstory Archives, New York Public Library, Regenstein Library at University of Chicago, Schlesinger Library at Harvard University, Schomburg Center for Research in Black Culture, Sophia Smith Collection at Smith College, Stanford University Library, Tennessee State Library, Wisconsin Historical Society.

So many people contributed to my long journey through this project. Benjamin Filene got me started on my journey in 1999 by introducing me to the field of public history and has continued to guide me in all related matters since then. He rightfully has earned "The Most Enduring Mentor" award. In the earliest stages, Robert Johnston guided me through the many ups and downs of nine years at the University of Illinois at Chicago (UIC). John D'Emilio modeled the perfect balance of serious scholar and engaged community activist. Norma Moruzzi was an exemplar of intellectual generosity during my doctoral training, and her gift of feminist mentorship will remain with me throughout my career. Bill Ayers inspired me as a model educator and tireless advocate for social justice, and helped me think more expansively about radical education. And this project simply would not have been realized without the informal yet ceaseless encouragement, support, and love of Laura Hostetler. She picked me up and dusted me off after innumerable grad school crises, ensured funding for my final years at UIC, commented on the entire draft and endless job letters and grant applications, and generally was the academic mother I needed. I still am humbled by the generosity of her mentorship and model my own graduate student support on hers, inclusive of pots of tea and recognizing my students as whole human beings.

The History PhD program at the University of Illinois at Chicago blessed me with many delightful, smart, and loving colleagues. From the early days of coursework, I had the best cohort imaginable: Libby Hearne, Adrienne Phelps Coco, Wayne Ratzloff, Amy Sullivan, and Greg Wilson. Other dear friends in the program also provided me with tremendous support, ready commiseration, and intellectual feedback, including Katie Batza, Mark Bullock, Theresa Christianson, Elizabeth Collins, Juanita Del Toro, and Emily LaBarbera Twarog. And I owe a very special thanks to my two partners in crime, conferences, archives, and so much more: Catherine Jacquet and Anne Parsons. You two especially made the experience enjoyable.

Acknowledgments

I owe an enormous debt of gratitude to the subjects of this book: the foot soldiers invoked by the title, namely the cultural warriors of the social justice movements of the 1960s and 1970s. Not only did they provide a fascinating narrative to research and recount, but they also shifted the terrain of American collective memory, making the past relevant for people of color as well as gender and sexual minorities. My field of public history stands on their shoulders and functions as a social justice practice in part because of their legacy.

Additionally, many souls have helped me maintain my sanity over the years of this project. Perhaps most significantly, five great danes snuggled with me throughout this journey, providing comfort and stress reduction: Lily, Gertie, Betsey, Zelda, and Matilda. To my mother, Luretta, who learned not to ask how that degree/dissertation/book was coming along. Dear friends have provided me with lodging for research visits and love to fuel me along the way: Alexia Bauer, Jessica Finley, Cindy Glass, Adam Grossi, Dara Ignacio, Michael and Amy Washburn, and Matthew Wogen. And the fine community at Tejas Yoga kept me sane during my graduate school years.

Lastly, I dedicate this book to two very important people: my former partner Jon Kelland and my partner Jenrose Fitzgerald. Although our relationship went through many different stages in the years it has taken to get here, Jon tirelessly cheered me on through two graduate degrees, countless public history projects, and so very many periods of doubt and struggle. For hundreds of takeout food containers, proofreading at so many stages, and always believing in me, thank you, Jon, and please always be my best friend. And although I have only begun building a life with Jenrose over the past couple of years, her social justice values have recommitted me to the importance of this story, and her presence in my life has alternately grounded and fueled me to stay the course and finish the book. As a recovering academic, she has contributed equal parts editorial skill, conceptual development, and insistence on living a life beyond the ivory walls. I thank you and love you so, Jenrose.

Clio's Foot Soldiers

Introduction

> Identities and memories are not things we think *about*, but things we think *with*. As such, they have no existence beyond our politics, our social relations, and our histories.
> —John R. Gillis, *Commemorations. The Politics of National Identity*

In the early 1970s, painting student Jocelyn Cohen, who was enrolled in a feminist arts program at California State University at Fresno, went looking for a postcard to send her girlfriend, who was, at the time, living outside of Cohen's local calling area. The couple had taken to sending each other notes to stay close while they were unable to make the hour commute that it took to spend time together. Frustrated by a lack of available postcards depicting women's experiences, Cohen and her partner, Nancy Poore, embarked on a twenty-year endeavor to research, print, and distribute historical images and stories of women's experiences to feminists across the country through their nonprofit endeavor, the Helaine Victoria Press.[1] From a single desire for historical recognition and representation, a rich thread of second-wave feminist collective memory emerged.

Like Cohen and Poore, we all draw upon a wide variety of sources to make narratives about the past. Each day, throughout the day, we understand our present experiences in the world based on our knowledge of past events. The social movements of the 1960s, 1970s, and 1980s sparked powerful transformations in the consciousness of subjugated peoples. African Americans, women, gays and lesbians, Native Americans, Chicanos, and other marginalized groups transformed their communities into much more forceful political presences, but along the way their efforts also inspired a desire for and a production of identity-based history. Movement participants found that their new consciousness led not only to the call for social and political equality, but also to a longing for narratives of collective struggles and successes, both present and past.

This book contextualizes the efforts of activists within the Civil Rights, Black Freedom, Women's Liberation, Gay and Lesbian Liberation, and Red Power movements who functioned as community historians. In each case, they developed new and honed existing memory practices to nurture collective narratives of the past that served their contemporary political goals. Usually working with minimal resources, often with little or no formal training in history or education, they researched, archived, authored, and presented their community histories in a variety of formats. Although not all of these agents viewed their work as formal history-making, all sought to craft a useable past that couched their newfound political identities in a legacy of shared resistance with those who came before them. Additionally, they performed historical interpretation in public forms before any professional field focused on such existed, serving as part of what one historian has called the "genealogy of public history."[2] Indeed, they were proto-public historians.

While activist historians served their communities and movements first and foremost, they also engaged mainstream liberal institutions like archives, universities, and public schools in a variety of ways. First, they critiqued the failure of mainstream organizations to address their communities' needs. Second, they pressured liberal institutions to be more inclusive as they worked within community-based venues. Third, they used their positions as professionals working within libraries, archives, and universities to shift institutional policies and practices toward inclusion and multiculturalism. Lastly, they formed new community-controlled organizations that paralleled mainstream institutions.

Individuals came to memory work from a variety of backgrounds. Activists within the Civil Rights movement tended to be community organizers first and cultivators of collective memory second, as exemplified by the grassroots educational projects of Septima Clark, Esau Jenkins, and Myles Horton in the Civil Rights movement.[3] After these projects were established, organizations such as the Southern Christian Leadership Conference engaged academic historians like Martin Duberman and Staughton Lynd to contribute to the formal curriculum and texts.[4] Black Power leadership was responsible for initiating larger projects of historical education within the movement, usually as alternatives to mainstream grammar, secondary, and postsecondary institutions. Black Power activists who espoused highly varied political orientations such as Malcolm X,

Elijah Muhammad, Howard Fuller, Huey Newton, and Ericka Huggins all developed history curricula as part of their efforts to build Afrocentric institutions that paralleled mainstream educational structures.[5]

Women's Liberation activists also built historical projects that were generally less formal and institutionalized initiatives. Feminists like Jocelyn Cohen, Judy Chicago, and Laura X initiated projects engaging women's history themes that flourished into significant collective endeavors and attended to movement-wide education needs, although community history work was also taken up by feminist academic historians like Gerda Lerner. Likewise, many Gay Liberation activists had a connection to academic history, as people like John D'Emilio and Gregory Sprague worked simultaneously to bring LGBT studies into the academy as they also developed community resources. Still others like Joan Nestle, Deb Edel, and Jonathan Ned Katz worked entirely outside of academic institutions to promote popular historical consciousness within the community. Lastly, American Indian activists reclaimed historical and cultural authority away from the federal government through the development of sovereign educational institutions, the symbolic and physical reclamation of place, and the production of pan-tribal cultural traditions. Some Native activists working in the American Indian Movement and larger Red Power initiatives cultivated tribal colleges to repair the cultural damage wrought by a century of church- and government-controlled boarding schools, while others claimed entitlement to and authority over historically significant spaces and practices like tribal lands, spirituality, and dance traditions.[6]

Collective memory activists cultivated many different kinds of projects to promote historical consciousness within their movements. Through their work, popular historians established community-based organizations like archives, libraries, universities, primary and secondary schools, and adult education programs. Activists also produced materials such as school curricula, children's literature, scholarly and popular books, historical postcards, resource guides, microfilmed collections, and professional guides for grassroots archivists. Community historians also used visual and performative projects like art installations, multimedia slide shows, theater, and film to share their research. Some activists developed new archival practices as they sought to collect, preserve, and catalog historical materials, as part of their goal to promote research and democratize access to historical materials within their communities. Still others organized conferences and similar gatherings to foster conversations about these memorial practices.

As this study tracks the genealogical origins of public history within social movements, I focus my exploration on expressly public interpretations of the past. The field of public history attends to "the many and diverse ways in which history is put to work in the world."[7] Put into practice, public history is the professional umbrella term that has emerged to encapsulate museum work, historic preservation, oral history, archival work, material culture conservation, digital history, and many other deployments of the past in public venues. It differentiates itself from scholarly written history and tends to favor visual, aural, and other modes of engaging the past. The named field emerged in the 1970s during a period of overproduction of history PhDs. These young professionals married their academic training with public work, developing a professional code of ethics, best practices, and an overall professional culture of enthusiasm for the useable past. When I began graduate studies, the field explained its own history in this way, crediting the rise of social history with the focus on a populist interpretation of the past and the job crisis with the material conditions that produced this professional shift. At most, mid-century social movements were briefly invoked via a sentence or two, generally indicating that they had something to do with it as well. Finding this unsatisfying, I sought to establish the particulars, seeking examples in which marginalized groups demanded ownership over their own historical narratives and forms. What follows is the result of that inquiry.

To locate connections between the work of social movement activists and the forthcoming field of public history, I chose case studies that either had a performative or visual focus, or, when looking at more traditional educational environments, served to create a separatist or parallel institution that incorporated community control and claimed new forms of cultural ownership over their past. The case studies included here have several things in common. First, I have developed case studies from projects that left significant archival records. Second, I consider a breadth of topics to reflect the wide array of narratives articulated by activists. Third, this range of projects illuminates what I call *memory practices,* the forms and strategies employed by community historians. Tracking the different kinds of memory practices demonstrates the creativity and resourcefulness of activists in weaving identity-based history into the activities of their larger movements. I do only engage scantly with K-12 curriculum, movement publishing, and more traditional written history forms, as these sit outside the heart of public history, and a key point of my analysis is to demonstrate that social movement activists acted as proto-public historians. By looking comparatively at this work, we see how these movement-based efforts have connections to the professional fields of historic preservation, archival conservation and arrangement, museum education, exhibit development, and multimedia versions of public history. Last, I highlight projects that make an explicit connection between the retelling of past collective experiences and the construction of new political identities. Since there are many more community-based projects that remain unexamined, perhaps this work will inspire further analysis of the functions of collective memory in social movements.

While this book enriches the historical literature on community memory, grassroots organizing, and cultural activism undertaken by Civil Rights, Black Power, Women's Liberation, Gay Liberation, and Red Power movement activists, it primarily seeks to broaden the notion of what is legitimate historical authorship to include efforts made beyond the walls of the ivory tower. By tracing how activists authored historical narratives that both significantly impacted their communities and shifted cultural authority toward the communities themselves, these historians raised the question of *Who can speak for whom?* on community historical matters. As the scholarly practices of social and public history, with their populist and democratic impulses, began to shift historical intellectual production toward being more inclusive, community historians were also a democratizing force for historical representations in marginalized communities. So, to fully understand the progressive impulses in academic and public history circles in the second half of the twentieth century, we must look beyond the well-meaning historians within universities and museums and recognize how activists like those identified here also shifted the terrain of legitimate historical authorship.[8]

Historical narratives naturalize our social structures by providing a sense of belonging, and in this way, they function very effectively to support the nation-state and other existing social structures. Activists in social movements often considered themselves, and were in effect, stateless, having been systematically denied the advantages of full citizenship enjoyed by their straight white male counterparts. African Americans had lived for nearly four centuries in the North American colonies and the United States with little to no political representation, first through *de jure,* then *de facto* means. Women had been enfranchised for less than fifty years prior to the birth of second-wave feminism, and even at mid-century only a small minority enjoyed significant economic and social autonomy from male-dominated institutions and society. Gays and lesbians had only just begun to understand themselves as a legitimate part of the national community during the latter half of the twentieth century, and then only in small numbers and isolated geographies. They had also very recently witnessed a kind of civic death through the intensive policing of homosexuals in the postwar era and the ousting of gay and lesbian employees from the federal government through McCarthy-era congressional investigations. Native Americans had experienced a complicated relationship with the federal government since first colonial contact, and for much of the twentieth century had struggled to secure a beneficial relationship with the Bureau of Indian Affairs.

If, as some scholars have argued, shared symbolic structures like those that constitute mass media are tools that create an imagined community, then history is the binding agent in that community.[9] Although individuals within these communities varied significantly in their investments in mainstream society and American democracy, the early manifestations of these movements generally encompassed identities that were outside of the legitimate nation-state. Although only portions of these movements overtly engaged in the rhetoric of nation-building, their respective collective memory projects illustrate a desire for autonomy in response to the political and cultural exclusion that they experienced in mainstream American society. In many ways, the identity-based social movements of the mid- to late twentieth century were projects in cultural sovereignty and self-determination, and like any nation-building endeavor, they deeply embraced the power of historical narrative to legitimate and coalesce community. As the movements aged, most community history initiatives moved toward the mainstream, seeking to engage wider publics and to link their narratives into national history.

As politically and culturally marginalized communities, American women, people of color, and sexual minorities shared struggles, strategies, and rhetoric with anticolonial struggles around the world. The civilizing powers of Europe had colonized the past through the hegemon of scholarly history, a narrative that explained the Orient as backward and infantile and the Occident as noble and benevolent.[10] Historian Dipesh Chakrabarty points to the Western construct of academic history and its failure to understand non-Western (and by extension, Western marginalized) experience.[11] Chakrabarty's and other postcolonial historians' ideas are helpful in interpreting the practices of American social movement activists who created new historical knowledge as a cultural intervention against academic history, which they faulted as reproducing the social hierarchies against which they were fighting. These activists intuitively felt what postcolonial scholars demonstrated in scholarship—that the histories legitimated by the state and the academy wrote their efforts, their agency, and their impact out of the past. Activists usually found mainstream academic accounts failing to explain important historical experiences such as black resistance during slavery, the presence of same-sex-loving couples, the survival of Native communities and traditions, or women's participation in public life. As a result, they critiqued the research and interpretive methods of academic historians and rewrote their communities' historical narratives to include instances of reform, resistance, presence, and perseverance.

As another cultural intervention, activists worked against the silencing effects of what one historian has called *archival power*.[12] Movement historians created new methods for researching their pasts, at times relying on nontraditional sources, reading archival traces against the grain, and collecting documents that mainstream archives and historians had ignored or overlooked. Recognizing the discursive power of archival collections, community historians shifted archival practices to include materials that represented the experiences and lives of the marginalized and that also broadened the pool of possible sources of historical information. Although earlier marginalized groups had certainly engaged with their histories before this period, within the context of global anticolonial struggles, this new generation of activists wove historical discourse throughout the movements. Social movement leaders understood that the institutional ownership of historical narratives was another form of imperial power and subjugation, and that demanding cultural ownership of such was a critical act in their own liberation. As leaders of these movements borrowed—sometimes explicitly, sometimes indirectly—language and ideas from the global struggle for self-determination, they were certainly influenced by the call for direct democracy and its related demand for cultural ownership.

This book relies on the work of other scholars who have considered the significance of historical narratives, archiving, and community education in social movements. My analysis builds on their scholarship, demonstrating how mid-century social movements functioned like other forms of oppositional cultural movements.[13] Likewise, I am much indebted to the analytic power of *collective memory*, as it provides me with a framework for recognizing the social and discursive nature of shared remembrances. I take as a foundation other scholars' arguments that collective memory is both mediated by and productive of mass culture. Indeed, the activists discussed in this book clearly made similar assumptions about the transmission of their ideas, as well as the importance of inserting their pasts into popular discourse.[14]

The contours of collective memory are as much about the present as they are about the past, or, as one memory theorist has put it, "a set of ideas, images, feelings about the past . . . [to be found in] the resources they share."[15] Similarly, I use the concept of *memory practices* to describe the enactment of collective memory, namely research, archiving, and communication efforts put forth toward the production of oppositional histories.[16] I use this term to frame the activities that activists undertook to rewrite dominant historical narratives and to lay claim to a past that historicized their contemporary struggles and provided a foundation for new political identities. To do so meant refuting historiographical traditions that interpreted African Americans, women, queer folk, and indigenous communities as lazy, intellectually inferior, characterized by pathos, helpless, morally questionable, and plagued with myriad other negative characteristics. Activists conducted research in secondary and primary sources; collected and preserved historical materials; collaboratively produced interpretations; and crafted public educational forms ranging from traditional fine art to ephemera, from newspaper articles to formal movement school curriculum. These memory practices used what would later become embraced as public history methods of research, interpretation, and exhibition to author and share stories of the past celebrating strength, resilience, autonomy, innovation, resistance, and leadership.

Although this book compares movements that have much in common with one another, it also attends to their differences, in the recognition that the historical experiences of each community inform the way they contemporarily interpret their own history. To that end, this book is organized by the respective movements, tracing the developments of new memory practices and analyzing the historical narratives by each identity. Chapter one considers how African American Civil Rights leadership built collective memory within the movement, emphasizing narratives of resistance under slavery and achievement and leadership after the Civil War. I examine Highlander Folk School's Citizenship School Initiative, tracing how activists developed their curriculum into an organizational tool for the Southern Christian Leadership Conference and the Student Nonviolent Coordinating Committee's Freedom Summer efforts. Chapter two looks to the Nation of Islam for the development of a distinct collective past that blended the enslaved past with Islamic traditions and African symbols to produce a new hybrid narrative.

It also considers how Black Power leadership rhetorically used the past in speeches and liberation school curriculum in order to channel political anger and educate children about the injustices of the past.

An inquiry into Women's Liberation in chapter three considers how the women's movement used visual arts, informal educational projects, and curricular interventions to reframe women's history as one of resistance and accomplishments. By demonstrating centuries of leadership, accomplishment, and activism by women, activists crafted a new feminist identity based on historical precedence. Chapter four looks at Gay Liberation's claiming and construction of a queer past. Like the Women's Liberation movement, LGBT activists used community-based history to build collective memory through popular education efforts such as slide shows and the development of community-based organizations. Chapter five traces similar efforts in the Red Power movement, tracking the development of tribal colleges, the contested role of heritage in powwow culture, and the rhetorical use of Native American history in movement literature and initiatives as an act of resistance against the cultural genocide of the federal government, particularly the Bureau of Indian Affairs.

The conclusion considers the repercussions of these efforts during the culture wars of the 1980s and 1990s, when identity-based struggles entered mainstream institutions of cultural representation. The outcome of the activists' efforts to claim history in the 1960s and 1970s manifested in debates over historical authority and ownership over curriculum, education policy, and cultural representations in museums and other cultural texts. But perhaps just as significantly, these claims to historical authority provoked a conservative backlash *because* they had successfully changed the terms of historical and cultural authority by cultivating the notion that communities should speak for themselves in public narratives.

This book endeavors to tell a history of individuals who desired to change the world they inherited. They understood the power of the past to explain the present and to reimagine the future. They recognized that culture was a key front in their struggle for liberation, and they knew the power that identity held for building political community. They understood that mainstream institutions had not represented their struggles and victories in a favorable light, and they redefined the terms by which liberal institutions interacted with their stories, their artifacts, and their representations. And they provided a basis for the more democratic museum and public history practices that would emerge in the following decades.

Dr. Staughton Lynd training volunteer teachers to teach history to Freedom School students at the second SNCC orientation in Oxford, Ohio, June 1964. Herbert Randall, McCain Library and Archives, University of Southern Mississippi.

CHAPTER 1

In a Long Line of Protest

The Civil Rights Movement and a New Collective Memory

If a race has no history, if it has no worthwhile tradition, it becomes a negligible factor in the thought of the world, and it stands in danger of being exterminated.

—Carter Woodson

Within the Civil Rights movement, collective memory served as a new and important tool of community mobilization. Although black intellectuals had been authoring and preserving their history throughout the late nineteenth and early twentieth centuries, most such efforts primarily came from the elite who focused on narratives in support of the project of racial uplift and respectability politics.[1] Informal kinds of collective memory existed in community events like festivals and parades, yet a wide-sweeping commitment to the transformative potential of a more full black history emerged only within the struggle for racial equality in the 1950s and early 1960s.[2] During this time, community leaders established citizenship and freedom schools across the South to promote voter registration and participation, and as a base for demanding other kinds of equality through the rhetoric of citizenship.

The memory practices brought forth by Civil Rights activists were primarily movement education initiatives that also asserted the right to citizenship for blacks.[3] These projects advanced central goals of the movement, namely to empower all black citizens toward realizing cultural, political, and economic parity with whites. Most of these leaders also attended to questions of power within the movement, often actively promoting grassroots leadership and a widespread and multi-authored collective memory. These leaders drew on two main traditions in their collective memory narratives and work. First, they produced narratives that placed their contemporary struggle in the context of racial struggles of the past, making connections between their efforts in the 1950s and 1960s and the resistance of enslaved people, the work of abolitionism, and the struggles for rebuilding the American racial order during the Reconstruction era.[4] Second, they drew upon grassroots organizing and popular educational traditions from the labor movement, especially the use of music, to transmit collective memory that challenged mainstream American historical narratives. Both of these traditions manifested in curriculum content and design and approaches to school leadership in the citizenship and freedom schools, and would lay a foundation for popular education taken up later in the Black Power, Gay, and Women's Liberation movements.

The Legacy of Black Education

For those who sought to change racial relations in the United States, education had long been embraced as a fundamental tool toward that goal. Enslaved blacks, abolitionists, and slaveholders all understood the radicalizing and effective power of literacy, and as a result, reformers embraced education as a central tool in transforming racial politics during the Reconstruction era. Likewise, northern white philanthropists poured money into southern black educational institutions during and after Reconstruction, believing education to be the first step toward economic and social equality. Yet, even as they provided black students with much-needed educational opportunities, black institutions of higher education (which would later become known as historically black colleges and universities, or HBCUs) often ended up unintentionally reproducing systems of racial inequality by constructing a separate but equal system that offered black students a significantly inferior education.[5]

A leading figure in the early-twentieth-century struggle for racial freedom, W. E. B. Du Bois devoted much of his writing and activist efforts toward improving black education. Du Bois placed black education at the forefront of the struggle for racial justice, prioritizing the development of educational opportunities as "the very first step toward the settlement of the Negro problem."[6] Du Bois envisioned that the *Talented Tenth* of the black race would form a leadership core that would produce solutions to racism, poverty, and equality by virtue of their vision and intellect. The roles of authority and leadership were quite clear for Du Bois—they would flow from "the top downward . . . [as the] Talented Tenth rises and pulls all that are worth the saving up to their vantage ground."[7] These early black efforts to claim and articulate a proud and useable past certainly predated the Civil Rights movement of the 1950s and 1960s, yet many of the earlier efforts made toward preserving and researching black history embraced a similar social hierarchy as Du Bois's. In his vision, intellectuals would provide leadership, and such vision and direction could be fostered only through formal schooling and universities.

In the early twentieth century, black intellectuals began to expand the production and dissemination of black history. The 1910s were a particularly rich decade for such work, with Arthur Schomburg founding the Negro Society for Historical Research in 1911 and Carter Woodson establishing the Association for the Study of Negro Life and History in 1915. Shortly thereafter, in 1916, Woodson began publishing the *Journal of Negro History* as an outlet for scholarly research on the black past. Schomburg, born in Puerto Rico in 1874, immigrated to the United States in 1891. A passionate archivist, he avidly collected documents and art related to the international African diasporic experience. In 1926, the New York Public Library purchased Schomburg's extensive collection and named him the director of the Harlem library branch, where the collection was made available to the public.[8] Woodson was born to formerly enslaved parents in New Canton, Virginia, in 1875, and grew up poor, attending school sporadically during childhood. Woodson began his formal education at the age of twenty, finally earning a PhD from Harvard at the age of thirty-seven, only the second African American to ever do so. During the latter half of his career, Woodson turned away from scholarly and elite projects, choosing instead to work on a more popular promotion of the black past, founding Negro History Week in 1926, an annual event aimed at the cultivation of collective memory in black communities.[9]

Although intellectuals played a key role in the cultivation of black history in the late nineteenth and early twentieth century, widespread popular forms of collective memory flourished as well. First commemorating the end of the Atlantic slave trade, then emancipation at the end of the Civil War, black Americans celebrated their freedom widely through parades and rallies. Speeches given at freedom festivals throughout the nineteenth century, during both the antebellum and post-Emancipation eras, harkened to individuals and events that underscored Christian values and promoted respectability for black citizens. In addition to their efforts to create a proud public culture for black Americans, organizers explicitly linked the need for shared history to the process of identity-building. In these more popular efforts, forgetting the slave past became as important as remembering other aspects of collective historical experience.[10] By diminishing the significance of enslaved experience to black history, intellectuals articulated a past that was built on cultural achievement and individual laudable attributes rather than on more dishonorable experiences of subjugation and shame. While these isolated efforts contributed toward the early development of black collective memory and the work of Schomburg and Woodson provided an important base to all of the black history efforts that emerged later in the century, a well-developed and wide-reaching national black history narrative would emerge a few decades later, as part of the efforts of Civil Rights activists.

Citizenship Schools and the Highlander Folk School

Although founded by white southerners, the Highlander Folk School was perhaps the most significant institutional home for the early cultivation of black collective memory. Myles Horton and Don West founded the Highlander Folk School in the foothills of the Appalachian Mountains near Monteagle, Tennessee, in 1932, in order to address deep poverty and inequality in the Appalachian region through adult education. Inspired in part by the Danish Folk School movement, Horton and West aimed to empower and mobilize both black and white impoverished communities by providing free educational resources for residents. Beyond providing much-needed educational opportunities and cultural conservation efforts, Highlander worked closely with labor organizations and local people to build coalitions among coal miners, woodcutters, textile workers, and farmers in the area as part of a small but committed tradition of southern progressivism.[11] In 1937, the school allied with the Congress of Industrial Organizations, which inspired other labor organizations to engage the school's workshops for union leadership training. During the 1940s, the school's racially integrated workshops began to attract negative attention, as state and federal agencies began to redbait Highlander leadership, charging them with running a "Communist training school."[12] After an overnight raid by the state of Tennessee in 1961 that closed Highlander and revoked its charter, the school reopened shortly after as the Highlander Research and Education Center, first in Knoxville, then in 1972 moving to New Market, Tennessee.

Throughout the school's history, Highlander staff cultivated grassroots leadership within their programs. In the early 1950s, the school initiated a three-year Community Leadership Training Project in Alabama and Tennessee, an initiative that an experienced school staffperson hoped would give community leaders "a better understanding of the nature of a democratic society and the individual's role as a citizen."[13] Built on the tenet that a vision for the future needed to come from within a community, Highlander experimented with various models for civic action and leadership training during the 1940s and 1950s. During this time, Highlander staff struggled to find an appropriately hands-off role in regard to local issues.[14] Through the development of the citizenship school model, Highlander would greatly improve on these issues, in part due to the pivotal role that adult educators and Civil Rights activists Esau Jenkins, Bernice Robinson, and Septima Clark played in the development of the program.

The Civil Rights era was a rich one for Highlander, as the citizenship schools proved to be the most successful programmatic manifestation of Highlander's values. Initially conceived as a project to increase voter registration by preparing adults for the literacy tests that kept southern blacks from being able to vote, citizenship schools became a springboard for other educational efforts. Although the staff had always desired that the school be a racially integrated space, it wasn't until 1942 that Highlander held its first mixed event, after which Highlander more fully committed to multiracial organizing. In 1953, staff shifted the school's direction away from poverty in general toward racial justice by focusing on school desegregation workshops. When the Supreme Court handed down the *Brown* vs. *Board of Education* decision in 1954, Highlander had already fostered conversations to prepare activists for the process.[15] Additionally, Highlander itself, with its populist and socialist ethos, was also invested in cultivating oppositional collective memory. The popularity of the workshops led to an unprecedented growth in the number of participants, and as a result, activists like Septima Clark and Esau Jenkins travelled to Highlander to take part in their training programs.

Septima Poinsette Clark was born in Charleston, South Carolina, in 1898. Trained as a teacher, she first worked as a teaching principal in 1916 at a small rural school on Johns Island. There she developed a deep connection to the community and nurtured a commitment to working for racial and economic justice. In 1947, Clark moved back to Charleston to teach in the public school system where she worked until 1956, when state law banned school employees from engaging in Civil Rights activism.[16] Firmly committed to the movement, Clark chose to leave her position and took up organizing work on a full-time basis. Clark had learned of the integrated workshops at the Highlander Folk School in 1952 when she went to a meeting on childhood education at the black YWCA in Charleston. In June of 1954, Clark wrote a letter to Myles Horton, requesting a scholarship to an upcoming "Workshop on Segregation," as she wanted to "organize a group from various clubs to use the training" offered by Highlander. Clark introduced herself in her application as a well-positioned community leader, noting that she held "offices in three interracial groups," a position from which she could marshal "their support to work out a program for the community."[17] Horton immediately granted her a full scholarship via telegram a mere three days after she posted the letter in Charleston. Clark went to Highlander on two occasions during the summer of 1954; at the first she met Rosa Parks, and at the latter she introduced Johns Island resident Esau Jenkins to Highlander so that he could participate in a workshop on the United Nations. At this second event, the idea for the first citizenship school circulated between black community leaders Clark and Jenkins and the white Highlander staff. Throughout the development of the schools, grassroots leadership was at the heart of the initiative and, indeed, a central part of its success.

From the beginning, the schools emerged from local efforts to obtain educational resources. Jenkins was born on Johns Island in 1910 and spent the majority of his life there, connecting with Clark first as her student, then as a collaborator. As an adult, Jenkins supplemented his farming income by running a transportation business between Charleston and the island. In this capacity, Jenkins acted as an informal tutor for Johns Island residents, helping them to pass the state's literacy tests as he shuttled residents during the forty-five-minute drive to and from their jobs in Charleston. According to Clark, Jenkins had single-handedly registered two hundred people to vote between 1948 and 1954, voters who then used their newly enriched citizenship to ask for improved roads, schools, and school buses.[18] The popularity of these "classes" led him to envision a more formal educational environment that could better address the widespread illiteracy in the coastal islands and facilitate political agency for the residents.[19] In 1956, Jenkins, Clark, and Horton initiated the first formal class and planted a seed for grassroots education that would become the model for movement education across the South.

As conversations progressed around the development of a program on Johns Island, Highlander staff initially deferred to Jenkins and Clark in dealing with local response and promoting the school.[20] After the initial groundwork for the school was laid, Highlander staff became more engaged in developing the program, working closely with Clark and Jenkins to get the school off the ground. To this end, Miles Horton and his wife Zilphia began a yearlong series of visits in 1954 to the first citizenship school on Johns Island as planning was underway to purchase a building for the school.[21] By 1955, Clark was driving local representatives to Highlander for conferences on leadership and desegregation, as well as producing a film series about the islands. With financial help from Horton, the Progressive Club secured an old schoolhouse and remodeled the building into a cooperative grocery store and meeting/classroom space.[22] In January of 1957, the first formal citizenship school met, led by Bernice Robinson, with fourteen adult students. Robinson was a local hairdresser who had attended Highlander workshops with Clark. Although at first reluctant to take on the role of instructor, she was persuaded by Clark and Jenkins that even though she had no formal teaching experience, her connections to the community gave her the best preparation for the work. Robinson proved to be an excellent choice, as her role in the community, combined with her respectful classroom demeanor, facilitated her students' trust at a time when attending the school was extremely risky. In light of Robinson's success as a teacher, Highlander staff continued to rely on her expertise as the program grew, employing her as a mentor for other citizenship school teachers and asking her to write a manual for training new instructors.[23]

Although Highlander staff remained committed to the principles of local control and autonomy in the development of curriculum for the citizenship schools, at times their vision for the schools conflicted with the on-the-ground realities faced by Robinson and other teachers. Septima

Clark served as intermediary between citizenship school teachers and Myles Horton, a relationship which at times resulted in Clark and Horton having to "shout it out."[24] Although these conversations initially produced conflict, Horton always ceded final authority to local leadership.[25] As Clark led the expansion of the schools, she too found herself modifying her views to recognize local needs. When school expansion took her outside of South Carolina, she found that as an outside organizer she "had to let them talk to [her] and say . . . whatever they wanted to say."[26] Similarly, even though she was a local, citizenship school teacher Bernice Robinson developed her lesson plans in tandem with her fourteen students, who requested writing lessons for filling out forms, as well as reading literacy for election laws.[27]

Citizenship school teachers used materials that reflected the balance between the larger goals of the movement and the on-the-ground needs in South Carolina. When Highlander drafted the first formal workbook for the schools, the chapters echoed these newly learned lessons on local autonomy. This first guide included the history and policies of Highlander, background on South Carolina's election laws, and sections addressing the subjects requested by students, such as how to fill out forms and address local officials.[28] As Highlander staffers developed a library for teachers to use in the citizenship schools, titles focused primarily on reading and writing primers alongside introductions to American government, including the now-venerable *Government by the People* and the secondary-level U.S. history textbook *My Country and Yours*.[29] Teachers used booklets like *The American Constitution; Your Flag;* and *You and the U.N.* to provide students with a civics education that mirrored that received by white children in the public school system. Handouts also provided background on the First, Fourteenth, and Fifteenth Amendments, to give participants a background in traditional civics as well as grounding in the black struggle for electoral and democratic power.[30]

While the citizenship schools' curriculum under the purview of Highlander stuck closely to literacy and local politics, black heritage was also incorporated in less formal ways through the musical heritage of the Sea Islands. Throughout the folk school's history, Highlander staff embraced the power of music and singing as an organizational strategy that also served as a collective memory practice. Before coming to Highlander, Zilphia Mae Johnson trained as a professional musician at College of the

Ozarks. In 1935, she first visited Highlander with the intention of preparing for labor union work, but fell in love with and married Myles Horton, formally joining the school as music director.

Highlander's emphasis on cultural preservation was a perfect environment for Zilphia Horton to merge her passion for music and radical politics. She initiated cultural outreach programming as well as provided musical curriculum for the residential programs, as workshop singing became an integral part of the Highlander experience. Horton herself had a bit of a documentary impulse, as she often collected sheet music for traditional folk songs on which she noted new leftist lyrics, which then were mimeographed and handed out at labor strikes. In 1939, she oversaw the publishing of a collection of such songs for the United Textile Workers of America entitled *Labor Songs*. Although Zilphia died tragically in 1956 of an accidental poisoning before the founding of the first citizenship school, she left an indelible imprint on the movement. Before her death, she institutionalized music into the Highlander culture. In her role as music director, Horton herself regularly added new lyrics to old folk songs, adapting them for contemporary movement purposes. The most famous example of this adaptation was the Civil Rights anthem "I Will Overcome," a song that had been popularized by Methodist congregations in the early twentieth century and then later appropriated by labor leaders. In collaboration with folk singer Pete Seeger, she changed the lyrics to the more unifying "We Shall Overcome," and the song became a favorite at Highlander meetings and rapidly spread throughout the larger movement, ultimately serving as a sort of anthem to stir activists' emotions.[31]

After Zilphia Horton's passing, folk singer Guy Carawan took over her position as music director, and in this capacity he continued to deepen Highlander's use of music in movement-building and collective memory. Born in 1927 in California, Carawan moved to the South in 1959 to work with Highlander. He was both an ethnographic scholar and teacher of folk music, but in his work at Highlander, Carawan also became passionate about the role of music in building social movements. In 1960, he met Candie Anderson, a student who was visiting Highlander from Fisk University in Nashville, and the pair married soon after. His role in movement leadership increased as he taught songs at organizing events, compiled lyrics to movement anthems, and distributed mimeographed songbooks at sit-ins and conferences.[32]

Carawan's passion for folk music matched well with Highlander's work in the Sea Islands, where a rich local music tradition had flourished for many years. After meeting Esau Jenkins and hearing of his citizenship school efforts, Carawan took up residency at Johns Island on Christmas Eve of 1959. Carawan spent several months living with Jenkins, conducting an evening singing program on the islands as well as documenting the area's traditional music. That winter he developed a singing program for the citizenship schools with both cultural preservation and pedagogical aims. Out of this endeavor emerged the Sing for Freedom workshop, first held in late summer of 1960. The initial workshop focused on putting the beatitudes to music and rearranging old spirituals to include "new words of freedom replacing the old words."[33] An old slave song that promoted faith during times of struggle pleaded, "throw me anywhere, Lord, in that old field," a song often accompanied by a dance called the "Buzzard Lope," making reference to a graveyard while also promising peace and glory in the afterlife. Student Nonviolent Coordinating Committee (SNCC) Freedom Summer workers substituted "jail" for "field," refashioning the song from providing hope during long hours of agricultural work to sustaining movement energy during long hours in southern jails.[34] Similarly, "We Are Soldiers in the Army" transposed "holding up the blood-stained banner" of the Lord's army to "holding up the freedom banner" of the Civil Rights movement.[35] By changing the lyrics to traditional spiritual songs, activists developed a memory practice that connected their contemporary struggles to those of generations of enslaved ancestors as it also transmitted cultural heritage to a new generation.

Under Carawan's guidance, in 1960 the citizenship schools formally included singing activities as part of their curriculum. Starting with schools on Edisto, Wadmalaw, North and South Johns Islands, and on the north side of Charleston, Carawan traveled from school to school for singing sessions, events in which he took both a passive role as learner and ethnographer and an active role as music teacher. Sessions began with thirty minutes of instruction in new songs, after which he opened the floor for requests for old favorites. Participants took turns leading songs, and sessions would often end with testimonials that professed "how the songs have helped give [participants] the faith and determination to hold on and overcome their many hardships and to come through them still full of love for their fellow men."[36] Such recollections of the music workshops echo the relationship between the former spirituals and secular freedom songs; what had once been a religious form was now secularized and politicized for the struggle for racial equality. Carawan also noted that the elite black churches proved to be the least useful in locating folk cultural traditions. Rather, it was in the rural churches in the isolated parts of the Sea Islands, which practiced less hierarchy in services, that the folkways of testimony, prayer, and song—many of which were not included in the hymnbooks—flourished.[37]

Coming out of the workshop in 1960, Highlander produced a mimeographed songbook entitled "Sing for Freedom" that featured songs connecting the slave past to contemporary struggles. One song linked contemporary freedom efforts with the struggle for emancipation, remembering how 'our folks have been in bondage we could not equalize, today our chains are broken . . . the freedom train is coming . . . just let us work together."[38] Choruses included references to John Henry, the mythic black rail laborer, as well as freedom lyrics sung to traditional Negro spirituals. Another song entitled "John Brown's Body—Negro History Week Song" connected present struggles to a heritage of past freedom fighters: "In the roster of our heroes is a great and shining throng / Negroes famed in Art and Science, famed in History and song / and the freedom road they opened is the road we march along / the truth goes marching on."[39] With the inclusion of singing programs into the rest of the curriculum, citizenship school students linked their cultural heritage to their political future as well as understood their own struggles on a continuum between their ancestors' efforts toward freedom and a future imagined as equal.

Carawan understood his role not only as a cultural organizer within a political movement, but also as a documentarian and archivist. During his first visit, Septima Clark and Esau Jenkins took him to meetings and church services, where he observed the region's distinct form of "shouting" spirituals, an experience that left him inspired to preserve the musical traditions of the islands. In 1963, Guy and Candie Carawan returned to the islands to develop a more substantive cultural preservation program, committing themselves to the conservation of "the oldest and purest Afro-American music known to be in existence in America today."[40] Out of their research, the Carawans produced *Ain't You Got a Right to the Tree of Life?*, a book of photographs, biographies, and music from the residents of Johns Island. They also created recordings of musical performances and promoted local musicians, in an effort to keep the musical traditions of the islands alive.⁴¹ Guy Carawan's work not only served to integrate current movement politics into familiar cultural traditions but also to weave heritage into the movement's vision for a racially just future. Furthermore, his efforts created an archive of a folk music tradition, preserving it for future generations.

Later workshops brought together volunteers from the Council of Federated Organizations, the Georgia Sea Island Singers, Alan Lomax, and others together to further enrich the political movement with a sense of the cultural past. Lomax, an ethnomusicologist and folklorist who travelled around the South recording local folk musicians, saw a direct connection between the development of racial pride through black cultural heritage:

> A few of these songs have served the Negro people directly in the freedom movement; they have been transformed into the "freedom songs" which provide the morals for the movement. Yet, in spite of this fact, most Negroes today feel rather ashamed of their musical heritage. . . . This movement should provide them with the audience and the appreciation they so richly deserve. They in turn can provide the movement with the treasure of their talent and their songs and make it, not only stronger, but culturally rich and at the same time more firmly rooted in the Negro community.⁴²

The "shame" noted by Lomax stemmed from the dismissal of black culture from mainstream white society—the belief that black cultural forms reflected a lack of education and finesse. This shame was also a byproduct of class divisions within the black community, which created a judgment against folk art forms that extended across American society. A young folk singer, Len Chandler, recalled that at a "Sing for Freedom" workshop held at the Gammon Theological Seminary in Atlanta, some younger participants "seemed ashamed of the 'down home' and 'old time' music" and that "slave songs seemed out of place at a 'sing for freedom.'"⁴³ In contrast, Carawan, Lomax, and many of the workshop participants viewed the preservation of music heritage as a form of black cultural pride. Such preservation served an important role in the struggle for political justice, a gesture that built on early-twentieth-century work to document folk music.⁴⁴

In October 1965, Highlander sponsored a Conference for Southern Community Cultural Revival, which included a workshop on Negro Folk Music. Alan Lomax spoke at the event, which included participants from the Newport Folk Foundation (a sponsor of other festivals and conferences) as well as freedom movement organizers from South Carolina, Mississippi,

Alabama, and Louisiana. The event underscored the importance of music and protest for Highlander. An article written for the *Southern Patriot*, a newsletter of the Southern Conference Educational Fund, introduced African American folk music heritage to a new generation of activists: "The moving force comes from young Southern Negroes who have come out of the freedom movement. Possessed of an inner freedom and sense of dignity won in struggle, they no longer feel ashamed of traditions of the past and have suddenly discovered a beauty and strength in the culture of their forefathers. They have determined that it not be lost."[45] Highlander staff saw musical heritage not only as a bridge between white and black activists, but also as a way to empower "downtrodden rural Negroes" as teachers and leaders in the movement via the transmission of their cultural knowledge.[46] Such sentiments predated the formal emergence of a named *Black Power* ideology but certainly reflected the growing emphasis on identity as an organizing strategy.

Highlander activists understood that traditional music could play an important role in the production of political identities. A report generated by conference participants underscored the connection between cultural heritage and political action as it committed activists to "enriching the newly aware and modern Negro with a sense of identity in his own and American culture."[47] Such efforts were necessary because "the Negro has been brainwashed, turned against his cultural heritage because of white-dominated teaching in the schools . . . and because of the distorted way in which his music has been presented by the mass communications industry."[48] The "Statement of Intent" also demonstrated how participants understood the importance of preserving distinct African American cultural forms as an act of resistance to assimilation, entreating "the Negro community to come alive in its own spirit and on its own terms . . . political and economic progress does not have to mean conformity."[49] Cultural preservation served not only as an intergenerational bond, but also as an assurance against cultural homogeneity in an era of liberal improvement.

The Next Era: The Southern Christian Leadership Conference and the Citizenship Schools

As the state of Tennessee continued its war on the Highlander Folk School, Myles Horton and Septima Clark transferred the administration of the citizenship schools to the Southern Christian Leadership Conference (SCLC) under the directorship of Martin Luther King Jr. Even before the political pressures on Highlander grew, the school leadership had considered transferring the program to another organization due to the immense growth that the schools experienced. Clark followed the schools, accepting a position with SCLC as director of education when the program formally transferred in 1961. Bernice Robinson also followed the program to SCLC, working on voter registration campaigns and implementing new citizenship schools. Within two years, the program boasted 9,575 graduates out of 277 classes from eleven southern states.[50] Under the aegis of SCLC, the citizenship schools assumed a new level of prominence in the southern Black Freedom struggle, a shift that also moved away from grassroots efforts toward more centralized, national projects.

SCLC's desire to expand the citizenship school program led to the creation of a unified curriculum that increasingly used heritage as a teaching tool. To this end, the organization published a thirty-three-page booklet entitled "Citizenship Workbook" for use in the schools. Citizenship school participants were all given the same materials from which to learn math, reading, writing, and history. This new standardized workbook included the purpose and history of the schools, community organization tactics, reading and writing exercises, handwriting tutorials, vocabulary lists, instructions for filling out money orders and other forms, math lessons, religious justifications for enfranchisement, and freedom song lyrics. This was a remarkable amount of material for adult students who possessed little if any literacy, a fact that demonstrates that SCLC envisioned the schools playing a pivotal role in mobilizing southern blacks into the movement. In the organization's view, "political, economic, and social progress" rested on "the importance of education."[51]

Black history assumed a prominent role in the new curriculum.[52] The introduction framed the schools as the endpoint of the freedom struggle that began with the arrival of the first enslaved Africans in 1619. The essay traversed the conditions of slavery, the possibilities and disappointments of Reconstruction, the failure of the seven decades following Reconstruction to produce racial equality, the appointment of the Civil Rights Committee by President Harry Truman, and the struggle for racial justice via the Civil Rights movement.[53] For the first time, participants in the citizenship schools explicitly connected their own personal role in the long historical struggle against racial inequality. As students were invited to make their own personal connection to slavery and racial struggle through time, they also linked their own participation in "a new kind of school, a new approach to learning" to the freedom struggle taking place in the streets.⁵⁴

Even though black cultural heritage worked its way into earlier curricular manifestations through songs and reading passages, SCLC's curriculum formally incorporated black history throughout its content. Five of the nine pages of reading examples contained within the booklet included history lessons on black heroes in the American past. Readers learned that "slavery was a degrading experience for the Negro but the progress of the last one hundred years and the rugged determination to be free makes our heritage glorious."⁵⁵ Throughout this section, narratives of historical struggles blossomed with rich detail, but ultimately the stories served contemporary struggles. For example, Revolutionary War soldier Crispus Attucks—shot in the so-called "Boston Massacre" of 1770—was presented as an early black hero, indeed "one of our first freedom fighters."⁵⁶ The curriculum positioned him not only as a figure of black history but also as a national martyr, as he "was the first man to die for our country's freedom," an act that would be best commemorated "by giving our vote."⁵⁷

For many students, the value of the schools included learning about black history, as well as moving them toward enfranchisement. Amid reports of political and literacy outcomes that boasted the impact of the schools, one young student declared, "attending the citizenship school helped me to learn the contributions made by Negroes. I am a senior in Richland County High School and never heard of Benjamin Banneker, Harriet Tubman or Sojourner Truth."⁵⁸ Although political goals were the first outcome of the citizenship schools, a richer sense of black history was undoubtedly shared by graduates of the program.

As the movement increasingly embraced voter education as a means to widespread grassroots mobilization, the Southern Christian Leadership Conference recruited more volunteers—most of whom were predominantly white students from the North—to work as educators in the expanding schools. Application forms for teacher training outlined desirable qualifications candidates should possess: at least twenty-one years old with strong reading and writing skills and "an interest in helping adults help themselves," as well as "persons with practical skills who could be taught to teach."⁵⁹ In 1965, SCLC also encouraged "retired teachers, businessmen, housewives, beauticians, tradesman [*sic*], etc.)" to apply for positions for Summer Community Organization and Political Education (SCOPE).[60] Freedom Summer's political education efforts had resulted in over 17,000 new attempts at voter registration, and SCLC sought to continue building this momentum with SCOPE during the following year. Volunteers chosen for SCOPE attended an orientation session, during which time they were given courses in southern politics with required readings in black history.[61] By importing leadership from the North, SCLC shifted the focus away from local grassroots leadership toward an interracial and broad-based demand for black enfranchisement.

SCLC's commitment to nonviolent struggle in the South required a past that emphasized a trajectory from slavery to full citizenship; the struggle for voting rights was a key issue in that story. This vision was based on a liberal view of social change, that rational appeal to a democratic society could produce racial equality. SCOPE's promotional brochure couched the project's mission squarely within the historical struggle for racial equality:

> After the slaves were freed 100 years ago, Negroes were allowed to freely vote. We had Negroes in the government and were on our way to rising from slavery to first class citizenship. We soon would have had equal jobs, education, housing, and political power. Federal troops from Washington were in the South to see that Negroes' rights were respected as human beings. There were as many Negroes as whites in many parts of the South and soon we would have had as much voice in government as the whites. White Southerners realized that they would have a "good thing" if they *could keep Negroes uneducated and without political power* [emphasis in original]. They would have the best jobs and all the political power for themselves. It would be almost as good as slavery. So a deal was made in Washington. The federal troops were pulled out of the South. We were unprotected.[62]

For SCLC leadership, the black historical struggle for political agency had intellectual roots in the Reconstruction era, and the movement would surely claim victory on this issue a century later through the efforts of citizen education. In this version of the failure of Reconstruction, the first wave of southern black political enfranchisement had failed due to the weakness of the federal government, leaving black citizens vulnerable and victimized. The second wave of contemporary activism would succeed due to the mobilization of grassroots activism and education, at last fulfilling the task of black liberty.

Even after the Civil Rights Voting Act ensured black enfranchisement, SCLC continued with its citizenship education program and the curricular emphasis on black history within the promotion of grassroots leadership and economic development. South Carolina citizenship school field supervisor Benjamin Mack lectured regularly on the topic, and his notes were featured in staff newsletters to inspire other teachers. Mack accused textbook authors of omitting black achievements, leaving nothing "for children to respect except white people," depicting blacks "as happy-go-lucky slaves sold on the auction block or picking cotton," and presenting Reconstruction as "the worst period in American history because Negroes found their way into government." He also opined that this curricular denial of black history "took away our identity and said we were nothing," and that the movement needed to raise awareness of this history because it "inspires us to do better. It gives us pride and dignity."[63] Although Mack's work with SCLC fit squarely within the mainstream intervention imagined by the Civil Rights movement, his comments about black history hint at the cultural activism that would mark the Black Power movement's engagement with history. As the Civil Rights movement saw a fuller enfranchisement of black citizens who still failed to experience social equality, leadership shifted the political goals from electoral politics toward cultural and political radicalism, demanding cultural autonomy for black communities, often using history as a tool for the development of racial pride.

Without a doubt, the impact of Highlander and the birth of the citizenship schools on the Civil Rights movement was extremely significant. SCLC organizer Marian Wright Edelman remembered Septima Clark's efforts with Highlander as providing a "training infrastructure" to SCLC's voter registration campaign, which she credits as "a process that transformed southern politics."[64] Voter education served not only to enfranchise thousands of black citizens across the South but also mobilized and politicized a grassroots base that provided a groundswell for other movement goals. As the citizenship schools developed within Highlander's and SCLC's institutional structures, their curricular forms evolved to reflect some of the tenets of each organization. Both Highlander's commitment to developing local leadership and the informal flexibility of the citizenship schools generated a curriculum that was only beginning to incorporate the black past into movement work. Highlander's use of songs in movement-building demonstrates how the organization's staff understood the emotional power of a collective past to mobilize individuals for the realization of movement goals. As SCLC expanded the schools in an attempt to expand movement force and political power, they shifted the curricular focus to draw more significantly from history for both reading content and movement inspiration. At the same time, SCLC leadership downplayed the significance of local leadership in favor of coalition-building with northern white academic communities, a choice that served as bedrock for the mass educational campaigns that came shortly thereafter. While this shift moved historical understanding toward a more universal narrative of black American experience, it also formalized black collective memory, validating a unified perspective via a standardized curriculum that fostered a less personal and less local sense of the past that had been promoted by the schools under Highlander's leadership.

A New Direction for Collective Memory: The Freedom Schools

While the citizenship schools were focused on adult education, a parallel movement of grassroots education for southern youth emerged. In 1961, as the newly formed Student Nonviolent Coordinating Committee (SNCC) facilitated voter registration efforts in the South, volunteers worked with high school students to stage a walkout at the Burgland High School in McComb, Mississippi. The action was a protest in support of Brenda Travis, a student who had been expelled for participating in a sit-in earlier that year. When administrators refused to address the problems raised by the protests and ordered students to return to class, SNCC leaders established a short-lived "Nonviolent High" that gave black students an alternative to the repressive environment from which they would have been expelled for participating in future protests.[65]

This event sparked discussions about other ways the movement could expand its educational efforts, a conversation that culminated in a 1963 proposal that declared "the development of a comprehensive educational program imperative" to the continued mobilization of grassroots activism.[66] The resulting freedom schools were an alternative free school project in which Civil Rights activists educated black southern students who had received substandard educations in public school systems. This initiative echoed both the long-standing faith in the role of education in racial uplift as well as a growing disenchantment with liberal institutions, which SNCC felt "sacrificed important elements of education and socialization."[67] The Council of Federated Organizations (COFO) and SNCC began to facilitate freedom school curriculum in various locations, but by the end of 1963, it had become apparent that a more comprehensive plan was needed, as isolated voter registration initiatives were proving ineffective. To this end, SNCC field secretary Charlie Cobb formally proposed Freedom Summer, a suggestion that resulted in the Curriculum Planning Conference in spring of 1964.

The schools were conceived of as an alternative to the Mississippi public school system, which movement leaders identified as a key tool of racial oppression, but they also provided an opportunity for activists to further instill narratives of the past into movement-building efforts. Planners imagined that the freedom schools would offer students an improved academic experience, but also—and equally important—give students a background in nonviolent resistance and social movement heritage, as the experience would "give them the perspective of being in a long line of protest and pressure for social and economic justice."[68] As a result, the curriculum emerged with an unprecedented emphasis on giving students "a better image" of themselves through the transmission of their "Negro heritage."[69]

Freedom school curriculum planners came to the project already possessing a strong commitment to history. Planners included Staughton Lynd, professor of history at Spelman College, and Septima Clark and Myles Horton, who had been pivotal in embedding history into early movement education efforts.[70] SNCC director Ella Baker was also central to the effort; in 1927, Baker, who herself had grown up listening to her grandmother tell stories of slave revolts, had organized a Negro History Club at the Harlem Library, one of many that appeared in cities across the United States.[71] As a result, freedom schools continued on this path, infusing curriculum with important moments of black history and producing curricula that explicitly contained substantive Negro history lesson plans. In 1964, teachers, clergy members, and other volunteers met in New York City to prepare the curriculum.[72] Participant Sandra Adickes recalls how Mississippi Freedom Summer staff poured over curriculum materials, revising and reworking language to "create an educational model capable of raising the consciousness of the black youth of Mississippi."[73] These efforts produced several hundred pages of materials, several units of which either explicitly engaged black history or wove historical analysis into current political themes.

Changes in the curriculum also echoed a shift in organizational strategy, namely from one of literacy training based on local needs and experiences to a formalized regional effort that could mobilize communities across the south via a national black heritage narrative. As an organization, SNCC was focused on leading the movement nationally while Highlander had been more attenuated to local conditions, a difference that was seen in the shift from a commitment to regional musical heritage toward a more formalized national curriculum. Planners relied on both traditional primary and secondary sources as well as incorporated units on southern power relations, leadership development, and nonviolent action. To bring the planners' ideas to fruition, Barbara Jones, a black volunteer from SNCC's New York chapter, and Bea Young, a white volunteer from the Chicago office, wrote outlines that white New Left activist and historian Staughton Lynd then incorporated into the final draft of the curriculum.[74] All volunteers who staffed forty-one freedom schools across Mississippi during the summer of 1964 were given copies of the curriculum, as well as training in how to implement the content.

The *Guide to Negro History*, a copy of which each staff member received, provided instructors with an introductory text that introduced the essays and encouraged them to adapt this contextual information to their needs. The first section included readings on the *Amistad* case and African history, slave trade and revolts, abolitionism, and U.S. presidential engagements with slavery. Beginning with *Amistad*, the authors wanted to recover heroic tales that were "so lost in the mainstream of history (along with most important aspects of the history of the Negro)," and by doing so would set the tone for the freedom school curriculum. They began with the *Amistad* story (the 1839 slave revolt in which recently enslaved captives from Sierra Leone commandeered the ship for a brief period) because "within this story can be found most of the major issues to be included in the subsequent curriculum."[75] The next section, entitled "The Origins of Prejudice," traced the legal status of slavery through the American Revolution and the development of the U.S. Constitution, and another section, entitled "Negro Resistance to Oppression," charted the 1791 Haitian Revolution and quotidian forms of resistance during enslavement. Reconstruction received its own unit, a narrative that divided the period between four plans, the last of which led to the present moment of struggle for voting rights.[76]

In addition to underscoring the significance of reclaiming such narratives, authors made an explicit connection throughout the material to contemporary movement goals. Teachers were also encouraged to "discuss with the students some of the Great African empires such as Ghana, Mali and Songhay, the African universities, the politics of these African states and the important African inventions, such as the smelting of iron; or they can simply discuss the organization of African life before its complete destruction by the slave trade."[77] This emphasis on African culture and politics foretold the movement's increasing emphasis on Black Power and its growing focus on African heritage, going beyond the simple goal of voter empowerment toward the production of an identity that enthusiastically turned away from white European culture.

Curricular accounts of slavery and Reconstruction underscored the agency of black subjects. The essay described the conditions of slavery as dire and oppressive while emphasizing some important dates for this period that underscored resistance to slavery, including the births of Frederick Douglass and Harriet Tubman (1817 and 1820, respectively); revolts by Denmark Vesey, John Brown, and Nat Turner; and the white abolitionist activism of William Lloyd Garrison and Henry David Thoreau.[78] While the curriculum intermingled white abolition work with slave insurrections, it also noted that black activism was much more militant than its white-led counterparts and emphasized that "protest is nothing new for Negros."[79]

The *Guide to Negro History* consistently brought the struggles of the past into the present movement, locating a useable past within the narrative of post-Civil War struggles for equality. The Reconstruction section drew connections between contemporary struggles and historical narratives as it attempted to answer how the black vote was granted and then lost. In this section, curriculum authors argued that the failure of the period lay in the economic imbalance between whites and blacks and the inability of the federal government to enforce the Reconstruction amendments. The segment entitled "Myths about Reconstruction" made an intervention into historians' interpretation of the era, charging academic history with presenting "the most distorted period in the writing of American history." In particular, the authors challenged the academic portrayal of Congressmen Thaddeus Stevens and Charles Sumner as "vengeful fanatics."[80] Finally, the curriculum focused on local history in a section titled "Reconstruction in Mississippi."[81]

Over time, individual freedom school instructors and their students helped shape the curriculum as they added their own research. Staughton Lynd, then director of the freedom schools project after overseeing the development of the curriculum, advised instructors that their "curriculum should be built around the political platform the students themselves create" during the months following Freedom Summer.[82] For Lynd, grassroots decision-making was a critical piece of movement education, much like the tenets of movement education established by Highlander in the citizenship schools. To this end, many instructors added history curriculum to the collection of teaching resources. In the opening notes of their curriculum, teachers from the Jackson Freedom School aimed "to explore the history of the Negro on the American scene in the hope of developing in the students an added appreciation of the strengths and weaknesses of American patterns of race relations. Special concern should be given to Negro contributions to the culture, to white reactions, and to political problems for the future in light of knowledge of the past."[83] Their curricular addendum also offered a bibliography and outline of twentieth-century Negro history. Other contributors also interacted with the curriculum as a kind of scholarly conversation and accumulation of knowledge. Otis Pease, a white professor of history from Stanford University working with the freedom schools, contributed research on "The Development of Negro Power in American Politics Since 1900." He prefaced his paper with an invitation to dialogue, as he acknowledged that his argument made "no claim for completeness or total objectivity. [Rather, he] look[ed] for discussion, argument, and even replies distributed similarly in a spirit of dissent."[84] Although Pease wasn't himself a scholar of black history, he volunteered for the project as an expression of his commitment to social justice.[85] Pease understood that writing movement history provided an opportunity to engage living memory, and as such he envisioned a more democratic process of knowledge production than traditional academic history allowed. His commitment to local needs carried throughout the curriculum plans, as his pedagogical proscriptions left instructors with room to adapt to individual and community needs within the freedom schools.

In addition to discussion and lectures on black history topics, theater served as an important pedagogical tool for the expression of collective memory. Historian and playwright Martin Duberman authored a document-based drama entitled *In White America* that was staged for freedom school participants. In one scene used by freedom school teachers, a Ku Klux Klan member stood trial for lynching a local black man, followed by actual testimony given in 1907 to Congress by U.S. senator Ben Tillman from South Carolina.[86] This scene provided exposition on the failure of Radical Reconstruction and the history of legislative complicity in the South. Duberman was an activist scholar, teaching at Princeton University, and an abolition movement historian. The play featured vignettes interspersed with a narrated timeline of Reconstruction, lynchings, and Civil Rights history. In response, the freedom school at Milestone, Mississippi, wrote and produced its own play, dramatizing scenes from black history and ending with a powerful treatise on the past and the present:

> I am the American Negro.
> You have seen my past: you have known my past.
> And you have seen the trouble I've seen.
> Today we have seen many men die
> Because they stood for their rights.
> Today we have seen three men disappear
> For joining our fight.
> Tomorrow many more will die.
> And many more will suffer,
> But we've begun and we are not turning back
> And someday, somehow, we shall overcome.[87]

Likewise, freedom school teacher Sandra Adickes recalled that her students eagerly embraced the opportunity to reenact revisions of dominant American history, as they dramatized the invention of the cotton gin not by Eli Whitney, but by plantation slaves. Adickes's use of role-playing in the classroom also allowed students to express contemporary political anger at "adults they believed were too compliant with segregation."[88] This sentiment echoed the frustration felt by many Civil Rights activists who felt that the complacent older generation had failed to meaningfully push back against Jim Crow and that younger activists possessed the vision, tactics, and determination to finally make meaningful change in racial relations.

In addition to curriculum planners, volunteers on the ground increasingly found a desire for black history. An unnamed freedom school teacher in Hattiesburg, Mississippi, lamented that "the students are taught nothing of their heritage. The only outstanding Negroes they are told about are

Booker T. Washington and George Washington Carver. They learn nothing of the contributions Negroes have made to our culture or anything else which could give them any reason to disbelieve the lies they are told about Negroes being unable to do anything worthwhile."[89] While some looked to the black past for inspiration and pride, others used the history of slavery to energize participants toward the goal of freedom. Lucia Guest spent Freedom Summer in Ruleville, Mississippi, a small town that was also the birthplace of Fannie Lou Hamer, where Guest recalled using an innovative role-playing method to teach history lessons. Beginning with a scene depicting the middle passage on a slave ship, Guest directed students to sing contemporary freedom songs as they pretended to be slaves.[90] In another case, students enrolled at the freedom school at Priest Creek Missionary Baptist Church in Hattiesburg prepared a performance of Duberman's *In White America* to be staged at a local community center, although the performance was cancelled due to rumors of an attack by local whites.[91] The use of drama was one of the more innovative memory practices deployed by freedom school teachers, giving students an opportunity to imagine themselves as part of their shared past.

Other portions of the freedom school curriculum made connections to historical themes outside of black history. An essay entitled "Nonviolence in American History" linked contemporary struggles, Quaker history, and abolitionism to Henry David Thoreau's interpretation of the American Revolution and Thomas Paine's political treatise *Common Sense*.[92] Still another case study drew parallels between Nazi Germany and the southern slaveholding past: "The very exaggerated character of the Nazi experience should serve to bring into clearer focus an understanding of realities latent or only partially observable in Negro history and in the South today."[93] In several places, the lesson plan prompted teachers to draw connections between enslavement and totalitarianism, including asking students to draw connections between "an event from Nazi Germany and one in Negro history."[94] In another case, teachers drew analogies between "Nazi methods of arrest and transport" and "descriptions of captures of Negroes in Africa."[95] These curricular and pedagogical strategies provided students with a larger context of exploitation in which to understand their own political realities and histories. For southern youth who had grown up with a narrative of the benevolence of slavery, the connection between their forefathers' and foremothers' enslavement and an uncontested icon of amoral Nazi exploitation and cruelty was crucial to the development of their political consciousness.

The embrace of the emancipatory possibilities of the past also went beyond freedom school curriculum. SNCC's newsletter, *the Student Voice*, from February 18, 1964, featured a sketch announcing Negro History Week on the back cover, promoting "Negro History, a basis for the new freedom."[96] The accompanying image showed a suit-clad black man striding out of a book encircled by chains. It is unclear if the book has bound him or liberated him, but the caption makes it clear that knowledge of Negro history is the means by which freedom can be obtained. As Civil Rights began to fade as the prominent ideology within the larger Black Freedom movement, the connection between collective memory and liberation was firmly entrenched in black communities and provided a basis for Black Power's shift toward heritage as identity and political legitimacy.

Conclusion

Manifesting both on the ground and in cultural politics, the Civil Rights movement in part distinguished itself from earlier collectivist efforts toward liberation in its abiding commitment to and widespread impact on grassroots organizing and mobilization toward the goal of full black citizenship. One of the key tenets in this shift was the role of the intellectual, a turn that would reframe the larger black history narrative and set a precedent for the democratized use of history in the liberation movements that followed. In the early twentieth century, black intellectuals like W. E. B. Du Bois envisioned social change through a racial uplift model that mirrored a more traditional social hierarchy via the talented tenth. Through education and social promotion, Du Bois and others imagined a black elite that would provide direction for the rest of community. Frustrated at the lack of change brought on by this model and its inherent elitism, Civil Rights activists brought a new definition of leadership to the black freedom struggle, promoting grassroots direction and authority throughout the movement. The model of leadership activated by the movement might best be understood, at least from its roots in the Highlander model of organizing, as a conscious cultivation of *organic intellectuals,* a term coined by the Italian Marxist theorist Antonio Gramsci.[97] For Gramsci, the proletariat needed to cultivate its own group of intellectuals, a sub-community that would bring informal knowledge and analysis to lead the struggles for economic and social justice.[98] Although Martin Luther King Jr. came to function within the movement as a traditional center of leadership and power, leaders like Septima Clark and, to a somewhat lesser level, Bernice Robinson and Esau Jenkins, were among countless others who began their work on the local level, yet ultimately shaped the movement, infusing black collective memory into the larger political struggle.

By decentralizing authority within the movement, Civil Rights activists laid a foundation for the use of history in social movements that would follow. Through the validation of local knowledge and the embrace of folk traditions, they also sought to democratize education as they cultivated a group of movement intellectuals. Such decentralized leadership also shifted the position of collective memory within the black community, laying ground for the identity-based demands for cultural ownership that began to emerge from other movements. The interpretation of the past no longer simply served the movement in an organizational capacity, but varying interpretations would lead to much ideological debate across camps, as we will see in later chapters. At this critical turning point, movements began to disregard elite historical authority and develop a democratic approach to the acquisition and sharing of historical knowledge.

As the Black Freedom movement focused attention on northern and urban racial injustices, Black Power rhetoric and ideology grew and connected these struggles to the larger trajectory of Civil Rights struggles. The Watts Riots in Los Angeles during the summer of 1965 and the riots that spread across Chicago, Detroit, Newark, and other cities after the assassination of Martin Luther King Jr. fueled a growing disenchantment with nonviolent resistance. King himself had begun to connect the southern Civil Rights struggle to northern urban poverty and struggles for racial justice, a move that fueled the shift toward Black Power within the larger movement.

As Black Power ideas began to ascend within the struggles for racial justice, Septima Clark and others shifted the narrative of black history, using it to illuminate new emphases within the movement and to mobilize communities toward Black Power ideology and activism. As Clark witnessed the growing focus on identity as the Black Freedom movement shifted from a focus on Civil Rights to Black Power, she expressed concern that identities not become an end unto themselves. Couching her emphasis on the past as a civic inquiry into the nature and possibility of a true American democracy, she underscored that "Black History is not simply 'soul food' and 'soul music' as some of its misinterpreters have suggested,"[99] but rather called for the "control over our institutions . . . of the telling of our story" as she positioned black history as a key site of cultural contestation. Here Clark identified a critical turn in the use of collective memory within liberation movements—interpretive ownership of the past served not only as a site of cultural self-determination but also, and explicitly, one of political power. This turn toward black ownership of cultural narratives and resources mirrored the direction that SNCC, the Nation of Islam, and the Black Panthers moved in—cultural self-determinism. As the arc of the larger Black Freedom movement turned toward the values and rhetoric of Black Power, the production, interpretation, and dissemination of historical narratives became an important front in the struggle for racial justice.

Although not as focused on individual identity as other movements, Civil Rights activists developed memory practices that served the goals of the movement, shifting them from the more locally focused use of folk music to a more nationally efficacious standard curriculum. By weaving black history into curriculum, teachers and administrators of the citizenship and freedom schools connected black southerners' efforts to claim full citizenship to the struggles of their enslaved, newly freed, and Jim-Crow-bound predecessors. Teachers from the citizenship schools connected their literacy lessons to communal pasts even as singing schools' curriculum linked musical heritage to present-day struggles. The effect of these efforts was a more broad-based black collective memory that directly linked the struggles of the past to contemporary demands for social equality and full citizenship. Although the intellectual and cultural tides within social movements increasingly placed greater emphasis on history as a foundation for identity, the bedrock laid by Civil Rights activists provided a basis for a prominent role for history within social movements and set the stage for a heritage-based identity politics that followed in other movements and culminated in the late-twentieth-century culture wars.

President Howard Fuller talking to a student outside Malcolm X Liberation University in downtown Durham, North Carolina, around 1971. Durham Civil Rights Project, North Carolina Collection, Durham County Library.

CHAPTER 2

Knowledge of Self

Liberation and Education through Black Separatist Collective Memory

> The number one thing that makes us differ from other people is our lack of knowledge concerning the past. Proof of which—almost anyone else can come into this country and get around barriers and obstacles that we cannot get around; and the only difference between them and us, they know something about the past, and in knowing something about the past, they know something about themselves, they have an identity.
>
> —Malcolm X

Black Power activists used similar memory practices to their Civil Rights counterparts, like movement schools for both children and adults, but they also developed new strategies, including the rhetorical incorporation of black history elements in speeches and movement newspapers. Like Civil Rights leadership, Black Power activists wove historical narratives into curriculum designed for edification and movement-building. But where Civil Rights deployed education primarily toward the goal of realizing full citizenship for black Americans, Black Power constructed a transnational heritage that served in the development of a separatist political identity. These efforts worked on the cultural level, using historical narratives to claim an autonomous sense of self for black Americans, an act of consciousness development that served as the outcome itself, not only the means to an end.

Black Power radically reformulated the use of history within the struggle for racial justice, away from lauding black Americans who stood as community heroes during and after slavery and toward a narrative that linked contemporary blackness to a Pan-African heritage. This new approach also reimagined the U.S. struggle for racial justice as in solidarity with global liberation struggles, a realignment that altered both collective memory narrative and envisioned political goals. When Student Nonviolent Coordinating Committee Chairperson Stokely Carmichael in 1966 popularized the term "Black Power" in front of a crowd frustrated with the failures of integration, the phrase set more liberal-minded organizers like Martin Luther King Jr. ill at ease, but it resonated deeply with a younger generation of activists who shared frustration at the rate of change set by integrationist activism.[1] Civil Rights activists had used black history primarily to connect mid-century efforts to past struggles for social equality and full citizenship. The birth of the citizenship and freedom schools under the auspices of the Highlander Folk School, Southern Christian Leadership Conference, and the Student Nonviolent Coordinating Committee had employed historical education toward the goal of social and political parity. In contrast, the Black Power movement used history to build cultural formations that celebrated racial difference by lauding blackness.[2] In a session called "Culture: Black Awareness and Love" at the first Black Power Conference in Newark, New Jersey, in July 1967, participants outlined the need for scholarship on *both* African and Afro-American history, calling for both "black interpretations in history" and eradication of "white distortions and myths."[3] This call echoed the intellectual foundations of Black Power and Afrocentric black history that had been laid in the previous few decades by the Nation of Islam. The mythological origins articulated in Nation of Islam leader Elijah Muhammad's theology had generated a fascination with African origins; similarly, Malcolm X's urgent rhetoric about black history provided the movement with a link between the burgeoning Black Power identity and African heritage. From the movement's outset, leaders underscored the importance of reframing black history as a transnational narrative that emphasized the era before U.S. enslavement.[4]

One of the ways that the Black Power movement distinguished itself from the Civil Rights movement was the production of and emphasis on a retooled black identity. To this end, Black Power activists used movement education to cultivate a Pan-Africanist sense of self that supported the movement's goals of not only racial pride but also cultural and political autonomy. Activists and organizations envisioned that the transformation of political relations in the U.S. depended upon black communities and individuals reimagining themselves as autonomous from white society.

Black Power activists built this new identity on a reformulation of black American historical narratives, emphasizing the centrality of African heritage to world history and celebrating the cultural heritage of the African past. Black Power activists transmitted this cultural pride through a variety of memory practices including speeches, formal curriculum, and movement newspapers.[5]

Although Black Power leaders began to claim interpretive ownership over black history, the idea of cultural and political separatism had much earlier roots in the Black Freedom movement. Marcus Garvey's establishment of the Universal Negro Improvement Association and African Communities League in 1914 established a basis for Black Power ideas and cultural forms.[6] By connecting Garvey's early-twentieth-century movement with the black activism in the late 1960s and 1970s, one can see continuity across the twentieth century while also attending to the different characteristics of each institutional formation of Black Power.

Culturally focused activists within the Black Power movement deployed a wide array of memory practices to achieve the goal of Afrocentric identity formation.[7] In particular, three institutional manifestations of black collective memory stand out as embodiments of the values of the Black Power movement. In the first instance, the Nation of Islam and its founder Elijah Muhammad crafted a historical narrative that supported the separatist political program through a reimagined sense of black self, one that shifted away from the black American slave past toward a history that emphasized black racial pride, even superiority. This narrative, much like Marcus Garvey's use of history during the earlier part of the twentieth century, crafted a Pan-African consciousness and identity in support of a black separatist political vision, and as such, inspired movement members to build parallel institutional forms and cultivate community ownership of their history.

The second instance is the Malcolm X Liberation University (MXLU), a Pan-Africanist university that emerged out of student protests at Duke University in North Carolina. Although historically black colleges and universities (HBCUs) had educated black students since Reconstruction, many of the new black nationalists found HBCUs inadequately educating them for self-determination, an ideological tenet necessary for the political project of Black Power. The establishment of MXLU gave Black Power activists the first higher-educational space in which to realize the goal of cultural nationalism.

Finally, collective memory efforts within the Black Panther Party provide a third example of the ways the values of the Black Power movement informed the production of a new political identity built upon a reworked narrative of the black past. To this end, Black Panther leadership used the party's newspaper to create and transmit a collective memory that served to supplement the socialist revolutionary agenda of the party, a project that was realized by explaining slavery, racial oppression, and American experience through a materialist lens. In a manner similar to their other movement counterparts, Black Panther liberation schools used historical narratives to cultivate the critical-thinking skills they imagined necessary for the next generation of Panther leadership. Although the Nation of Islam espoused a very different political project than the leadership of MXLU and the Black Panthers, each of these case studies offers insight into the ways that mid-twentieth-century social movements engaged the African past and the legacy of U.S. enslavement. In all three instances, activists revised the dominant historical narratives to construct a political identity that demanded cultural autonomy from mainstream American society.

Nation of Islam and the Historical Self Knowledge

Although the founding of the Nation of Islam predated the term *Black Power*, the organization nonetheless laid crucial bedrock for the activists who came later by making black separatism intelligible, if not perhaps even inevitable. From the ashes of Marcus Garvey's nascent black separatism, the Nation of Islam (NOI) emerged not only as a new religious and quasi-political organization but also as a beginning of a black collective memory that was Afrocentric and supportive of cultural and political autonomy. The self-determining demands of the Black Power movement in the 1960s took cues from NOI's earlier collective memory groundwork. Although Booker T. Washington, W. E. B. Du Bois, and Carter Woodson had been using black history toward the goal of racial justice during the earlier twentieth century, the Nation of Islam took this work in a different direction as it developed historical narratives in service of an explicitly separatist political identity. The NOI origin narrative placed Afro- and Asiatic black experience at the center of human history. This prehistory served to de-emphasize black enslaved experience and also served to foreshadow the emergence of NOI itself, lending an inevitability to its political project of nationhood and separatism. NOI leadership used memory practices that transmitted this newly crafted heritage to all generations of the organization's membership through sermons, newspaper articles, and the University of Islam schools.

The deeply impoverished slums of Detroit, Michigan, offered fertile ground from which the Nation of Islam emerged in 1930, when a newly arrived door-to-door fabric salesman began preaching a new religion to his black clientele. An entrepreneurial and charismatic leader, Wallace Fard called on his new followers to reject Christianity as a religion of their oppressors and return themselves spiritually to their own origins by embracing his retooled version of Islam. Developing an origin myth that blended elements of Christianity, Judaism, and Islam, Fard explained the history of race relations while also justifying the black separatist political program he was developing. Fard's date of birth, national origin, and ethnicity are shrouded in mystery; much more is known of his successor, Elijah Poole. Born to a poor sharecropper in Sandersville, Georgia, in 1897, Poole worked various jobs until he met Fard in Detroit in 1931. An early convert, Poole quickly endeared himself to Fard, and was sent to Chicago in 1932 to found the Nation's second temple, at which point Poole also assumed the surname "Muhammad." When Fard mysteriously disappeared in 1934, Poole assumed leadership of the growing organization.[8]

Elijah Muhammad believed that the first step in black self-determination was embracing a self-definition that was separate from white culture. He argued that "knowledge of self" kept black Americans from "enjoying freedom, justice and equality . . . [which] belongs to them divinely as much as it does to other nations on the earth."[9] Central to the project of "a true knowledge of self" was a revision of black history that would refocus the narrative away from unsatisfactory figures lauded by white historians to African heroes and a transnational sense of history:

> So-called Negro History is all slave history. . . . Muslims extoll, in the place of Booker T. Washington, Richard B. Allen, etc., the fighting men and women of the black man's past such as Hannibal of Carthage and King Menelik of Ethiopia whose small army in 1856 inflicted a resounding defeat on the mighty forces of imperial Italy at the Battle of Aduwa. . . . According to the messenger, the black man's history will begin only and when he stops groveling, begging, cringing in fear before the white man, still his master, and stand [sic] on his two feet as a full-fledged man with pride of self and race.[10]

For Muhammad, there was nothing useful or even correct about black history that was centered in the United States. As long as the black community embraced narratives of the slave past, liberation would be forestalled. By reframing the narrative of human development around black experience, Muhammad inverted the narrative of racial hierarchy that justified white supremacy and claimed blackness as the pinnacle of human greatness. For Muhammad, black history was far more than just a tool of identity; in fact, it was the key to understanding and overthrowing white racial power. The heritage claimed by Fard and Muhammad lent legitimacy to black separatism, NOI's millenarianism, specifically the belief that black Muslims were destined to assume supreme power on Earth. Fard asserted that God viewed his congregation as "members of the original people or black nation of the earth. . . . [L]ong before the white man himself was a part of our planet, we were the original people ruling the earth, and according to the Holy Qur-an, we had governments superior to any we are experiencing today."[11] Not only did Muhammad's myth serve to generate identity and racial pride but it also established the black diaspora as the origin of humanity as a whole.

During Muhammad's life and leadership, the origin story embraced by NOI remained mostly consistent to Fard's historical narrative. According to the doctrine, black people originated in Asia, but first possessed smooth hair and delicate features. As the story went, "original man" appeared seventy-six trillion years ago, then shifted into the deity form of Allah. One of the twelve clans of black humanity, the Tribe of Shabazz emerged as the first civilized African people. A member of this tribe named Yacub was predestined to betray his people, an act realized through a combination of sorcery and science. Afterwards, Yacub crafted a race of white people who came to dominate the twelve black tribes. For this story, Fard drew upon elements from both Judeo-Christian and Islamic theology, crafting a mythology that was a sort of useable past of American and Islamic influences.[12] Beyond serving as a historical explanation for racial difference and conflict, this theological myth also foretold the coming of a savior who would complete the twenty-five-thousand-year cycle with a renaissance of black separatist civilization: "We have arrived now at the day we call six thousand years from the creation of the white man's world. And now, according to the prophecy and your own understanding of history, the truth must be told."[13] That truth, of course, was the inevitable ascendency of a superior black civilization led by Fard and Muhammad.

NOI's origin myth serves to explain a history of oppression while simultaneously providing liberation from that legacy. By locating the birth of humankind in blackness, the organization built a sense of racial pride, even superiority, as it claimed a kind of ownership over the entirety of human civilization. The myth of Yacub served several important purposes toward changing black heritage from a tale of victimization to a purposeful trajectory. First, Yacub himself explained the transition from an era of black social power and cultural achievement to one of colonialism, slavery, and exploitation, rejecting the "civilizing" narratives of much white-authored history without portraying black culture as weak or pathological. Second, the inclusion of the "white devil" justified NOI's call for black separatism as it demonstrated the moral bankruptcy of white culture. Third, the millennial structure lent an imperative to the movement, which served the Nation's recruitment efforts as it offered poor urban blacks a proud, culturally and politically prosperous future that had been foretold for centuries. Imaginative as the narrative was, Muhammad's articulation and promotion of a historic backdrop that outright rejected Eurocentrism provided an important foundation from which later activists could reject, rework, and then reclaim black history on their own terms.

As knowledge of self was fundamental to transforming the inner worlds of NOI converts, NOI foregrounded education as a fundamental movement-building task. NOI held special appeal to those who had been or were currently incarcerated, as it aggressively marketed a formula for personal transformation to respectability, and as a result, the movement attracted large numbers of followers in prisons. The program laid out by Muhammad required adherents to reimagine themselves shaking off the ideology of white America. Premised on the idea that recent converts had internalized the hatred projected on them, the Nation's program included an unlearning of the black slave past and a relearning of African historical experience. Muhammad faulted mainstream schooling for failing to "teach us the knowledge of self. We have been to the schools of our slave-master. We have been to their schools and gone as far as they allowed us to go. That was not far enough."[14] For Muhammad and his followers, mainstream American culture was irrevocably tainted with racist ideologies. Thus, claiming ownership over the form and content of education was a means to self-respect, a drive for nationhood, and the development of the skills needed to be economically independent from mainstream society.

The disdain that Nation of Islam leadership held for "the schools of our slave-master" transformed into pragmatic action through the establishment of the University of Islam (UOI), the educational arm of NOI. Although the schools held an important place in the organization during the late 1950s and 1960s, the early years proved especially significant for the development of collective memory in the curriculum. Just before his disappearance in 1934, Fard founded the first school in Detroit. As one of the church's earliest programs, the University of Islam initially instructed fourth through twelfth graders, ultimately expanding its curriculum to encompass students as young as preschool age. The school quickly attracted parents who wanted an Afrocentric and positive educational environment for their children, and as a result, the school provoked anxiety in the mainstream, even national, press. An article in *Time* from 1934 described how "Negro moppets have been disappearing in batches from Detroit's public schoolrooms."[15] The article covered an external investigation, which led to arrests of teachers and administrators for "contributing to the delinquency of minors."[16] When Detroit officials sought to close down the school, Muhammad and his adherents committed more deeply to oppositional educational work.[17] In the following years, NOI opened several more University of Islam campuses across the country.

The prescription of appropriate comportment was a key part of the school's curriculum. Teachers instructed students in the conservative gender roles espoused by the Nation, a social framework and hierarchy that was extremely important to the doctrine of the church. Girls wore long dresses and covered their heads in scarves while taking additional domestic coursework called "Muslim Girls in Training." Female students also adhered to a strict doctrine prohibiting high heels, makeup, and dancing with anyone other than a husband. Young men supplemented their training with courses to prepare them for membership in the Fruit of Islam, the church's paramilitary organization. Muslim women's history was also highlighted in the newspaper, lamenting, "it is indeed sorrowful to hear our people exclaim that the Muslim woman is a backward product of Islamic Society."[18] The status of women in the Nation of Islam had received much criticism from outside the organization. Critics derided NOI's expectations for women's dress and comportment as placing women in a subservient role. In response to charges such as these, the article invoked the twelve-hundred-year-old example of Zodeidah, a philanthropist who supported Muslims on pilgrimage and also was a noted engineer, as the article that served "to locate the past greatness of women and to inspire black women" in the present.[19] NOI leadership ardently defended their doctrinal teachings on women, lauding women as important members of the community but also placing them under the control of men.

Both Nation of Islam leaders and their critics within mainstream American society understood the power in the oppositional historical narratives being taught at the University of Islam. In 1962, Illinois State Senator Arthur Gottschalk toured the University of Islam in Chicago. Gottschalk had called for a state investigation into the school, charging the institution with fomenting race hatred in school children based on the history curriculum taught at the school. For the two years prior, the school had refused routine inspections from the Cook County Superintendent of Schools, presumably to shun the judgment of the white educational establishment, as NOI's national secretary grounded the accusations in "the fear by some elements that they cannot control the black man's education."[20] After growing pressure from the press, national secretary John Ali invited the senator to tour the school.

Coverage of the senator's visit in NOI's newspaper *Muhammad Speaks* invoked both Cold War ideology and racial strife. The opening paragraph of one article referred to the senator's perceptions of the school as if it were "behind the walls of the Kremlin" and stated that the anticipated visit had stirred "lynch fever" in the larger white community.[21] Photos from the visit featured the senator examining students and their reading materials, with captions noting that the curriculum included several black history textbooks to enrich the students' understanding of the past. The article also underscored the importance of economic theory, noting that both American and Arabic models were taught to students. For UOI administrators, curricular choices echoed moral choices that reflected the goals of the movement: "We teach the history of the Black man, which is not taught in the public schools. We are trying to . . . bring them back to their culture and give them roots."[22] The senator remained hostile during the tour, and the exchange failed to persuade Gottschalk, who vowed to continue his fight to close the institution.[23] Gottschalk continued his campaign for a few months, insisting that school administrators repudiate the teachings of Elijah Muhammad, a demand that administrators unflinchingly rebuffed. A few months later, Gottschalk's bill died in the Senate, and the issue faded from the limelight.[24]

Beyond training the next generation of NOI citizenry, the organization's leadership was also proud of the academic successes of its students. A 1963 article in *Muhammad Speaks* boasted of college placement of recent graduates as attesting to the impact of the Muslim curriculum."[25] But movement members also prized the academic institution for its role in furthering the racial and class uplift mission on which NOI prided itself. The school offered rehabilitation for youth who had fallen into undesirable company and behaviors, in a way similar to NOI outreach to adults in comparable circumstances. In 1964, Willie X recounted his teenage salvation through the UOI. Rescued from underage drinking, armed participation in a street gang, starting fights, and chasing girls, Willie was unequivocal about the source of his redemption as he declared the university "the best school in the United States or the world."[26] The University of Islam also understood its work as a reformer of the behavioral problems arising from the ills of white education.

The Nation also actively critiqued mainstream educational institutions in its newspaper. NOI members regularly read articles that criticized mainstream curriculum and textbooks. In one case, L. P. Beveridge Jr., editor of the black protest magazine the *Liberator*, charged the entire educational complex with perpetuating white supremacy: "There is in the United States today," he declared, "a national conspiracy to indoctrinate our children with white supremacist propaganda. This conspiracy operates quite openly; it is condoned by most parents' organizations, officially approved by most school boards and indirectly subsidized by federal, state and local governments. It is able to reach every school child in the country with its insidious chauvinist literature. I refer to the multi-million dollar textbook publishing industry."[27] For Beveridge and others, school curriculum reproduced racial ideologies by not acknowledging that blacks had endured "four hundred years of absence from our own people."[28] Coverage in *Muhammad Speaks* also occasionally applauded developments within scholarly history that enhanced interpretations of black Americans' contributions. A 1964 article lauded historian John Hope Franklin's work, commending his scholarship as both author and planner of university curriculum that represented blacks in a favorable light. At the same time, the article withheld comment on Franklin's more liberal political inclinations.[29] The embrace of Franklin's work by *Muhammad Speaks* was likely due to the leadership of Malcolm X in the paper's production. By 1963, Malcolm had begun to embrace orthodox Islam, which also fostered in him a more inclusive worldview that increasingly tolerated the more integrationist ethos of the Civil Rights movement. Additionally, the paper increasingly served a black leftist and even communist readership, during which time there was an increase in coverage on black history topics.

Instructors at the University of Islam entwined collective memory and political ideology throughout the curriculum. The student enrollment unit required that new matriculates be able to answer questions regarding the original man, the colored man, the population of the original nation, population of the colored people, land use for each of these groups, and age of various world religious systems. The expected answers ensured that students had internalized the story of "the Asiatic Black Man," or the original human inhabitants of earth, the production of the colored man through Yacub's mischief, and the omnipresence and eternal nature of the Nation of Islam in contrast to the more youthful Buddhism and Christianity.[30] Once they demonstrated an aptitude for these foundational myths, students then advanced to the full curriculum. Although the specter of transatlantic slavery hung over all of NOI's historical narratives, the intellectual focus of UOI's curriculum oriented students away from U.S. history and toward that which came before the middle passage.

By the time of Muhammad's death in 1975, there were over forty Universities of Islam across the country, proving an effective institutional arm for recruitment and the reproduction of the membership's values and ideology. Upon taking the helm of the organization after his father's death, Wallace D. Muhammad sent out a memo to all mosques recommitting his energies to the enhancement of the universities.[31] Wallace was a product of NOI's educational system, and as such had both personal and professional commitment to its excellence.[32] Under Wallace's direction, the schools were renamed the Clara Muhammad Schools, in honor of his mother. UOI lessons encompassed a broad array of values and knowledge espoused by the Nation. By this point, a single packet of lessons contained training on the Nation's organizational structure, including the Fruit of Islam and the Muslim Girls training groups; the history the Qur'an; the geography of Africa; a question-and-answer reading aptitude script that inculcated NOI's racial ideology; and a historical lesson on Yacub and the original nation.[33]

NOI's engagement with historical education also went beyond the schools' doors. Readers of *Muhammad Speaks* followed other popular education initiatives within the Black Freedom movement. In 1963, the paper lauded the efforts of Boston's freedom school to "place Negro history in its proper perspective in relation to American history."[34] The paper also congratulated the efforts of the members of Chicago's Amistad Society, among whom numbered high school teachers and undergraduate history majors working to educate broadly on African American history topics.[35] Similarly, coverage of Chicago School Board protests celebrated the efforts of activists involved in the action, charging that white-authored history about black experience "omits the contributions of Negros in an effort to convince Negros that they have no heritage."[36] The newspaper's support was surprisingly unequivocal, given the Nation's efforts to emphasize an African past while downplaying black enslaved historical experiences. Such wholehearted celebration of all aspects of the black past reflected Malcolm's growing tolerance and equanimity toward the larger movement.

As important as formal historical education was to the Nation, perhaps the most significant, and certainly the most intimate, ritual of collective memory was the practice of renaming. In *Message to the Black Man in America,* Elijah Muhammad equated slave names with linguistic shackles and charged his followers with taking a name reflective of their African heritage. Many in the early Nation dropped their surnames in favor of "X," memorializing the eradication of identity under slavery. Adherents also increasingly took up Islamic names, including "Muhammad," "Ali," and "Shabazz." According to Muhammad, freedom could never be known until black folks understood themselves on terms outside of white society: "After nearly a hundred years of freedom, we are still representing ourselves by the names our slave-masters called us. . . . It is time for us to learn who we really are, and it is time for us to understand ourselves."[37] For Muhammad, heritage was a fundamental condition of citizenship, and thus true liberation could only come with followers personally and intimately claiming their African heritage.[38]

Perhaps one of the richest examples of the Nation's success in cultivating a collective memory that served a separatist political goal can be found in the personal journey of Malcolm X. The enthralling historical narrative preached by Elijah Muhammad inspired an early and important convert to engage richly with black history. Malcolm Little was serving time in a Massachusetts state prison in the mid- to late-1940s when he met a devoted member of the Nation of Islam. After a rapid conversion to

NOI's doctrines and faith, Malcolm began a project of self-education, as he vigorously set to reading books that spanned a wide array of historical subjects. He delved particularly into black history, both U.S. slavery and global black experience. Malcolm's search led him to H. G. Wells, W. E. B. Du Bois, and Carter Woodson, all of who gave him a background in pre-slave-trade African empires, slavery and colonialism, and early black struggles for freedom. Malcolm's anger increased as he continued his readings, and his newfound knowledge fueled his identification with the Nation of Islam: "Not even Elijah Muhammad," he wrote, "could have been more eloquent than those books were in providing indisputable proof that the collective white man had acted like a devil in virtually every contact he had with the world's collective non-white man."[39]

Through early Afrocentric history, Malcolm found inspiration for organizing and building the Nation as well as a rhetorical basis for the change he preached to the rapidly growing congregations. Upon leaving prison, Malcolm took his newfound passion for history into his role as an NOI leader, often using history in his sermons and recruitment efforts.[40] Malcolm's passion for scholarly historical research also marked a shift in the historical narratives within the Nation; through his sermons and editorial hand in the Nation's newspaper *Muhammad Speaks,* collective memory within NOI deemphasized Elijah Muhammad's origin myths and began to include more black American history.

In 1963, as Malcolm learned of Elijah Muhammad's secret affairs, he nurtured a growing mistrust in Muhammad's teachings and began to further develop his own interpretation of the collective black past. In 1965, just weeks before his assassination, Malcolm X gave a speech on African American history as part of a three-part lecture kicking off the platform for his new project, the Organization for Afro-American Unity. Malcolm started the first lecture in the series with thoughts on the importance of history, used the second speech to address the current state of racial politics, and planned the third to address his political program for the future, but the last speech was precluded by his death. Malcolm's sentiments on black history took on even more importance after his assassination, as they stood out as part of his final ideas and legacy for racial change. This series of talks at the end of his life quickly became foundational to the nascent Black Power movement, with Malcolm assuming a position of "secular sainthood."[41]

Less master narrative than thematic essay, Malcolm X's speech both called for a better understanding of black history within the black community and served as a criticism of dominant white versions of black history. Here Malcolm's thoughts reframed African American history away from the American slave past toward one that emphasized the glories of ancient black civilizations. Malcolm also took issue with commemorative practices around black history. Although Negro History Week had been celebrated since 1926, Malcolm charged the uncritical acceptance of the event as indicative of white hegemony: "[D]uring this one week they drown us with propaganda about Negro history in Georgia and Mississippi and Alabama. Never do they take us back across the water, back home . . . so Negro History Week reminds us of this. It doesn't remind us of past achievements, it reminds us only of the achievements we made in the Western hemisphere under the tutelage of the white man."[42] This charge echoes a common refrain within NOI discourse, as both Malcolm X and Elijah Muhammad often referred to the "so-called Negro." They both felt that "Negro" indicated only African American experience within the national context of slavery and instead preferred to use "African." By extension, framing black history only within the U.S. context not only cut off significant parts of black experience, but also defined such only within the terms of enslavement.

For the purposes of cultural nationalism, the benefits of reframing black history away from American "Negro" experience and toward a universal history of black humanity were multiple. Attending to black history as a whole reclaimed a past that was capable of generating racial pride. As race categories proved tenuous and shifting across time and space, a part of Malcolm's historical project was to lay claim to peoples who were previously considered Caucasian or Asian. Malcolm claimed Sumerians, Moors, Egyptians, and peoples from the Indian subcontinent as "high civilizations" that predated European counterparts and provided a proud legacy for black Americans.[43] These civilizations gave white society traditions around clothing, food, architecture, universities and pedagogy, and other social achievements. One of his more interesting and original arguments was that the invention of gunpowder broke black cultural superiority and self-rule. Through this tool of domination, white slave traders created the institution of American slavery, eradicating the high moral fiber of West African societies through enslavement by what Malcolm considered the dregs of European society. "The founding fathers from England," he argued, "came from the dungeons of England, came from the prisons of England; they were prostitutes, they were murderers and thieves and liars."⁴⁴ From the pulpit, Malcolm X regularly entreated his congregation to proudly reclaim an African heritage that told a story of superiority over European historical narratives.

As Malcolm X provided a bridge between the earlier theological separatism of the Nation of Islam and the secular cultural focus of later Black Power projects, his contributions transitioned black collective memory from the cosmological focus of NOI's origin myths toward an emphasis on "the black race's historical greatness."⁴⁵ Malcolm charged Black Power activists with reclaiming historical authority, lamenting that history "has been so 'whitened' by the white man that even black professors have known little more than the most ignorant black man about the talents and rich civilizations and cultures of the black man of millenniums ago."⁴⁶ Although Malcolm would not live to realize his demand for the revision and authorship of black history, others would take up the charge in his name only a few years later.

A University for Black Power

From the beginning of the movement, Black Power activists identified intellectual production as an important site of struggle for the movement. Higher education quickly became a target for that very contest, and activists brought memory practices to bear on the development of Pan-Africanist liberal-arts-styled curriculum in the Malcolm X Liberation University. By the late 1960s, campuses witnessed a swelling of dissatisfaction among students and communities of color.⁴⁷

Newly formed black student associations at campuses across the country brought the activism of the Black Freedom movement into the classrooms, curricula, and campuses of both state and private institutions of higher education. Within this milieu of higher education activism, a group of students at Duke University in 1969 found themselves dissatisfied with the educational environment for black students, first protesting at Duke, then leaving the school to found an Afrocentric university. After occupying the Allen Administration Building on Duke's campus, fifty activists assembled an informal education group, calling their protest activities the Malcolm X Liberation University (MXLU), and provided the Black Power movement with its first separatist institution of higher education. While their counterparts at mainstream institutions shaped the future of humanistic and social scientific intellectual production, organizers and students at MXLU sought a more direct, community-based solution by establishing an institution of higher education that fully was by black Americans, for black Americans.[48]

Duke University's Afro-American Society had been working on black student grievances for three years in February 1969, when they asserted a demand for a black studies program from the university administration. Although Duke administrators initially agreed to start the program, they refused to cede to student demands for black student representation on the program's advisory board. Upon finding university administration unwilling to negotiate further, more than 50 percent of the black student population decided to withdraw from Duke and form a grassroots organization.[49] Local activist and community organizer Howard Fuller served as advisor to the group and helped organize a leadership committee, drawing from local student bodies as well as black educators from area colleges and leaders. Interest in the school blossomed, and organizers scrambled to build a full-time institution out of the informal organization.

The vision for MXLU first and foremost was to train young people for the task of liberating the black diaspora. Early planning efforts situated the university squarely within the movement for the equality of black people everywhere:

> The revolutionary struggle of Africans in this country has reached a level where there must be total understanding of the relationship between Black people in this country and the whole Pan-African liberation struggle.[50] . . . [We] must develop a Black Revolutionary Ideology, crystallize and project positive self-awareness for Black people, and create an educational process that builds and disseminates concepts and techniques to the Black community.[51]

The link that organizers made between U.S. racial and anticolonial struggles across the globe both sought to address systems of oppression that operated beyond national lines and rhetorically worked to create a transnational blackness that sought political self-determination in diverse geographic locations.

Although leaders made easy distinctions between mainstream, white-majority universities and the vision for MXLU, the relationship between the new school and existing HBCUs remained less clear. School

Knowledge of Self 55

documentation does not reveal the administration's views on their black mainstream counterparts. However, Fuller kept in his records another treatise on the need for a community-led institute of higher education, a booklet published by the Southern Student Organizing Committee (SSOC) entitled "Towards a Black University." A fairly radical affiliation of students from southern universities, SSOC members were, interestingly enough, mostly white. Although explicitly fighting against racial inequality and broad educational reform, SSOC members nonetheless embraced their southern background, using the Confederate flag as a backdrop for the icon of a white and black handshake as the organizational logo.[52] Within their preamble to the proposal, SSOC outlined a position that racial equality would absolutely "require radical changes in many of America's present institutions."[53] Throughout several paragraphs of the introduction to their proposal for a new Afrocentric model of education, SSOC charged HBCUs with perpetuating an intellectual ghetto and failing to address the material and class issues that black youth faced. Moreover, HBCUs mimicked white institutions, which failed to include a curriculum that engaged black culture in any meaningful way. Even more egregious to this group, HBCUs assumed the eradication of blackness, as they worked toward "the goal of the Negro college[, which] was to liquidate itself when the great day of Integration arrived and to resurrect itself as a white entity."[54] For SSOC, HBCUs' commitment to racial uplift whitewashed their cultural background as they trained black students to be more "white," thus failing to address the educational needs of their community. Though MXLU's founders did not publicly take such a strong stand against their black educational counterparts, the inclusion of this in Fuller's planning documents indicates, at minimum, interest in this criticism.

MXLU's organizers understood their work as a response to an educational crisis that was larger than the needs of the student body at Duke University. In the spring of 1969, after the first informal course had been organized under the new university's purview, a planning committee formed to engage broader representation from various state and private universities in North Carolina and sought to develop a full-fledged institution of higher education. Planners appealed to faculty at various institutions in April to participate in brainstorming sessions for the new Black Power university, raising questions "about the practice of teaching history, political science, sociology, psychology, economics and other non-scientific courses" as "the student—especially the Black student—finds it difficult to relate his total college experience to the problems of race and poverty in our society."⁵⁵ While structural racism within coursework was a major concern, equally troubling was the lack of connection between university education and attention to social problems within the black community, an educational challenge that planners intended to rectify.

In May 1969, representatives from several institutions of higher education came together for a three-day conference in Bricks, North Carolina, to plan curriculum, infrastructure, and policies for the new university. Participants from Bennett College, Duke University, East Carolina, Elizabeth City State University, North Carolina Agricultural and Technical University, North Carolina Community College, North Carolina State University, Shaw University, St. Augustine University, University of North Carolina at Greensboro, and Wake Forest University submitted recommendations for the institutional goals of MXLU in the context of what their home institutions failed to provide for black students. During planning sessions, participants hashed out ideas for leadership composition, social and curricular goals, and faculty and student recruitment.⁵⁶ Coming out of this event, an interim committee then oversaw the implementation of the session's recommendations into the new university, which opened a few months later. Committee members came from a variety of backgrounds, including Student Nonviolent Coordinating Committee (SNCC) activist Cleveland Sellers, university instructor T. D. Pawley, Cornell University staff member Faye Edwards, writer Robert Brown, activists Jim (Kwame) McDonald and Frank Williams, MXLU director Howard Fuller, Federal City College's black studies program director Jim Garrett, and eight students from supporting campuses.⁵⁷ Although international rhetoric and identity increasingly characterized the Black Power movement, local needs remained the first concern of MXLU's form and function at this point.

Organizers set out to design a curriculum that would, among other things, incorporate the historical struggles of the black community, weaving heritage throughout the curriculum. Out of sixty-two courses proposed by the planning conference, a vast majority tended toward engaging the past, with titles like African History, African Slave Trade, Study of the White Movement, Imperialism and Exploitation, Study of Minorities in the U.S., Study of Revolutionary Leaders, Afro-American History, various language and literature topics, and a number of courses on the history of black education, economics, and religion.⁵⁸ Planners imagined from the start that cultural heritage would be a key factor in creating social change through a transnational African identity, even as they critically engaged with a history of poverty, prejudice, and exploitation in the United States.

On an October Saturday morning in 1969, 3,500 community residents turned out to the Hillside Park in Durham, North Carolina, to celebrate the birth of an institution of black higher learning that shunned the earlier movement values of integration, preferring instead the goal of self-determination. The day-long celebration included a parade through Durham, a Pan-African festival, and a long list of speeches given by leading figures in the burgeoning Black Power movement. The program's highlight most certainly was the appearance of Betty Shabazz, widow of the slain leader for whom the college was named and the "First Lady of the Black Nation."[59] The speaker's platform also featured leadership from community institutions such as the television show *Black Journal*, the Center for Black Education, and sponsoring organization the Foundation for Community Development (FCD). Courtland Cox, executive director of FCD, used the opportunity not only to celebrate the achievement of MXLU's opening but also to call for even more efforts toward the development of Afrocentric education: "The fact is that this is just a start—where is our Black high school? The question now is where is the Black kindergarten? The question is where are the Black technical schools? Where are the Black agricultural schools? Where is every aspect that governs our mind from the cradle to the grave?"[60] More than just a singular community resource, administrators positioned MXLU as a beginning of a new era in black grassroots education.

Although MXLU opened with great fanfare and community support, the school's popularity wavered during the four years it operated. Less than a year after opening, President Fuller announced that the university would be moving fifty miles from Durham to Greensboro, North Carolina. Although Fuller explained the move as arising from a need for more spacious facilities, rumors circulated that the support from Durham's black community had begun to erode. By the third academic year, the *Greensboro Record* ran a four-part article depicting the school as a committed gathering of young Pan-African leaders. Although mostly sympathetic, the article ultimately suggested that the school served African needs more than African American needs, as it presented a tight-knit community of activists engaged in day-long training sessions that looked more like military training than a Socratic debate about lived struggle.[61] The separationist ethos of MXLU was also at odds with more integrationist energy in Greensboro, and thus the Afrocentric university failed to cultivate full community support in either location. Still, MXLU continued to educate students, strengthened in part by an alliance with the Federation of Pan-African Institutions, an organization of other Afrocentric schools ranging from elementary through higher education.[62]

Ultimately, the shuttering of MXLU in 1973 was due to an amalgam of issues financial and ideological. In a 1974 article, the *Black World* described the failure of MXLU as a casualty of long-standing debates in the Black Liberation movement between Marxist and Pan-Africanist visions for racial justice.[63] Certainly, a split in the larger Black Freedom movement emerged in the early 1970s, with groups like the Black Panthers addressing the needs of urban black Americans, and Pan-Africanists like Fuller and poet Amiri Baraka focusing more on international activism as a means to solving racial struggle on a global level. Like most groups working outside of mainstream institutions, MXLU also struggled during its entire duration to raise sufficient financial support. As a result, Fuller found himself primarily in the role of fundraiser, a marked change from the direct-action organizer he had been just a few years earlier. Although it might be tempting to dismiss MXLU as a transitory failure, the school served as a manifestation of the values of the Black Power movement and as a significant experiment in black separatist education. As MXLU administrators struggled to build and sustain a separatist, Pan-African university, other activists extended the Black Power movement to mainstream college campuses across the country, demanding and establishing black studies courses, faculty, and programs, eclipsing projects like MXLU.[64] The 1970s served as a fertile period of cultivation in both the streets and in the classroom for black historical narratives that supported self-determination and racial pride. By the 1980s, the "golden age of African American history" had arrived in the academy, as the field came to enjoy increasing legitimacy and vibrant intellectual production."[65]

Although MXLU was a short-lived institutional manifestation of collective memory for Black Power, it nonetheless reflects an important moment and ideology within the movement's engagement with black history. Envisioned as a learning space for the study of Pan-African heritage, planners realized the vision put forth by Malcolm X just before his death—a scholarly institution that would undo centuries of black history as written by white academics. By planning a curriculum that wove African heritage throughout its course offerings, MXLU advanced a memory practice that offered postsecondary training centered on black collective memory.

Black Panthers: No Understanding without Knowledge

Founded in Oakland, California, in 1966, the Black Panther Party (BPP) was a grassroots response to police brutality toward the city's black population. Both the party's political efforts and cultural interventions sought to address the social and cultural needs of the black urban poor. Even as the Panthers set out to distinguish themselves from other Black Liberation groups, the party echoed the long-standing tradition within the black community that underscored the importance of education.[66]

Like many of their predecessors and contemporaries in the Black Freedom struggle, the BPP embraced collective memory as a tool for building community, identity, and political momentum, deploying a wide array of memory practices throughout party activities and discourse. The Panthers wove historical narrative into the rhetoric of the party through speeches, through the party newspaper and literature, and through the establishment of community schools. Much like Elijah Muhammad, Malcolm X, Stokely Carmichael, and Howard Fuller, the Panthers understood themselves as having an imperative to teach community and party members, young and old, about the historical experiences of African Americans. Like the Nation of Islam, the BPP's historical narrative shifted over the course of the party's existence. During the early years, the party's history had a unique arc, emphasizing a materialist interpretation that placed slavery within the rise of global capitalism and emphasized four centuries of brutal economic exploitation. As a result, early instances of collective memory-building served the party's Marxist agenda and sought to fuel revolutionary energy. By the party's demise in the mid-1980s, however, both content and form had shifted toward increasingly liberal goals as it engaged more with public schooling and emphasized a humanistic love and racial pride, moving somewhat past its original revolutionary aims.

In all of their initiatives, the Panthers created a national political party and culture that allowed for local input. All BPP leaders received training on party background, including a curricular unit that answered, "What is the history of the Black man in America?"[67] Rather than narrating the founding specifics of the party, the training gave a crash course in world history, which argued that religious differences between Europeans and Sub-Saharan Africans led to the slave trade. According to training materials, imperialists had explained their civilizing mission to Sub-Saharan Africans on the basis of their pantheistic faith, missionaries having preached that Africans from the northern half of the continent were "good" Africans because they primarily were monotheistic.[68] Much like the Nation of Islam and MXLU, the historical narrative of the Panthers located the origins of the party within the context of pre-European contact in Africa. Their Marxist critique charged that imperialists "raped Africa economically," a violation that left the U.S. black population subjugated through an understanding of black history as the extraction of capital.[69] Although somewhat echoing other Afrocentric origin narratives, the Panthers distinguished their engagement with black history by framing it squarely within a Marxist interpretation of history.

Like their leadership counterparts in the Nation of Islam, Black Panther Party leaders also used the group's newspaper the *Black Panther* to cultivate collective memory in an effort to build membership and mobilize their communities. Party leadership used the newspaper as a pedagogical tool, regularly including articles on a wide variety of topics related to party ideology that wove in historical themes. The nature of the BPP as, in part, a defensive front against police brutality placed the organization in the legal spotlight much more than NOI, and a significant number of articles dealt with these legal struggles. Yet even within coverage on intense police repression and extreme corporal struggles, authors connected their analysis to history:

> The American Historian has a way of justifying this system by using Germany as the most vicious enemy against mankind; this is perhaps true for the people of Jewish descent. But when we really check this shit out, starting with the genocide of the Indians, the 50,000,000 Black people slaughtered by the oppressors when taken against their will at the point of guns, over 400 years ago, right here in America. Then reminding ourselves of the genocidal and imperialist war against the Vietnamese people, the burning of Black on the sacred cross of Christianity. Then it becomes easier to relate to the chieftains of fascism, imperialism, racism, and Bobby Seale's demand for his right to self-defense.[70]

Party membership certainly read *the Black Panther* to keep up on the party's political struggles, but they also received a revisionist history lesson as part of the context for their contemporary moment. In the above example, the paper's coverage of Seale's trial as one of the Chicago Eight, a group charged with conspiracy to incite a riot at the 1968 Democratic National Convention in Chicago, made an occasion to educate party membership on black history in the United States. Beyond presenting an oppositional history, the article's author also critiqued the failings of contemporary mainstream historical knowledge.

The party's raison d'etre was, in fact, very much based on history. Beyond the ten-point platform, the Black Panthers' guiding manifesto, the party understood itself as part of a longstanding tradition of black physical resistance:

> Throughout our history black men with guts and nerve have stood up to challenge this system with bullets and pamphlets: Men like David Walker who wrote an appeal to the slaves to organize and overthrow their masters by any means necessary, was murdered because his ideas were "dangerous." Henry Garnet who taught that submission to slavery was wrong and that black people should forget those who cautioned them about force and who said that the lord would provide. Garnet said that God helps those who help themselves. All the way down through our history men like Garnet have been ignored.[71]

The collective and often unremembered past offered inspiration, precedence, and mandate; by invoking narratives of resistance during slavery, Black Panthers intertwined their political work within a history of black resistance, naturalizing their agenda and legitimating their political project.

True to the party's commitment to serve the radicalized *Lumpenproletariat* (a Marxist term invoking the underclass of extreme poverty and criminality), the Panthers reached out to prison populations with adult education courses. Among these efforts, the party developed two significant programs at the medium-security prison in San Pedro, California, and the federal penitentiary in Leavenworth, Kansas. At both sites, activists from outside of the prison formed study groups with incarcerated men that echoed the nascent black studies programs popping up on college campuses across the country.[72]

Both study groups generated intellectually rigorous, in-depth group discussions based on assigned readings. While the San Pedro group brought African American history into a broader course on black culture, the Leavenworth Afro-American history study group undertook an impressive curricular plan that blended lectures, discussions, photographs, and film.

Many of the discussions focused on positioning black experience squarely within the political history of the United States: The Colonial Experience, Black Cargoes, The Peculiar Institution, The War to Make Men Free, Reconstruction: The Great Experiment, The Roots of the Northern Ghetto, The Great Migration. Other weeks focused on questions of resistance to white hegemony, including: The African Legacy, The Crusade Against Slavery, The Genesis of the Black Revolt, Washington vs. Du Bois, The Era of the New Negro, The Civil Rights Movement, and the James Baldwin book *The Fire Next Time*. The curriculum finished on more sociological themes: Myths and Realities, The Black Man in America, and The Quest for Identity.[73] In distinction from the Afrocentric narrative of the Nation of Islam, the narrative arc of the BPP course clearly put black experience front and center in American history via monographs of mainstream academic scholars such as John Hope Franklin, Basil Davidson, Kenneth Stampp, Martin Duberman, and C. Vann Woodward.[74] Although instructors framed the course as political education, the books read by prisoners could have mirrored a graduate course in one of the growing black studies programs emerging across the country.

One of the most significant ways that the Panthers complicated the militant stereotype and radical movement paradigm was through their survival programs. These inner-city community initiatives included provisions such as free breakfast for school-age children, senior assistance, clothing distribution, self-defense classes, health clinics, and sickle-cell anemia testing; through these projects, the party provided for the material needs of the communities as it worked to politically organize in a radical and revolutionary direction. Their programmatic efforts would not only produce new and parallel institutional forms but would also echo the larger movement's integration into liberal processes that would characterize the identity politics struggles of the 1980s and 1990s.

Arguably the most successful of the survival programs were the liberation schools. The BPP first established informal educational groups for children in 1969, teaching everything from basic literacy to black history. One party member explained, "we recognize that education is only relevant when it teaches the art of survival," a sentiment that echoed the influences of earlier educational theorists like Jean-Jacques Rousseau and John Dewey, with a bit of a Black Panther twist.[75] Like other contemporary alternative educators, the Panthers embraced the educational reform tradition of child-centered learning and pragmatic education while also engaging the unique needs of urban black children and the larger political goals of community self-determination. In 1969, the party opened schools in Oakland, San Francisco, and New York, projects that often served as extensions of the BPP's breakfast program.

More than just edifying diversions for youth lured in by free breakfast, party leadership viewed the schools as an important part of the party's work. The schools served as a manifestation of Point Five from the Panthers' Ten-Point Manifesto: "We want decent education for our people that exposes the true nature of this decadent American society. We want education that teaches us our true history and our role in the present-day society."[76] From the beginning, party leadership envisioned the schools as transmitters of black history and revolutionary culture. The most rudimentary schedule of the first school offered the following weekly plan: "Monday is Revolutionary History Day, Tuesday is Revolutionary Culture Day, Wednesday is Current Events Day, Thursday is Movie Day, and Friday is Field Trip Day."[77] For the BPP, creating a revolution required an education that encompassed both histories of oppression and resistance, as well as provided an engagement with present struggles and needs.

The success of and demand for the schools led the party to transform their initial and more informal educational efforts into a fully institutionalized education initiative. In 1970, BPP chief of staff David Hilliard developed the idea of a full-time liberation school, which would shortly thereafter open as the Intercommunal Youth Institute in 1971. School leadership changed its name to the Oakland Community School in 1973, and it ultimately became the longest lasting BPP school. The school was an immediate success, quickly reaching capacity at 150 full-time students and maintaining a wait-list, sometimes as large as four hundred names, among which were even yet-to-be-born children. The school, directed by Ericka Huggins and Donna Howell, provided students with a tuition-free residential education. Initially financed by the sale of the Black Panther newspaper, a funding committee called the Each One, Teach One Foundation organized in 1973 to cover tuition and expenses for the entire student body.[78] The majority of students were African Americans, yet the school population also included Mexican Americans, Asian Americans and even a small minority of Caucasians. Students wore black and blue uniforms, which mirrored adult BPP member uniforms. Majeedah Rahman, director of curriculum, saw the school as striving "to create a learning environment that promoted revolutionary thought, community service and cultural awareness."[79] She also recalled that she based some of the school's curriculum on the cultural and educational revolutions in China and Cuba from 1957 to 1976. This emphasis on multiculturalism distinguished BPP schools from their other nationalist counterparts like MXLU, as Panther schools first emphasized an international class awareness rather than Pan-Africanism.[80] Through the curriculum, Panther leadership transmitted the party's commitment to international solidarity with marginalized people of color across the world to the next generation.

The schools became not only a space for resisting mainstream schooling, but also an expression of a different philosophy of education. School leadership integrated black history into the entire curriculum. As minister of education and director of the Oakland Community School, Ericka Huggins vociferously embraced the intertwining of education and history, declaring "that my mind and heart immediately go back generations to the enslavement of Africans and I think of how brutal [conditions were if] we wanted or were found to be learning to read, to write, to think critically . . . and I know you know what happened if we did. . . . It hasn't changed much."[81] Huggins had a passionate interest in the role of education in marginalized communities from an early age. After growing up in Washington, D.C., she studied education at Lincoln University in Pennsylvania in 1967, at the same time that Charles Hamilton and Stokely Carmichael penned their movement-defining book *Black Power*.[82] At Lincoln, Huggins met her future husband John Huggins, with whom she headed to Los Angeles to join the Black Panther Party, shortly thereafter moving into leadership positions within the party. After John was gunned down in 1969 by members of a rival black nationalist group (the US organization), Ericka continued to serve as a leader within the party. During the next few years she founded the New Haven BPP chapter and liberation school, wrote for the party's newspaper, and moved back to the west coast to direct the Oakland Community School from 1973 to 1981.[83]

BPP educators gave much thoughtful attention to pedagogy in the schools. While curricular choices were very important, the promotion of critical, antihegemonic thinking was as important as the content of the lessons. To this end, at a ceremony dedicating a new iteration of the liberation schools, Bobby Seale echoed Howard Fuller's earlier sentiments on the role of education for the black community, this time with a focus on elementary and secondary education: "We're not here to teach our children WHAT to think, [sic] We're here to teach our children HOW to think." Central to their vision was the promotion of critical thinking about historical narratives.⁸⁴ Party Chairwoman Elaine Brown also intended that the school's work focus more on developing the next generation of revolutionary citizens than on the simple transmission of party ideology, that the school was "not a freedom school or a liberation school in the sense that we teach the children rhetoric," but rather BPP aimed to show "that Black, poor children are educable."⁸⁵ Administrators also recognized that their schooling efforts emerged in the broader context of growing progressive educational projects, such as the free school movement, yet they also made clear that the liberation schools were not simply an extension of the primarily white-led education reform movement; they shunned the term "alternative school" in favor of the more uplift-oriented "model school," intentionally refusing to further stigmatize their students, many of whom had been deemed substandard by mainstream schools.⁸⁶

Under the leadership of Huggins, the Oakland Community School offered not only an alternative to mainstream white-controlled schools but was also a manifestation of a community institution based on love and care.⁸⁷ The school was housed in the Oakland Community Center, a grassroots-funded hub of BPP community programs. Along with kindergarten through sixth-grade students, Oakland residents seeking medical care, senior services, adult education, and martial arts training frequented the center.⁸⁸ Huggins sought to cultivate an antiauthoritarian learning environment, using yoga and peer justice systems to deal with conflict and problem behaviors rather than the hierarchical authority found in most mainstream schools. Teachers also encouraged self-expression and utilized engaged, hands-on learning techniques at a time when such pedagogical approaches were anything but the norm for poor urban children.⁸⁹

Although teachers integrated black history throughout the curriculum year-round, the month of February provided special opportunities for the celebration of black historical achievements and struggles. Each year the school sponsored black history bees, calling them a "friendly competition about the history of our people from Olduvai Gorge to Jonestown."⁹⁰ During the month, the school's newsletter featured a Black History Month calendar, highlighting the birthdays of Frederick Douglass, Langston Hughes, Rosa Parks, and Huey P. Newton.⁹¹ The festivities culminated in 1980 with a special program called "Pass the Freedom, Please." During the performance, students dramatized George Washington giving medals to slaves who fought in the Revolutionary War, a dramatic activity that integrated blacks into the origins of the American nation. American history units further revised the national narrative, incorporating materials such as a research paper on black politicians during Reconstruction and a twentieth-century interracial working-class history unit including a satirical comic book on John D. Rockefeller and interviews with contemporary union representatives.[92]

Beyond curricular innovations, administrators nurtured an educational culture that immersed students in the collective memory denied them in mainstream American schools. Upon accepting their position, teachers were given a manual that outlined expectations for pedagogy, curriculum, and student-teacher interaction. In a section on the physical environment of the classroom, teachers were instructed to maintain a colorful bulletin board in their classrooms, where they were encouraged to use themes of black history. The school also maintained a calendar that observed numerous holidays, including national U.S. holidays as well as days that celebrated the history of marginalized communities like International Women's Day to recognize the historical struggles of women worldwide; May Day as a moment of remembrance for class struggles of the past; and Malcolm X's birthday as a connection to the larger Black Power movement and history of U.S. racial struggle.[93] The inclusion of such holidays reveals the school's commitment to liberatory politics focused on all marginalized people and reflected the Panthers' identification with other liberation struggles across time and space, and highlights the efforts of some of the party's membership to build coalitions across national lines.

Over the years, curriculum at the school became increasingly more standardized. By 1978, the reputation of the school and its successes had spread to larger educational circles and local school districts. Enthused by the attention drawn to the school, administrators sought to copyright the school's curriculum in an effort to maintain control over the its design.[94] As the school continued to flourish, leadership began to seek more creative ways to finance their endeavor. Federal funding for educational initiatives had increased over the previous decade, as part of President Johnson's Great Society programs, and by 1982, the Panthers had become significantly more hospitable to partnerships with the government. As a result, administrators undertook the significant task of bringing the school's curricular structure in line with California state standards. This initiative provided school administrators with an opportunity to design a more comprehensive history including "the history of the chattel slavery of blacks as well as the slave-like exploitation of Spanish-speaking peoples and Asians in the U.S. [and] the migration of Native Americans," as well as "Harriet Tubman and Julius Caesar; Ethiopia and the British Empire; China before and after 1949 and France before and after 1789."[95] This topical list reflected both an identification with other marginalized peoples and the creation of a historical narrative that was organized around political oppression and revolution. Administrators also revamped the social science lesson plans, with geography units containing assignments to study housing needs in Oakland, and world studies lessons that brought in guest speakers on land reform in Cuba and engaged students in an examination of the origins of the caste system worldwide.[96]

In American history, planners divided the curriculum into three periods: Revolution through 1873; Imperialism and War: 1873–1938; and War, Suspicion, and Rebellion: 1932–1968. Antebellum and Reconstruction gave students "the opportunity to hold a mock debate between the Abolitionists and slave owners," while the Imperialism unit included the reading of "Mighty Rock," a text that satirized the Rockefeller family.[97] Here too the curriculum strayed from traditional U.S. periodization, emphasizing the contradictions between the Revolution, slavery, and Reconstruction through the first period (it is particularly noteworthy that Reconstruction's rise and fall is included here); the growth of the United States as a world power in the second; and subversion and repression in the third. The most contemporary unit engaged an array of Panther political causes and included a visit to a union hall, a tour of a Japanese American concentration camp, and listening to personal accounts of Civil Rights movement activists. With this rich historical curriculum, the school continued to educate party members' children until 1982, when it closed, the final remaining program of the BPP.

The significance of the BPP's educational initiatives lay in the impact it had on the ownership of black history within the movement and community. The Black Panther Party used a wide variety of memory practices, from articles in *the Black Panther* to the development and evolution of the liberation schools, practices that echoed their political goals of transforming the cultural and economic realities of African Americans through a political agenda that linked the struggles of marginalized people and rejected capitalism and imperialism. Like their movement counterparts in the Nation of Islam and Malcolm X Liberation University, BPP leaders began with a strong commitment to radical change and increasingly embraced over time a more liberal agenda of humanistic inclusion.

Although historians have traditionally demarcated the Civil Rights and Black Power movements along liberal and radical lines, perhaps it is more useful to focus on the various approaches to the question of racial difference, especially as manifested in the cultural front of the movements. Civil Rights leaders largely sought racial equality through the goal of removing social, legal, and cultural differences between whites and blacks. While Civil Rights groups generally sought to create significant change through a nonviolent reform of mainstream American society, at times they embraced forms of self-defense that many considered "violent" while also seeking to create new community-controlled institutional forms. Black Power activism proved equally complex, as activists strove for various kinds of separatism but also engaged existing institutional forms. Increasingly, activists framed their work within a rhetoric of racial pride rather than one that was simply critical of mainstream American society, a tactic that is perfectly compatible with political liberalism.

Conclusion

The Black Power movement, as a whole, reframed the struggle for racial change away from a demand for social equality and integration toward a forceful demand for political and cultural autonomy. Activists' calls for "self-determination" and "revolutionary struggle" took precedence over the desire to combat racism within existing institutions and legal structures.[98] Stokely Carmichael's battle cry for Black Power as a more autonomous direction for the Black Freedom movement sought the unification of all black people in the United States; a meaningful engagement with black heritage; and the building of a clear sense of community united in political, cultural, and economic goals.[99] At the core of this project was the transformation of black identity, and as a result, activists both sought to change the schooling of black students and to create more informal kinds of adult education through movement newspapers and community programs. While these initiatives emphasized a political identity that was more separatist than earlier manifestations in the Black Freedom movement, the emphasis on community-led education was a century-old tradition in black struggles for equality.[100]

Although these three institutional examples illuminate some of the more significant ways in which Black Power activists used collective memory as a tool for cultural nationalism and black autonomy, each of these institutions varied significantly from one another in terms of political visions and tactics. The Nation of Islam was in many ways politically conservative, in terms of its gender politics and economic/class views. The organization also relied on a very narrow model of leadership that was dependent upon charisma in the pursuit of separatist racial uplift. The leadership of Malcolm X Liberation University envisioned social change through cultural nationalism that reclaimed African traditions, identities, and values, while in practice sometimes giving less attention to the lived local struggle of black Americans. The Black Panther Party engaged highly disenfranchised and politically repressed working-class urban blacks in a Marxist program of social and economic revolution that sought to liberate all working peoples.[101] While all three deployed collective memory to support the movement's political goals, their respective memory practices produced highly varied programs and curricula.

Each of the three examples also differs from each other in terms of the narratives constructed. The Nation of Islam broke sharply away from contemporary black historiographical traditions by diminishing the significance of the legacy of American enslavement and by crafting myth and narrative to explain a collective African past that also foreshadowed their intended future. Later collective memory activism arising out of the Student Nonviolent Coordinating Committee (SNCC) and the Black Panther Party consciously incorporated the history of slavery while enriching it with other useful narratives of resistance and solidarity among other marginalized groups. The Malcolm X Liberation University balanced a historical narrative of slavery and exploitation with a Pan-Africanist cultural heritage in order to build racial pride. Likewise, the Black Panther liberation schools taught a Marxist version of black American history while connecting that experience with other marginalized groups. Across all of these examples, Black Power activists developed parallel institutional structures to promote memory practices that refuted dominant historical narratives in favor of narratives that supported cultural and political sovereignty for black Americans.

Helaine Victoria Press postcard featuring Gladys Bentley, a Harlem Renaissance-era musician. The original caption, penned by gay historian Eric Garber, reads: "The talented pianist and blues singer, was one of the most notorious and successful Black lesbians in the U.S. during the 1920s and 1930s. She performed at the fanciest New York nightclubs, had an active recording career, and socialized among trendsetters and visiting European notables. Born in Philadelphia, Bentley ran away from home as a teenager. Like many African-Americans of her generation, she traveled north to Harlem. She survived by playing piano and by inventing and singing scandalous lyrics to the tunes of popular melodies. For many years Bentley headlined at Harry Hansberry's Clam House, where she performed in a white tuxedo and top hat. Poet Langston Hughes noted that Bentley 'was something worth discovering in those days.' Throughout the 1930s Bentley continued her career, cultivating a large lesbian and gay following, but the repressive McCarthy Era forced her to 'conform' and deny her lesbianism. Despite this she never regained her former popularity." Postcard image courtesy of Helaine Victoria Press, Inc.

CHAPTER 3

A History of One's Own

Feminist Collective Memory in the Second-Wave Women's Movement

> The volumes which record the history of the human race are filled with the deeds and the words of great men. . . . [T]he Twentieth Century Woman . . . questions the completeness of the story.
>
> —Mary Ritter Beard

Like their counterparts in the Civil Rights and Black Power movements in the 1950s, 1960s, and 1970s, second-wave feminists crafted a community history that supported their vision for justice focused on gender equality. Their political struggle also was marked by a desire to construct a new, shared identity that was self-defined within their own community of womanhood. For second-wave feminists, a new historical narrative served as legitimation and as a tool of movement cohesion. Community historians looked to the past for narratives of women who had realized personal success, resisted patriarchal limitations, and worked for women's equality; these stories were then used to develop feminist consciousness and activism as they sought to transform gender roles in both public and private contexts.

As Black Freedom movement collective memory activists built institutions to educate their communities outside of mainstream institutions, Women's Liberation activists worked more informally, often germinating women's history projects within existing arts and educational institutions to make "women's work, movements, families, and loves visible to an indifferent present."[1] Women's Liberation collective memory projects tended to emerge when feminists interacted with mainstream institutions and found themselves frustrated with existing representations of women's history.

As a result, activists focused more on new research and collecting initiatives than their Civil Rights or Black Power counterparts. When activists founded separatist history projects such as women-only community archives, the organizations were generally short-lived, and their collections were subsequently integrated into mainstream repositories.

At the level of historical narrative, activists sought to reframe women's history as public, a revisionist effort that resisted the confinement of women's historical experiences to home and family. Community historians embraced the ideal of universal womanhood, crafting a historical category that was transnational and spanned economic class. Although they were often white and middle-class, collective memory activists within the women's movement often made efforts to transcend their privilege to craft a past that attempted to account for race, class, and ethnicity while breaking these social divisions in favor of promoting the primary identity of womanhood. So, although these activists assumed the colorblind tenets of the larger movement that women of color rightly challenged, many community history activists nonetheless made at least some efforts to be inclusive and acknowledge cultural difference in their work.

This chapter traverses collective memory practices put forth by a variety of activists and organizations. Women's Liberation activists collected historical documents, developed research methods for locating sources in traditional archives, and crafted narratives in a wide variety of media to provide the larger movement with a community history and a shared identity. Beginning with the movement-building process of consciousness raising, activists used projects like the Women's Herstory Library, Judy Chicago's *The Dinner Party* art installation, Helaine Victoria Press's historical postcards, and the Summer Institute on Women's History to develop memory practices that suited feminists' need for a proud past through both women's separatist projects and interventions in mainstream organizations.

The Seeds of Collective Memory in the Women's Movement

An organized desire for women's history emerged at the end of the first wave of the women's movement, sparked primarily by activist scholars working within the academy. In the early twentieth century, few women historians held academic jobs. Most women who managed to secure academic appointments felt professionally marginalized and were often disregarded by their male counterparts as serious colleagues. In response to what several women perceived as a hostile environment at the American Historical Association's annual meetings, Louise Fargo Brown and Louise Ropes Loomis founded the Berkshire Conference of Women Historians in 1930.[2] Loomis and Brown cultivated a professional association where women could form supportive friendships within the profession. This organization would go on to figure significantly not only in the establishment of women's studies within the academy, but also in nurturing the work of women's and Gay Liberation community historians.

Women's historians working in the early twentieth century recognized that a lack of archival sources severely constrained research and writing on women's historical experience. Emerging from first-wave feminism's successes in 1935, historian and archivist Mary Ritter Beard founded the World Center for Women's Archives in New York City. Supported by international suffrage activist Rosika Schwimmer, American feminist Alice Paul, First Lady Eleanor Roosevelt, and artist Georgia O'Keefe, Beard initially envisioned an archival repository as well as a university that would institutionalize women's history. Financial difficulties continually plagued the Depression-era project, and by 1940 the organization folded. Archives chairwoman, feminist author, and activist Inez Haynes Irwin entreated supporters to view women's history as integral to the larger movement and to uphold the archive's mission, suggesting that "every member of your Board and of the organization itself is a potential World Center for Women's Archives."[3] Upon the center's closure, the holdings were either returned to their donors or transferred to other appropriate archives. The libraries of several women's colleges agreed to maintain portions of the collections, including Wellesley, Barnard, and Radcliffe Colleges.[4] As significant as the development of such collections were to the emergence of women's history, this work reinforced a kind of top-down institutional organizing that tended toward the exclusive representation of elite white women. During the 1940s, women's college administrations continued pathbreaking yet limited preservation work, establishing the Sophia Smith Collection at Smith College in 1942 and the Arthur and Elizabeth Schlesinger Library at Radcliffe College in 1943.[5]

In the late 1960s, women's history and collective memory efforts resurfaced as part of the second wave of feminist activism. In the wake of the newly emergent collective political consciousness fueled in part by

Betty Friedan's *The Feminine Mystique,* women working in the early part the Women's Liberation movement began to take up the recently developed practice of consciousness raising (CR). Arising out of the mandate embraced by early radical feminists that asserted "the personal is political," CR became a tool for connecting individual experiences of depression, frustration, listlessness, and a lack of agency to larger social processes found in patriarchal societies. Women who participated in the process generally discovered that experiences they had previously understood as singular to them were often shared by many other women. CR participants often made connections to their mothers' or maternal ancestors' experiences, a connection that strengthened the idea of universal womanhood.[6] In 1967, a group of women formed the New York Radical Women, adapting a form of small group critical discussions from radical left organizations, who had themselves adapted such techniques from the Maoist practice of "speaking bitterness."[7] First calling them "rap sessions" or "bitch sessions," these early radical feminists brought the burgeoning practice to Chicago for the first national Women's Liberation Conference in November of 1968, where the practice spread to other local groups.[8]

Early guides to CR encouraged an informal connection between the personal and the collective past. In the 1973 *Women's Fate: Raps from a Feminist Consciousness-Raising Group,* women exploring CR were told that the practice "serves as an anvil for women to beat out a lifetime of ingrained hostility men have encouraged them to feel for each other. In small groups, the myth of the feminine bitch is destroyed. Women learn their history. They learn that *female is good* [emphasis in original]."[9] For these early proponents of CR, women's historical experience was key to moving beyond simply sharing their frustrations with each other and toward imagining movement action. Early radical feminist and Redstockings Collective member Kathie Sarachild wrote an outline for the first national Women's Liberation Conference, underscoring the importance of "discussing possible methods of struggle in a historical context."[10] For early radical feminists, history could provide not only legitimacy and explanations for women's oppression but also a tool for women to resist patriarchy. Although CR did not always explicitly encourage connection to women's history, the sense of long-term oppression that emerged from such discussions came from a place of personal history and often resulted in a sense of a shared historical experience that created space for the emergence of more grassroots historical projects. The collective identity produced by CR often moved participants from the experience of a group catharsis to a desire for further knowledge, inspiring reading groups devoted to topics such as women's history and feminist political theory.

Women in the movement were torn over the embrace of CR. This division remained throughout the 1970s as activists debated what the primary work of feminism was. Many felt that CR sessions did nothing to further the political goals of the women's movement; some even worried that such efforts detracted from action.[11] The New York Radical Women eventually split in part over the issue of CR, with the emergent Redstockings group claiming the CR torch.[12] This tension reflects a larger anxiety over the relationship between expressly "political" and the more nebulous "cultural" work, as some felt that the movement work needed to first attend to collective social issues like equal pay and access to abortion rather than the interior experiences of women. In what historian Alice Echols refers to as "the Politico-Feminist Fracture," early radical feminists struggled over the nature of the movement: was it to be a separatist space for activism led by identity work or was it to be a gender-conscious wing of the New Left?[13] Although the larger women's movement never came to full consensus on this issue, many groups began to veer toward the identity-based agenda. In the mid-1970s, leadership of the National Organization for Women (NOW) took an interest in consciousness raising as a tool for growing the movement and used it in recruiting new NOW members.[14] As CR's role in the Women's Liberation movement shifted from memory practice to organizational recruitment tool, women's desire for a shared history extended to other projects within the movement.

Although the practice of consciousness raising and the planting of seeds of desire for women's history were key activities for the Redstockings Collective, leaders of the group also rhetorically engaged women's history to ground their contemporary political work in a tradition of women's resistance. In one example, Kathie Sarachild invoked the classic *History of Woman Suffrage* to inspire and direct contemporary feminist struggles. Written by Elizabeth Cady Stanton, Susan B. Anthony, and Matilda Joslyn Gage, *History of Woman Suffrage* was a six-volume project first conceived of in 1881 and published in 1922 on the first wave of the feminist movement. Sarachild argued that first-wave feminists used history in movement-building and that they understood history "as movement, as development, as continuing struggle; a history of the present as well as the past—for the future . . . a history by the activists, those who write history to change history."[15] It is striking that second-wave activists like Sarachild not only placed themselves in a tradition of women's activism, but also in a tradition of community history-making. As Sarachild and many others believed, the task for the next generation of feminists was not only to generate social change but also to preserve the historical record for future generations.

As feminist consciousness and organizational development exploded in the late 1960s and early 1970s, the appetite for women's history also rapidly expanded across the movement. Cultural activists responded with a variety of projects and initiatives that told women's historical narratives in a variety of forms. Feminists undertook archival, fine art, pop culture, community education, and broad curricular projects to build a collective memory that would serve the political goals of second-wave feminism and reinforce the values of universal womanhood.

An Archival Basis for Women's History

Perhaps the first feminist to envision a major historical project arising out of Women's Liberation was a young woman, Laura X, who had found herself infuriated in 1969 with a male academic historian's dismissal of women's history.[16] Laura had asked her professor at the University of California at Berkeley to develop a course exploring women's historical experiences, to which he replied with a scornful dismissal that one could hardly find sufficient content to fill an entire semester. In response, Laura X and a few friends set out to prove him wrong, researching and writing a pamphlet entitled "Women in World History." Laura's historical curiosity had been first piqued on International Women's Day in 1968 during a screening of *The End of St. Petersburg,* a film that depicted a women's demonstration during the Russian Revolution.[17] Laura's excitement about the film reflected a new universal experience of womanhood embraced by second-wave feminism, one that imagined gender oppression as categorical struggle that transcended race, nationality, and historical era. At the same time, Black Power activists were exploring similar ideas around identity and nationhood, and the film fueled Laura's growing commitment to a transnational movement of women that paralleled that of Black Nationalism.

After publication of the brochure, Laura X set out to collect anything she could find on women's history, as well as actively documenting the movement of which she herself was a part. Finding a deluge rather than a dearth of information in the university library, she founded the Women's Herstory Library in Berkeley, California, as a women's separatist cultural organization to collect and preserve sources on women's history. Using her own inheritance and home to fund and house the rapidly growing collections, Laura and a growing group of volunteers broadly collected materials on women's historical and contemporary experiences and political resistance. Striving to "get [women's history] back and record herstory in progress," the library sought not only to collect women's historical materials, but also to right historical wrongs like "the woman who invented the cotton gin and got ripped off by Eli Whitney."[18] Although she sought to collect both traditional archival materials and documents from the blossoming second wave, she also included such unusual archival objects as photos of graffiti traces, old books on "tokology" and midwifery, and graduation books, anticipating the cultural turn that the larger movement and the interpretations of women's history would shortly take.[19]

Laura X's experience with her male professor who scoffed at the idea of women's history fueled the development of an archive that would provide the raw material for scholarly and popular historians alike. Although there were a number of archives and libraries in the northeastern region, the western portion of the United States lacked any such collection, and this group of Bay Area feminists threw themselves into the work of developing collections and documenting the new movement. By January 1970, less than a year after the organization's founding, the Women's History Research Center (WHRC) compiled and published a report on its developing collections. Thirteen pages of typewritten notes divided the collection topically by subjects such as politics, art, sciences, and professions and further organized the materials according to era and region, specifically identifying thirty countries across Asia, Europe, North America, and South America. WHRC staff concluded the guide with an amended quotation from the Declaration of Sentiments, a document produced by the Seneca Falls Convention in 1848, reminding second-wave feminists that "the history of mankind IS A HISTORY OF REPEATED INJURIES AND USURPATIONS ON THE PART OF MAN TOWARD WOMAN, HAVING IN DIRECT OBJECT THE ESTABLISHMENT OF AN ABSOLUTE

TYRANNY OVER HER. . . . P.S. 1/27/70 THE ONLY FUTURE IS REVOLUTIONARY FEMINISM [emphasis in the original]"[20] For Laura X and her colleagues, not only was the construction of women's historical knowledge an important form of activism, but they also located their historical work within the legacy of past generations of feminists.[21]

As the collections at WHRC rapidly expanded, the larger movement's desire for women's historical resources became increasingly evident through the growing number of research requests made to the organization. In only a few short years, WHRC amassed archives of all known Women's Liberation periodicals, a significant law library, a compendium on women in the arts, materials on women and health, a women's film guide, books, and topical files, as well as serving as a reference for other small press and ephemeral publications, resources that were eagerly used by feminists.[22] As word of the collection spread, staff increasingly struggled to keep up with research request correspondence, a flurry of inquiries that illustrated the increasingly popular desire for women's history within the movement.[23]

Women from all across the country corresponded with WHRC volunteers on a wide variety of topics, reflecting the diverse interests and issues on the minds of movement participants. Although WHRC served as a full repository of information on women, both contemporary and historical, many of the research requests focused on historic inquiries. Some were broad queries on women's past experiences, such as women in World War I, women's organizations in Atlanta between 1890 and 1920, American women during the Depression, New Jersey women in history, nineteenth-century British women, and working women in Philadelphia from 1900 to 1940. Many of the inquiries sought to recognize individual women activists and early feminists, such as Charlotte Perkins Gilman, Sylvia Plath, Mary Wollstonecraft, the Grimke Sisters, and Susan B. Anthony and the suffragists. Others reflected the values of second-wave feminism, looking for resources on women in experimental and utopian living communities of the nineteenth century, Mexican American women, and Women's Liberation in the 1940s (a rather ahistorical request that nonetheless testified to a desire for movement heritage and ancestry). Still others sought to uncover earlier women in unexpected places and social roles that defied their contemporary gender norms, such as women mystics, preachers, and witches in the seventeenth century, U.S. women who have declared for the presidency, women and war from 1607 to the present, and women in early American printing. Movement participants also drew upon the resources of WHRC to add historical depth to contemporary political issues, inquiring on a wide array of professional topics like working women, prostitution, women and politics, women in data-processing careers, women in psychology, and discrimination against women in college admissions. Researchers inquired about a variety of personal topics, such as mental health, child custody and lesbian mothers, problems of old women, rape, self-esteem, and lesbianism. Still others sought out answers to cultural and representational issues such as sexism in children's literature, advertising and women consumers, cultural differences in women of different countries, the sociology of the middle-class women's movement, and the Swedish Women's Liberation movement.[24]

Although the library primarily collected print materials, staff also endeavored to preserve other kinds of artifacts. Judy Busch, a musician who approached Laura about compiling women's folk songs after finding only a few in WHRC's "oral herstory" collection, believed that song was a particular kind of women's memory practice that transcended generations and cultures.[25] The coining of the term "herstory"—a term that rapidly proliferated and will emerge in debates discussed in the chapter on the Lesbian Liberation movement—echoed this desire to carve out a historical narrative that was squarely focused on women's experiences. Indeed, Busch believed that women transmitted historical experiences in less formal ways "because we've been denied education and writing materials for so long . . . the only way our story has been carried through time is via songs, 'wives tales,' lullabies and what has 'previously been slandered as gossip.'"[26] Working together, Laura and Busch collected songs and graphics penned by women, and they published their findings in a collection they called the "hermenal," continuing a playful tradition of feminizing nouns that were masculine-sounding, if not exclusively denotative of men.

During its relatively short life span, the Women's History Research Center institutionalized the desire within the Women's Liberation movement for grassroots ownership of movement memory. From 1968 to 1971, WHRC blossomed out of Laura X's personal collection, growing into a substantial community resource. First located in Laura's home in Berkeley, WHRC shortly expanded to employ a full-time staff that worked to continue developing the collection. By 1972, Laura's own funds had run out, and the organization came to rely on volunteer labor and work-study students from local colleges. As center leadership began to struggle to raise funds, Laura and others urged other women's organizations to collect and organize historical materials within their own communities, extending the collecting mission outward into the larger movement. WHRC staff especially encouraged others to collect newsletters, as they found them to be "very special historical documents. They frequently reflect the arguments which six months to a year later become national task force issues."[27] This urging underscored that staff were actively concerned about preserving their own historic moment as well as documenting the grassroots origins of major policy shifts. Much like earlier efforts to institutionalize women's history within academic libraries, WHRC staff sought to preserve and document women's historical experiences. Yet their desire to locate those materials in a grassroots archival organization collapsed under the weight of financial difficulties and small-organization challenges. Still, their efforts worked to instill in feminists the historicity of their own work as well as inspiring a diffuse commitment to document the movement as a whole.

A Cultural History of One's Own

While some feminists amassed historical documents as an archival basis for women's history, others claimed cultural space within male-dominated art museums and galleries, bringing women's collective memory into mainstream cultural institutions. In the early 1970s, visual artist Judy Chicago dedicated her own practice to the exploration of women's history. Having studied studio arts at UCLA where she earned BA and MA degrees, Chicago developed a feminist art program at California State University at Fresno in 1970, which sought to teach art skills to young women while simultaneously building feminist consciousness. Between 1974 and 1979, Chicago led the development of a collaborative art project called *The Dinner Party*, which sought to provide a master narrative of world history focused solely on women. A massive multimedia installation featuring a triangular-shaped table with thirty-nine place settings, *The Dinner Party* served as a feminist response to the all-male environment depicted in Leonardo da Vinci's iconic painting, *The Last Supper*. Chicago had first conceived of the piece as a more modest wall installation entitled *Twenty-five Women Who Were Eaten Alive by History*, but found herself enthralled by the expanse of women's historical narratives and shifted the plan to the much more dramatic oversized dining table. The triangular motif represented for Chicago a structure that was more feminine and egalitarian; as no one individual could be placed at the head of the table, Chicago selected the triangular shape to reflect the feminist goal of dismantling hierarchical structure.[28] Although historians have begun to locate Chicago's work among other significant outcomes of cultural feminism, the significance of *The Dinner Party* as a tool for collective memory is only now emerging.[29]

The Dinner Party told a revisionist human history, which placed women at the center of the narrative and as the primary agents of change. Although the idea originated with Chicago, hundreds of volunteers took part in the research, production, and promotional stages of the project. The project emerged from the ideological groundwork of the early portion of the second-wave movement: that patriarchal society oppressed every woman and that each had an intimate and personal connection to collective liberation. Similarly, Chicago embraced a collectivist process for both the research and production of the installation, relying on an army of volunteer researchers to pour through male-dominated historical texts to pluck out women figures who lurked in the background. This effort reflected movement values, as Chicago cultivated a separatist arts space that attempted to embrace the antihierarchical ethos of the movement. Set in a triangular shape, the dining room setting harkened to women's space of the hearth and home, and the place setting motif allowed Chicago to elevate feminine crafting heritage into fine art through ceramics and embroidery.

Like other researchers who struggled to find marginalized historical experiences in mainstream literature and archives, Chicago and her volunteers were forced to use creativity and rigor to research *The Dinner Party*. In the introduction to *The Dinner Party: A Bibliography*, she detailed the process by which women's history shifted from a personal interest to a massive educational and artistic project:

> I began to do research in women's history in the late 1960's in an effort to see myself in the context of women's rather than men's achievements. Discovering the enormous amount of information that existed about women, their work, and their lives, and realizing the potential power of that information started me on the journey which eventually led to the creation of The Dinner Party. Headed by Ann Isolde, team members slowly learned to "read through" the sexist biases of history which disguised, rather than illuminated, women's accomplishments.[30]

Chicago argued that dominant historical narratives obscured and distorted women's historical social roles and contributions, an oversight she wished to rectify. Chicago's own "reading against the grain" of historical sources paralleled the growth of social history in the academy, as scholars who wished to recuperate common voices began to critically engage with archives that had traditionally favored the powerful. Researchers' notes also reveal an engagement with other scholarly research, connecting their work to historical writing in diverse publications such as *Music Journal, the New Yorker, Ms., and the Science and Society Journal*, as well as with scholarly monographs.[31]

More than twenty volunteers spent over two years amassing research notes on the themes engaged by the installation. Massive file drawers of index cards detailed the lives of a wide array of artists, physicians and nurses, explorers, lawyers and judges, painters, playwrights, political figures, social reformers, philanthropists, educators, journalists, authors and orators, religious figures, historians, entertainers, athletes, natural and social scientists, and even "outlaws."[32] From this massive body of candidates, the research team selected thirty-nine individual women, each to be featured with her own place setting. Additionally, tiles naming 999 other notable women adorned the floor of the installation.

Promotional materials for the installation detailed the research and nomination methods deployed by Chicago and her twenty plus volunteers during two years of research:

> Ultimately over three thousand women were researched and then we began to make choices based on three criteria: 1) Did the women [*sic*] make a significant contribution to society? 2) Did she attempt to improve conditions for women? 3) Did her life illuminate an aspect of women's experience or provide a role model for the future? We selected 999 women who, we believed, represented a range of nationalities, experiences, and contributions. Our choices were limited by language barriers, fragmented information, and our own inexperience and biases. Our intention, however, was not to define women's history, but to symbolize it—to say that there have been many women who have done many things, and they deserve to be known.[33]

Chicago's language reveals a sophisticated scholarly approach to her work, including critical engagement with both her own research bias and the limited source materials that skewed her work toward European heritage. Chicago was in part also responding to the growing voices of feminists of color who charged the larger movement with failing to engage race. As a popular historian, Chicago's concern with broadly representing women's experience reveals both the imagined universal womanhood that was the project of cultural feminism and the progressiveness of her work at a point in the women's movement in which many white middle-class feminists failed to engage meaningfully with racial issues.³⁴ *The Dinner Party*'s main place settings included nonwhite female figures such as the Hindu goddess Kali, the Egyptian Pharaoh Hatshepsut, a Shoshone diplomat, explorer Sacagawea, and freedwoman abolitionist Sojourner Truth. Ceramic floor tiles also featured a number of figures from South and Central America, although African and Asian women remained somewhat underrepresented. Although *The Dinner Party* did not fully represent the totality of global women's historical experiences, Chicago's attention to the matter is noteworthy for her sensitivity toward this issue and her efforts to include a wider representation of women's history at a time when many academic historians operated with little concern for Eurocentric biases.³⁵

The dining room table in the installation provided the viewer with a structured account of women's history from Western antiquity to the present. Each side of the table presented thirteen women who fleshed out Chicago's periodization—*From Prehistory to the Roman Empire; From the Beginnings of Christianity to the Reformation;* and *From the American to the Women's Revolution*. In the first section, visitors learned about several goddess figures, including an unnamed primordial deity and Ishtar, the Assyrian fertility goddess, moving through time to the Greek scholar Hypatia. The second era included the canonized St. Bridget from Sweden, the medieval physician Trotula of Salerno, and the Italian Baroque painter Artemisia Gentileschi. The modern period spanned from early American settler and theologian Anne Hutchinson and British writer Mary Wollstonecraft to painter Georgia O'Keefe and writer Virginia Woolf. Likewise, the 999 tiles that decorated the floor enumerated Aztec goddesses, American anarchists, and Finnish epic heroines. Taken as a whole, the installation told a grand and seamless, if uncomplicated, narrative of the dawn of humanity through the inevitable conclusion of Western women's enlightenment and liberation.

Visitors responded to *The Dinner Party* with a variety of emotions, ranging from joy and exuberance to frustration and rage. Hundreds of notes of gratitude to Chicago and her team reflect how the installation positioned visitors' sense of self within a larger historical context. One visitor described the exhibit as offering "a sense of belonging—finally—to a dynamic, honorable group. There is a history; I don't exist in a vacuum."[36] But the sense of continuity that inspired some women provoked in others anger and frustration that their history had been denied for so long: "Why did it take so long? Why did we have to unearth these women buried and obliterated? Why do the power-holders even now try to keep such beauty and such strength and such worth invisible, denied?"[37] Still others found themselves motivated by the installation to further pursue women's history, as two visitors formed a study group to connect to their "own history—a sense of self, our place, and validation."[38] Visitors also responded to the exhibit with a desire for as many women as possible to see the project. Grassroots groups sprung up in cities across the country to organize local exhibitions of the event, often including ancillary programming and conferences on women's history as part of the opening festivities.[39]

The Dinner Party proved to be a highly effective instrument of a useable past, as educators relied on it as a text from which to teach women's history. William Monter, professor of history at Northwestern University, required forty of his undergrads to attend *The Dinner Party* when it was exhibited in Chicago. Students selected two figures from the place settings and two figures from the center tiles, writing on their impressions and the impact the installation had on them. Many students were profoundly moved by their encounter with the installation, recounting "an emotional mix of sadness, proudness, and happiness."[40] In another instance, a California high school teacher incorporated *The Dinner Party* into her curriculum with ninth-grade students, in which teens were required to write a "toast" to a female historical figure of their choosing. Each student researched one of the exhibit's featured women, then created an individualized table setting as a tribute to the figure. As part of their final presentations, students recorded their commemorative speeches and played them during a simulated banquet dinner. As one student raised her glass to Mildred "Babe" Didrikson Zaharias, she offered a heartfelt "thank you for the hopes, memories and dreams" that Didrikson's story had inspired.[41] For young women coming of age in the late 1970s and early 1980s, female role models were a critical tool in creating a new consciousness and identity for the next generation, a generation that second-wave activists envisioned as populated with self-possessed, fully empowered women.

Judy Chicago relied not only on empirical work to develop a connection to the past, but also engaged myth to further link feminist consciousness with a sense of a shared heritage in her project that followed *The Dinner Party*. Drawing on the material amassed by her volunteer research team, Chicago drafted an alternative history, again placing women at the forefront of human evolution. The draft became the content for an illuminated manuscript she titled *Revelations of the Goddess*. In her cosmology, the planets emerged from an abyss through a vaguely birth-like process that produced "the Vagina Primera," culminating in "one last wail sounded in the Universe as Gaea gave birth to Woman."[42] From this first woman emerged the human race, until "some of the sons of Woman grew restless" out of envy and desire for power.[43] This desire led to violence between the genders, resulting in the expulsion of the human race from the paradise they had once inhabited. Much like her counterparts in the Nation of Islam, the crafting of myth gave Chicago an opportunity to both explain current power relations and craft a teleological narrative of social revolution. In *Revelations of the Goddess*, Gaea allowed the transfer of power to men as the finalized punishment for women's desire for power. This shift had allowed for women's subjugation until a millennium passed and feminine wisdom returned through the restoration of Gaea as spiritual authority. The myth incorporates the narrative elements of *The Dinner Party* in the conclusion: "The true worth of my Apostles and my Disciples and their long toil for redemption, will neither be seen nor known until the day when I shall carry thirty-nine of my Apostles and nine hundred and ninety-nine of my Disciples to my side. Then shall we celebrate at a heavenly banquet when my daughters will at last arise from their servitude and be resurrected in glory."[44] It is the production of *The Dinner Party* itself, then, that signals the new utopian feminist era. Structurally speaking, this myth again parallels that of Yacub in the Nation of Islam's cosmology. In both stories, a fantastical narrative accounts for historical subjugation as it heralds a transformation of the social order. Furthermore, the space of both *The Dinner Party* and *Revelations of the Goddess* provided movement members with a civic engagement with an imagined community of unified womanhood.

Judy Chicago and her team of researchers and artists contributed to the development of a feminist collective past by cultivating memory practices that were collaborative and honored women's crafting traditions. By bringing women's historical narratives into male-dominated spaces, they infused the cultural sphere with women's experiences and talents. Although the production of *The Dinner Party* took place in a separatist manner, the exhibition itself took women's history into the public sphere, proving to be both a radical act of feminist arts production and a liberal intervention into the cultural sector.

Mementos of Womanhood

As mainstream institutions of art and archival collections received an influx of women's historical themes and stories, another pair of feminists were developing a much more personal intervention into women's collective memory. Founded in 1973 by Jocelyn Cohen and Nancy Poore, the Helaine Victoria Press (HVP) produced and distributed historically themed postcards that educated feminists on women's history for nearly twenty years. Cohen had been a student of Judy Chicago's in the painting program at California State University, where Chicago had piqued Cohen's interest in the history of women artists. Cohen and Poore had begun dating long-distance and had taken to corresponding via postcards to save on long-distance phone bills. Over time, the women found themselves frustrated with the dearth of postcards depicting women in a positive and non-demeaning manner. What began as an arts school hobby blossomed into a full-blown nonprofit endeavor, as the two women transformed themselves into self-taught community historians.

Feminists such as Cohen and Poore who undertook such projects worked within and against institutional frameworks that ignored or diminished the accomplishments of women throughout history. Their research first sought to identify women's historical experiences, then, as they became more sophisticated historical thinkers, sought to integrate them into a larger national narrative. Initially, the two women contracted with a professional press to produce an eight-card set that they had researched and designed. After growing increasingly frustrated with male press staff who were derisive about the postcards and offensive toward the women's work, they began to print the cards themselves in a graphic design space at California State University.[45] From the beginning, the women sought "to uncover women's history, to make those findings highly visible and affordable through a popular art medium, to enrich the field of postcard art and to help keep the craft of letterpress art alive,"[46] a vision that they fulfilled over seventeen years of researching, designing, printing, and distributing women's history postcards. Cohen and Poore undertook most of the work of the entire business, only employing minimal administrative help after a few years as the endeavor grew.

Cohen increasingly favored HVP work over her own art practice, and this interest prompted her painting mentor Judy Chicago to discourage Cohen from pursuing full-time work as a community historian and printer. Chicago and feminist arts program cofounder Miriam Schapiro had felt that the project wasted Cohen's painting talent, and Chicago saw Cohen "as a painter, not a politico."[47] Chicago's response was ironic, as Chicago herself was in the midst of realizing her own massive work exploring women's history. Still, Cohen disregarded Chicago's urging, and after graduation threw herself full-time into the work of running the press. In 1976, Cohen and Poore moved the press to rural Indiana, taking an opportunity to manifest the back-to-the-earth lifestyle they had come to admire. Upon moving to Indiana, both Cohen and Poore grew increasingly passionate about printing heritage as they reconstructed an antique letterpress on which they produced the postcards.[48]

When Cohen and Poore began to seek out images of women for the project in 1973, they found themselves frustrated with a lack of source material. Cohen had received a modest introduction to the history of women in the visual arts from Judy Chicago at California State University in the early 1970s, but otherwise had little experience in scholarly research, historic or otherwise. Cohen and Poore began their research process by pouring over what limited published sources on women's history they could find locally. When the pair felt that they had exhausted the existing literature, they began to undertake visits to archives to conduct original research, frequenting the Library of Congress and National Archives in search of new postcard images and background information for image captions.[49] They also visited academic libraries, including Wayne State and the University of Michigan. Although these libraries had collecting scopes outside of women's manuscripts and books, their holdings in labor history and anarchist collections proved fertile ground for identifying prominent women in leadership roles, and their research there ultimately inspired a series on women in the labor movement. After identifying themes and images for reproduction, Cohen and Poore often shot the images themselves on film, using the photos for postcard graphics.[50] The images they identified had often aged out of copyright protection, and the women felt that shooting new photographs from books gave them some freedom around copyright restrictions during their early years. As the business grew and they became more savvy researchers, they began to seek authorized reproductions from the archives themselves.

As Cohen and Poore grew familiar with the existing, if scant, literature on women's history, the pair found that library card catalogs offered little direction for pursuing their topics further. Similarly, they struggled to find interesting images to use for the postcards. Cohen recalled roaming through book stacks, searching almost randomly for useful historical images of women. After growing increasingly frustrated with libraries' limited holdings, they sought out-of-print books from used bookshops. Cohen and Poore's home and workspace began to overflow with books, as the pair immediately purchased any and all books they found on women's history. They began to sell their expanding library along with their postcards, including a catalog of secondhand women's history books in their mailings. Customers of the press purchased books spanning a wide variety of topics, such as *A Hilltop on the Marne* (a reproduction of the letters sent by an American spinster from her retirement home, which was inconveniently located in a World War I battle zone) published in 1916; a Victorian feminist comportment guide from 1893 entitled *What Can a Woman Do?*; the biographical *Frances E. Willard;* Rita Sackville West's *Saint Joan of Arc* from 1936; a 1928 version of the lesbian classic *The Well of Loneliness*, featuring an introduction by famed sexologist Havelock Ellis; 1886's *The Life of Nellie C. Bailey*, recounting the trial of a wife accused of murdering her husband; and the biographical novel *Judith of France,* which narrated the life of a ninth-century Saxon queen.[51] Such books impacted the movement's collective memory on two different levels: first as a resource for the development of the postcards' text and rich captions, second as the texts circulated through the larger community of feminists.

Like their counterparts in other social movements, Cohen and Poore became self-trained historical scholars with a knowledge base that was generalist but also possessed a notable amount of depth. Although the two women identified as popular historians, scholars in the fields of women's history and studies took note of their research. Ruth Perry, a humanities professor from Massachusetts Institute of Technology, wrote the women, commending them "because the information you cite on the back of your Mary Astell notecard is alright, which is more than many scholars in the field can manage."[52] Cohen and Poore sought also to develop significant context within the captions on the postcards, as well as short essays that were used to introduce the sets. During its existence, HVP published over two hundred distinct cards, many of them grouped thematically in numerous series. HVP's popular *Women in History* collection offered several sets that broadly highlighted a wide range of women's historical contributions. In other cases, series such as *Women and Ecology, Sisters of the Harlem Renaissance, Latina History and Culture, Women Library Workers, Women in Social Protest: The United States since 1915,* and *Bread & Roses: Women of the American Labor Movement* all introduced larger historical themes that advanced the movement's sense of a collective past.

By 1982, the partnership, both personal and professional, had dissolved, and Poore moved away from Indiana, leaving Cohen to manage HVP alone. Cohen would keep HVP alive until 1990, working collaboratively with a research team that included academic historians from nearby Indiana University, having moved all press operations to Bloomington in 1986. By the time that the press shuttered, Cohen felt that her intellectual production positioned her as "a forerunner in the field of women's studies," a self-categorization that was more than fair given the scope of her research and the broad dissemination of her work.[53]

HVP's historic postcards functioned as manifestations of collective memory via both graphics and text. Although the main utility of the postcards as a memorial practice was to circulate historical images in the promotion of a sense of shared female struggle, Cohen and Poore wanted to share the richness of their research findings with their audience. While both women cared deeply for circulating the historical narratives that the cards encompassed, as a former writer and editor Poore brought a meticulous eye to the cards' text. As a result, her captions included a careful and effective economy of context and narrative. The now-iconic image of Jane Addams and Mary McDowell carrying American and peace flags during a suffrage march was chosen as a postcard image in 1984, packing in over two hundred words and filling more than half of the writing space of the card. The "Bread & Roses" series from 1979 featured eight cards, each with a thick paragraph of biographical data, movement history, and a nuanced analysis of the larger political context of each featured woman.[54] Cohen recalled having to exert a great deal of restraint in the crafting of the captions, as she and Poore agonized over which details to omit from the text because of space considerations. This passionate commitment to sharing as much information as possible with their customers reveals the power that the historical narratives of resistance and power held for them.

The carefully hand-crafted cards themselves were a labor of love through which Cohen and Poore transmitted their growing knowledge of women's history. Upon moving to Indiana, the women purchased an antique press, trekking across the state to locate necessary components to set up their new shop.[55] Over time, they became more sophisticated printers and artisans who took on new challenges as they claimed a rarified place as women in the printing trade. The physical production of the cards was quite labor intensive, with one set requiring fourteen press runs, that is, fourteen distinct passes for each item to complete the full process. One particular run of a thousand sets of a series required Cohen and Poore to hand-glue the letter-pressed outer jacket of the series onto the boxes.[56] This dedication to detail produced images and objects that had a keepsake quality, encouraging customers to treasure the cards.

Unlike contemporary women's history projects like the Women's History Research Center and *The Dinner Party* exhibit, Helaine Victoria postcards operated on a much more intimate level of collective memory. More akin to consciousness raising, the postcards promoted a direct relationship between women's own experiences and the history of collective womanhood. Cohen and Poore envisioned the postcards as a medium for a popular and informal tool of movement education. In the folksiest of manners, an introduction to the postcard catalog outlined HVP's mission: "Why do this? Because we want to help remedy the shortage of convenient information in so many areas of history. We chose postcards because they are relatively cheap and tell the story quickly and memorably. And people see them along the way—sender, recipient, postal clerk and carrier. And maybe some of those people who see our cards and posters feel like going out to do something to help fix the world good and proper. That's our real purpose."[57] Cohen and Poore imagined their work as bringing women's history into some of the most personal spaces: hanging on bedroom walls and refrigerators, or serving as a gentle exchange between two friends who shared a desire to restructure gender relations but perhaps did not share a zip code. Customers wrote to Cohen and Poore, gushing enthusiastically over the cards and the connection that they made between the past and the present. One customer wrote that she "never expected to be moved to tears by a postcard catalog—and [HVP] did it *twice*."[58] Likewise, some women used the images and stories contained within the postcards to educate others; another customer expressed appreciation for the postcards "not only for myself, but as a means to introduce other women in a subtle way to women in history."[59] This casual sharing of historical narratives between feminists is perhaps the most decentralized of historical education within the movement, as the nature of the medium made informal, one-on-one education possible.

Branching Out with Women's History

Although much of second-wave feminism's early collective memory work emerged in grassroots organizations and as individual projects, as the 1970s waned, movement activism increasingly focused energy on reforming mainstream institutions. Likewise, as feminists increasingly gained access to higher education, they brought their reform ethics along with them into the academy. In this vein, the graduate program in women's history at Sarah Lawrence College hosted the Summer Institute on Women's History for leaders of women's organizations in 1979, an initiative that equipped movement leaders with scholarly training in women's history. The Summer Institute on Women's History nurtured a community of learners selected from diverse grassroots organizations in a residential setting that immersed feminist leaders in topics and debates on women's history. The event inspired delegates to take their knowledge beyond the bounds of the feminist movement, and their shared enthusiasm for the subject matter led them to support a local effort in California to incorporate women's history into school curriculum, an action that would ultimately lead to the establishment the first National Women's History Week and subsequently National Women's History Month. Although historians have begun to trace the rise of women's studies programs in the academy, the relationship between academic feminists and movement activists in the production of collective memory is underconsidered.[60] The Summer Institute on Women's History stood out from other collective memory projects in that it relied on academically trained feminists for leadership and sought to use existing feminist institutional structures to broadly cultivate historical knowledge throughout the movement. Yet the mission of the institute firmly grounded the work in a commitment to broad movement education at the grassroots level, even as it relied on mainstream liberal institutions.

With financial support from the Women's Action Alliance, the Smithsonian Institution, and the Lilly Endowment, academic historians Alice Kessler-Harris, Gerda Lerner, and Amy Swerdlow, along with graduate students from the Sarah Lawrence MA program in women's studies, planned and executed the residential event. Planners hoped that the institute would "bridge the gap between the theory and practice of feminism: to spread the knowledge of Women's History to activist women and to make Women's History an integral part of the life of women's organizations."[61] The institute's academic leaders, ranging from junior to senior members of the field, planned and executed a seventeen-day immersive learning experience that gave women activists a robust background in women's history, as well as a network of colleagues dedicated to bringing women's history into the frontlines of the struggle for gender equality.

Institute planners recruited for the seminar with the intention of attracting a diverse and passionate group of delegates, seeking "the broadest possible representation from the organized women's community."[62] While admission was competitive, forty-five participants were chosen on the basis of their record of leadership and activism within the movement, rather than more traditional selection criteria of educational background and record.[63] Despite drawing on a nontraditional crowd, the faculty planned "a very intensive curriculum, designed to give the equivalent of a 15-week graduate course" scheduled into a rigorous seventeen-day schedule.[64] Sensitive to criticisms within the women's movement regarding race and class, the institute consciously struggled to bring in a racially and economically diverse group of participants. Their outreach strategy sought to address some of the challenges faced by feminists of color: the invisibility of activists of color, lack of resources within working-class and minority organizations, and a lack of connections between mainstream organizations and smaller marginalized feminist groups.[65]

Curriculum for the Summer Institute on Women's History led delegates through a broad survey of American women's experience. Required lectures spanned an array of topics including: women's work, family life, activism, suffrage and reform, sexuality and control, modern feminism, and black women, while elective courses gave delegates the opportunity to delve further into these issues. Faculty prepared an eight-page annotated bibliography entitled "Basic Books in the History of American Women," encouraging delegates to extend their learning beyond the bounds of the sessions.⁶⁶ As part of the requirements of the institute, participants researched an individual project and presented their findings in small work groups, an assignment that gave delegates the opportunity to conduct original research. Participants were also encouraged to actively plan to incorporate their learning into their everyday movement work once they returned to their communities; one of the suggestions administrators offered to participants was to include women's history facts in newsletters, an inclusion that would weave feminist collective memory into the everyday interactions of women across the country.

In addition to concerns over diversity within the event's delegation, planners also strove to include women of color's history into the curriculum. One of the scheduled program days included lectures and discussions on working-class and black women, followed by evening programs that promoted awareness of the issues facing feminists of color. Although Kessler-Harris, Lerner, and Swerdlow had identified scholars of Native American, Asian, and Chicana women's histories, financial constraints prevented these scholars from appearing at the institute. Nonetheless, a few of these scholars did share their research via printed materials submitted beforehand that engaged the histories of Native American, Chicana, and Asian American women.⁶⁷ While conference organizers lamented a lack of funding to bring in scholars of color like Grace Lee Boggs, Lupe Castillo, and Clara Sue Kidwell to the conference, their final report also underscored that future events must prioritize the inclusion of minority scholars, not to "be added merely as token lecturers, but must be involved in all aspects of the educational planning of the institute."⁶⁸

Institute leadership demonstrated more sensitivity to movement debates around "the lavender menace." The term was coined by Betty Friedan in 1969, expressing an anxiety that if the women's movement were to be associated with lesbianism, the movement would lose mainstream acceptance and thus be less efficacious.⁶⁹ To counteract this, the institute included panels like "Lesbianism and the Cultural Tradition," a discussion which included a biographical examination of feminist lesbian Lakota Tillie Black Bear and black lesbian poetry and music.⁷⁰ Through the diversity of panel topics, planners demonstrated a commitment to inclusion that many of their movement contemporaries had yet failed to fully embrace.⁷¹

Just as planners hoped, institute participants found themselves inspired to incorporate history into their grassroots organizing upon their return to their home communities, inspired by this "genuine feminist community" who vigorously studied history and applied past women's struggles to contemporary movement goals. Participants reflected back on the value of their experiences, underscoring the importance of both "the study of women's history with wonderful teachers and role models and the opportunity to get to know so many wonderful women activists."[72] Participants also praised the overall structure of the institute, calling it "a valuable model for reaching women's organizations."[73] By employing feminist pedagogy to deliver the curriculum, the institute distinguished itself as an exemplar of community education, as well as a source of feminist collective memory.

The passion for women's history generated by the institute certainly led to newly inspired activists, but the most far-reaching outcome of the event was the creation of National Women's History Week. During the institute, organizers learned of a recent grassroots effort in Sonoma County, California, from delegate Molly Murphy MacGregor. The education task force of the Sonoma County Commission on the Status of Women in California had initiated a weeklong celebration of women's history in 1978, organized around International Women's Day. Inspired by this work, participants decided to extend the energy of the institute, taking a demand for recognition both into their own communities and to the national level. Institute participants organized campaigns in their communities to petition legislators and governors to recognize the week at the state level. The following fall, the Women's Action Alliance hired an intern to support the national campaign to pressure the U.S. Congress and President Carter into formally recognizing the week at the federal level, an initiative that passed in 1981. Support for the week coalesced rapidly, building on the successes of Black History Month, which was first recognized by President Ford in 1976, and, as Molly Murphy MacGregor said, because "they knew who to call and how to get things done."[74] Institute participants also produced programming in their home organizations to commemorate the week.[75] In response to further pressure from women's groups, Congress expanded the week to a month in 1987.

National Women's History Week provided collective memory activists with a project that likely had the largest impact of such movement education projects. MacGregor's initial vision was to promote awareness around women's history in elementary and secondary schools and provide resources to teachers participating in the commemoration. In 1972,

MacGregor became enraged when a colleague derided her proposed semester-long course on women's history. Much like Laura X's experience, scorn from a male colleague provided the frustration that fueled a major historical project. The National Women's History Week's project packet, produced by institute alumni, provided a guide for classroom activities; most of the fifty-one-page packet also offered organizing materials, including sample letters to educational professionals, women's organizations, and academic history departments; churches and religious organizations; and social and civic organizations, as well as sample press releases and public service announcements. Equally important as getting resources to teachers was the need to educate the local community on the importance of women's history.[76] Within a few years, the impact of the Summer Institute on Women's History had realized its goal "to spread the knowledge of Women's History to wider circles, into our museums, libraries, schools, [and] communities" through the establishment of national recognition for the importance of women's history.[77] Through these efforts, Women's Liberation activists handed down to the next generation a feminist identity that was inextricably linked to collective historical struggle and achievement.

Conclusion

Unlike their counterparts in the Black Freedom movement, many of the collective memory activists responsible for the development of a feminist collective memory individually had little institutional or scholarly bedrock on which to ground the development of community history.[78] Early efforts like the World Center for Women's Archives and the development of the Sophia Smith and Schlesinger Collections were either short lived, or the specialized nature of collections failed to speak to the next generation of feminist activists, many of whom were inclined toward building homegrown projects. As a result, the first stirrings of historical curiosity within the movement created a demand for grassroots researchers and new research methods. To this end, activists amassed collections on women's history and dug through mainstream collections to identify documents and images that illustrated a portion of women's historical experiences. As community history projects cultivated collective memory within the movement, activists' intertwined desire for history and a proud identity led many toward educational projects that went beyond the bounds of the movement. Some of the most successful Women's Liberation education projects often took a less formal approach than their movement education counterparts in the Black Freedom struggles. In these cases, instead of building traditional institutions of learning, these feminists often utilized more everyday means of transmitting collective memory through media like postcards, calendars, and newsletters. Additionally, as the majority of women still found themselves financially dependent on men, the movement's ability to maintain predominantly separatist institutions proved challenging. Although the WHRC emerged early in the movement as a promising cultural institution, Laura X and others were unable to financially maintain the organization, and the significant collections amassed in a remarkably short time were transferred to mainstream institutions. The National Women's History Project, founded in 1980 to support National Women's History Week, flourished, bolstered in part by support at the federal level. In the example of a more unconventional educational project, the postcards of the Helaine Victoria Press circulated from woman to woman through the mail or as gifts, sharing narratives of historical women's struggles between individuals. Additionally, interventions into mainstream institutions like *The Dinner Party* and the Summer Institute on Women's History worked on both intimate and cultural levels, bringing the personal development of identity into mainstream spaces like museums and schools.

Feminist activists were also attuned to the need to document their own movement efforts, bringing a kind of forward-thinking collective memory to feminists that might come generations later. A key part of the work of the Women's History Research Center was the active collecting of movement newspapers and documents, and this collection has proven a significant documentation of second-wave activism. Feminists of color were particularly aware of this as well, as they attributed their archival silences to both misogynistic and racist cultural attitudes. Black lesbian-feminist twin sisters Barbara and Beverly Smith recognized "as Black women, as lesbians and feminists, there is no guarantee that our lives will ever be looked at with the kind of respect given to certain people from other races, sexes or classes. There is similarly no guarantee that we or our movement will survive long enough to become safely historical. We must document ourselves now."[79] This concern, though forward looking, speaks of a particular relationship to the archives. The Smith sisters directed their activist energies toward black feminist publishing as part of Kitchen Table: Women of Color Press. Although publishing activism is not directly connected to the genealogy of public history as are other collective memory practices considered here, the Smith sisters' identification of historical silences echo the nascent public historians that appear throughout this book.

In other ways, the collective memory projects of Women's Liberation were distinct from their counterparts in other social movements. Feminist activists had long pushed back against the idea that a woman's place was in the home, shielded from the public sphere.[80] Although first-wave activists had made considerable gains in securing a place in civic life for women, second-wave activists still struggled against patriarchal cultural norms that discouraged women from participating in public life. This struggle is reflected in the shape of collective memory work in the movement, as projects like *The Dinner Party* and the Summer Institute on Women's History pushed women's history into museum and grassroots political organizations. Yet the work of the Helaine Victoria Press reflects another distinction in women's collective memory—that of a personal and intimate means of transmission. Cohen and Poore intended that the postcards be exchanged through friendships and one-on-one encounters, providing a conduit of collective memory that might suit isolated women or feminists who might not be inclined toward organizational work. In contrast to the Black Freedom movement, second-wave collective memory activism was distinctively more project based, less institutionalized, and relied more on personal relationships and intimate interactions.

Narratives deployed by feminist activists highlighted the values of universal womanhood yet also made efforts toward a multicultural perspective. Although most of the women involved in the efforts outlined here were white, many of them attempted to engage, if in a somewhat limited capacity, histories of women of color. Their narrative choices underscored women's participation in public life and highlighted tales of activism and earlier forms of solidarity among women. Taken as a whole, these stories served to position Women's Liberation activists within a long arc of resistance to gender oppression and underscore women's strength, resilience, and effectiveness in realizing change.

For all participants in the Women's Liberation movement, a basic shared goal was to elevate women to equal political, social, and cultural status with men. For so many women, one step in this process was to undo the internalized misogyny and perceptions of inferiority. This identity project took on many different fronts, from direct action events like the 1969 feminist protests against the Miss America pageant to a basic and prideful reclamation of women's bodies as beautiful and revered. Likewise, the collective memory practices of second-wave activists were bound up in questions of identity. A desire for a new autonomous sense of self drove activists to create narratives of the past, even as a growing knowledge of women's history generated a new feminist identity. While building organizations and producing informal education projects served an important and overt part of the movement's efforts toward building a feminist collective memory, some feminists tapped into the emerging social movement process of identity development to connect women to the past on a very personal level. With *The Dinner Party,* Judy Chicago and a league of volunteers crafted a massive visual display of historic women's achievements, creating a sense of women's heritage that visitors could engage with on a personal level, as they recognized their own achievements, talents, and struggles in other women's biographies. In a similar vein, the Helaine Victoria Press understood the complexity of the new feminist identities. Although their earliest postcards took on a rather broad idea of womanhood, the press later shifted its focus to explore the intersection of women's identities with race, sexuality, and class. At a time when the larger movement was still struggling with how to address such complexities, Cohen and Poore navigated such debates by promoting a diverse historical picture of women's experiences and activism.

In many parts of the larger movement, a clear line was drawn between grassroots organizing and structural activism. This division was less clear for community historians within the feminist movement, and there are many examples of academic women's historians and women's studies scholars who supported community history projects, demonstrating the relative fluidity between academic and community women's historians at this time. Helaine Victoria Press founder Jocelyn Cohen recalled many fruitful exchanges at the Berkshire Conference on the History of Women, a triennial conference that started in 1973 (in distinction from the fraternal/scholarly organization of female historians founded in 1930). The conference was itself a reaction to academic conservatism and sexism, as academic scholars mingled with popular historians like Cohen staffing booths at the conference.[81] Although the results were in part a demarcation between grassroots and academic history endeavors, this professional shift was part of the same foment that produced the wide array of popular memory practices examined in this chapter. The Helaine Victoria Press would later go on to work closely with academic scholars in the mid-1980s to develop some of the later series produced by the press. Likewise, the Summer Institute on Women's History provides a fine example of women academics applying their skills to movement activist causes and organizations, although academic feminists still maintained authoritative positions as teachers to frontline activists. Despite the significance of women's history memory practices to the second wave of feminism, by the 1990s there remained few community-based women's history projects, and most of the authority of women's historical narratives was assumed by academic women's historians. The National Women's History Project remains an exception to this, as a thriving organization focused on primary, secondary, and to an extent, popular education. By partnering with academic historians, educators, and policy-makers, the project quickly transformed from a grassroots initiative into an important educational nonprofit dedicated to enriching public school curriculum with women's history.

Through both research and educational efforts, community historians working in feminism's second wave produced a new feminist identity based in part on narratives of women's history. More personal and intimate than their peers in the Black Freedom and Gay Liberation movements, collective memory within the women's movement enriched a new feminist identity through dialogues with texts that were consumed individually and collectively. Although academic history claimed authority over women's history, grassroots activists created archives, conducted original research, criticized historiography, and educated the movement and beyond on women's historical successes and struggles.

Poster announcing a slide show lecture given by Gerber-Hart Library cofounder Gregory Sprague. Courtesy of the Gerber/Hart Library and Archives.

CHAPTER 4

Scripted to Win

Collective Memory in the Gay Liberation Movement

> We have a special need for history. Raised as we were in heterosexual families, we grew up and discovered our gayness deprived of gay ancestors, without a sense of our roots. We need to create and carry with us a living awareness of gay generations, to incorporate in our consciousness not only the organized struggle of our predecessors, but the everyday struggle to survive that our ancestors engaged in. We need to affirm and appreciate our past, not in some abstract way, but as it is embodied in living human beings.
>
> —John D'Emilio, *Body Politic,* February 1979

Like other movements of the 1960s and 1970s, Gay Liberation took cues from the direct-action tactics and democratic demands of earlier activists. Black Power, Red Power, the Antiwar movement, and Women's Liberation all had shared rhetorical forms, movement-building strategies, and demands for cultural representation. Gay Liberation activists followed suit, reworking the cultural forms to suit the needs of the movement and community. Shortly after the Stonewall Uprising in June 1969, in which drag queens, gays, and lesbians resisted police violence and repression, queer historians began working to share resources, build archival access and collections, and create a new body of historical knowledge. In the early 1970s, activists became amateur and sometimes academic historians, blurring the division between university- and community-based history. By the 1980s, however, two paths toward the institutionalization of LGBT collective memory took shape.[1] In some cases, the cultivators of collective memory sought to engage with existing institutions through a struggle for legitimacy within the academy and mainstream archival repositories. Others, however, worked outside of the institutions of dominant culture, establishing grassroots organizations that would be accountable only to the LGBT community.

Beyond simple recognition of the longstanding existence of same-sex-loving practices, a claim to the past was especially integral to developing a shared identity that was based on visibility and resilience. As many LGBT people had been disowned by biological family and thus estranged from more traditional forms of heritage, the need to craft a new lineage was fundamental to the success of the movement. By asserting the endurance of same-sex-loving practices and individuals, activists crafted both an internal sense of self and an external community image that linked resilience and strength to the LGBT community. In 1979, historian and gay studies pioneer Jonathan Ned Katz saw an explicit connection between the movement's struggle to shrug off the pathologizing narratives of psychiatry and the effort to find a place for gay and lesbian experience within the American past. Carrying the authority of the medical profession, psychiatrists had explained LGBT behavior as pathological and perverse. For Katz, developing historical narratives of success and happiness was an assertion of a historical presence and a legacy of resistance. Katz described the quest for origin stories as "an important contribution to our current struggle to dispossess the professionals and repossess ourselves," while simultaneously "finding spiritual nourishment in knowledge of our historical foremothers and fathers."[2] To this end, laying claim to the past provided not only the legitimation of both presence and precedence, but also contributed to the building of a proud identity inspired by those who came before.

As within other social movements of the era, memory practices varied across place and changed over time. The homophile movement of the 1950s and 1960s invoked prior same-sex-loving figures as a rudimentary step toward creating a public identity. The Daughters of Bilitis, a lesbian homophile organization active during the 1950s and 1960s, drew its name from a literary figure associated with the Greek poetess Sappho, an act that laid claim to the classic era of human accomplishment while also underscoring the literary focus of their monthly publication, the *Ladder*. Though not explicitly offering historical essays, articles appearing in the *Ladder* often mentioned other classic female literary figures, including references to their passionate relationships with other women. In one example, reprints of Sappho's poems lamented "with grief that so much has been lost."[3] These invocations, however, remained in the mode of excavating famous figures from the archive.

This simple call to the past served primarily to integrate LGBT history into mainstream historical accounts, as gays and lesbians began to claim well-known historic figures as same-sex-loving ancestors. Such early claims to gay and lesbian history stood in contrast to the cohesive cultural and social history that LGBT scholars would begin writing during the late 1970s.[4] The Stonewall Uprising and ensuing Gay Liberation movement shifted queer memorial practices away from simple reclamation of famous figures and moved it toward the exploration of a more populist and broad-based gay and lesbian history. As activists devoted to this work began to seek out narratives that would represent a wider array of past experiences, LGBT history mirrored the new social history by attending to the experiences of everyday same-sex-loving people.

In addition to articles featured in community newspapers, activists identified an explicit need for popular education for movement members. In the mid-1970s, activists and scholars, working both independently and in community organizations, developed a variety of queer memorial practices, including slide show lectures, conferences, films, and other programming to bring the new scholarship to the community. Many community historians developed their projects into books, videos, and exhibits, while others organized community archives and developed more institutionalized history projects. All such projects offer an important glimpse into how activists viewed their role as community historians and, more broadly, the significance of a useable past.

Collective memory activists deployed four significant strategies in the Gay Liberation movement. The first called for the cultural ownership of gay history, which gave rise to the founding of community-based historical institutions. Second, researchers and archivists developed new taxonomical forms and archival approaches to nurture and organize a body of knowledge about LGBT experience. Third, activists began to share their findings on LGBT history throughout the Gay Liberation movement, most notably through the popular education forms of slide shows and films. Lastly, as the movement built community-based organizations to preserve and interpret LGBT memory, some activists began to work to legitimate LGBT history within academic and other mainstream cultural institutions. These varied efforts were at times complementary, and at other times in conflict with one another regarding liberal and separatist approaches to cultural authority and ownership. Tension between community ownership and mainstream inclusion emerged more quickly and vociferously in this context than in other movements. In contrast to the Black Freedom and Women's Liberation movements, LGBT history had no presence in liberal institutions before the 1970s. Although rare, historians dealing with women and black historical experience were part of the academy before the 1970s, yet gay and lesbian historical experience was entirely absent from scholarly historical circles. As LGBT history began to emerge, gay and lesbian community historians struggled over whether community-based organizations or mainstream liberal institutions were the best repositories for the community's historical assets as they crafted a historical narrative that supported the identity-based goals of the movement. Regardless of this split, the development of LGBT history in both community and academic settings transformed in less than two decades from a few loosely affiliated movement intellectuals to a significant body of knowledge and constellation of institutional homes.

The Cultural Ownership and Institutional Development of Gay History

Prior to Stonewall, LGBT lives were all but eradicated from the historical record. At times, archival professionals destroyed evidence of same-sex loving experiences in manuscript collections, and museums, scholars, and other keepers of the past erased long-term partnerships from the historical record. As a result, the activists who came of age in the Gay Liberation movement grew up feeling isolated and without precedent.

The development of community history in the LGBT movement was inextricably bound with the cultural front of the movement, which sought to develop a new, proud political identity that relied on a historical narrative of presence and persistence. As activists increasingly used history to legitimate the movement, queer community history transformed from a simple excavation project into community-controlled ownership and authorship of LGBT history. Yet not all LGBT historians felt such mistrust, as one can see through John D'Emilio's words that open this chapter. While an individual's suspicion of liberal institutions might be attributable to myriad experiences and circumstances, it nonetheless illuminates the separatist impulse of some community historians, most notably lesbian activists who, as women, had much less comfort with mainstream organizations than many of their gay male counterparts. Additionally, the acts of claiming ownership of their own historical narratives and forming community-based cultural organizations were gestures of self-determination that echoed sentiments that emerged during the early days of Gay Liberation. Throughout the 1970s and 1980s, a preoccupation with the past flourished within the gay and lesbian community. Articles in popular LGBT newspapers and slide show lectures in community centers posed questions and offered answers regarding earlier same-sex-loving practices and people. Writers for community newspapers explicitly linked a claiming of the past with a demand for equal status: "as more knowledge about human sexuality and behavior has been discovered and disseminated, greater numbers of persons have begun to realize that not only is it okay to be, it is the normal lifestyle for some people."[5] To some extent, demonstrating the longevity of same-sex-loving experiences dismantled the perspective of the psychiatric profession and other "authorities" who pathologized gayness as sick, harmful to the individual, and destructive to society.

In March 1973, a handful of academics and community intellectuals gathered in a New York City apartment and found both personal and intellectual kinship with one another, as well as a desire to change the intellectual discourse about LGBT experience.[6] This informal meeting led to the formation of the Gay Academic Union (GAU), a critical network during the early years of LGBT collective-memory-building. The first GAU activists met that day to address the fear, hostility, and rejection they often experienced in the academy, as well as to begin networking around LGBT scholarship, although their efforts and interests were not confined by the walls of academe. Out of this network, several other lesbian and gay community-based history projects emerged, notably the Lesbian Herstory Archives in 1974 and The History Project in Boston in 1980. Although this first incarnation of the GAU itself was relatively short lived, it generated critically important social networks that came to be fundamental for cultivating queer collective memory.

One of the oldest and most significant lesbian-feminist history organizations in the United States, the Lesbian Herstory Archives (LHA) emerged out of the young Gay Academic Union proceedings in late 1973 or early 1974. Women members of the GAU who felt a need for a women-only space formed a consciousness-raising group to address both a political need for self-determination and a cultural need for lesbian history and representation. At the nexus of this early group was GAU cofounder Joan Nestle, joined by Deb Edel, Julie Stanley, Sahli Cavallaro, and Pamela Oline.[7] The five founders all came from well-educated backgrounds, although some of them claimed working-class origins and identities. Nestle, an English instructor from Queens College; Edel, a doctoral student in psychology; and Stanley, who had recently left a job in the English department at the University of Georgia, all were lesbian activists in their thirties. Oline, a practicing feminist psychotherapist, identified as a straight woman who devoted her life to activist allyship, and was also in her thirties. Cavallaro, an undergraduate psychology major in her early twenties, was the youngest member. As the group focused its efforts more on the collective queer women's past, its members began to pool their personal collections and actively preserve additional materials pertaining to same-sex-women-loving experiences.[8] For members of the LHA collective, the personal commitment to archival work did not end, however, with the donation and collection of materials. Rather, many of these women began to commit their labor and their leisure-time to the project. Perhaps most notably, founding member Joan Nestle cared for the entire archives in her Upper West Side apartment from 1974 to 1991.

Born and raised in New York City by a single mother, Nestle came out as a "Fem" in the late 1950s.[9] Her experiences in the pre-Stonewall lesbian community grounded her own sense of self in an earlier identity, even as post-Stonewall lesbians began rejecting the butch-fem labels and expressions of the earlier generation. In the early 1970s Nestle, unsettled that lesbian-feminism dismissed the significance of the butch-fem community and experience, determined to incorporate the earlier generation's experiences into the contemporary movement. During the years that Nestle maintained the collection in her apartment, the holdings grew from a few boxes to an archive filling several rooms of the apartment. Women from all over the world began to travel to the archives, and Nestle and other volunteers welcomed them, offering research support, camaraderie, and warm mugs of tea.[10] This intimate space of the archive echoed the ethos of lesbian-feminism, as LHA members were committed to creating a safe and personal space to preserve the community's collective past.

As LHA grew, members of the collective fiercely held to their commitment of being a grassroots organization in the service of lesbians across the world. To this end, in a conversation with other LGBT historians, Nestle underscored the importance of keeping the archive entirely separate from a patriarchal institution, insisting that lesbians "should be in control of our own materials, our own history."[11] Similarly, LHA prohibited men from using the space and collections, a policy that lasted through the

1970s and well into the 1980s.¹² The archive also maintained a strict commitment to a non-elite atmosphere. While LGBT researchers often found themselves barred from established institutional or academic archives due to a lack of institutional credentials, LHA upheld a policy of accessibility for all lesbians, a commitment that led to exclusion of non-queer women in addition to men.

Policies such as these produced an archival space that was as much a community center as it was a repository for historical materials. Book and slide show researchers comingled with recent mastectomy survivors who came to look at erotic images as a means of reclaiming sexuality.¹³ Throughout its organizational history, collective members remained committed to the archive as "a cultural institution which, though it plays a dynamic role in the Lesbian community, is, at its core, a safe, nurturing environment, a mixture of library and family album."¹⁴ This commitment led to the organization not simply serving as a historical resource for lesbians, but as a social and political organizing space as well.

In May 1975, members of the Lesbian Herstory Archives participated along with other lesbians from across the country in a consciousness-raising event organized by West Coast lesbian activists outside of Los Angeles. A group of eight women, including Jocelyn Cohen and Nancy Poore (who founded the Helaine Victoria Women's Press as a part of collective memory efforts within the Women's Liberation movement) spent a year in preparation for the Lesbian History Exploration. This event, claimed as the "first national lesbian separatist event," drew women from across the country for a weekend of festivities focused around building lesbian historical consciousness.¹⁵ Event planners gave careful consideration to the use of *history* versus *herstory*, ultimately settling on what some considered a masculinist word. The collective produced an invitational packet that included an explanation of several paragraphs on the Greek origins of the word, arguing that it, in fact, did not come from the masculine pronoun but rather from *istor*, meaning knowledge or learning. To this end, planners rejected the increasingly popular *herstory:* "We plan to include in the Exploration some way for women to give words to each other, to invent and share new words, and to reclaim lost woman-words. But we don't want to discard words at face value. We want to take our own history seriously, and we want to take seriously the history of the words we use."¹⁶

Planners imagined a wide array of uses for lesbian history within the lesbian-feminist movement, from the embracing of the difficulty of historical lesbian struggles to the development of a future political strategy of the movement as a whole. To this end, Jan Oxenberg, an organizer and filmmaker, acknowledged that a full understanding of historical lesbian struggles might prove unpleasant: "This event has to do with pain, incredible pain and rage. What we're doing is just dredging up crumbs from the past . . . like dragging the lagoon for dead bodies. What I really want from this event is *catharsis* [emphasis in original]."[17] While most of her peers in the movement talked about using the past as a means to build a proud identity, this comment marks a distinct new use of the past, as a means to process suffering and loss through a shared history marked by oppression and erasure. Still others strove to use such narratives as a means to political reinvigoration. Exploration participant Jo Hyacinthe, for example, was driven by past oppression to organize for change: "We're changing our scripting, we've always been scripted to lose, now we're gonna be scripted to win. I see a lull in lesbian feminist politics, it's not the time for marches or rallies—that was just the beginning . . . it's time now to create theory, get facts, [determine] where we're coming from, why, [and] where we're going."[18] This expansive, and at times unpleasant, engagement with the past contrasts sharply with the Daughters of Bilitis's reclamation of famous and laudatory figures. In only a decade or so, lesbian activists had begun to use historical narratives both as a process of healing and as a tool for political mobilization.

Regardless of the other movement ends it served along the way, event planners held community ownership as the most important outcome of the Lesbian History Exploration. Although most lesbians understood themselves to be part of the larger Gay Liberation movement, for many there was a need to carve out lesbian-only cultural space. This sentiment extended to lesbian history as well: "The orientation of the Exploration is Lesbian Prime, lesbians as a group rather than a sub-group."[19] This desire for historical autonomy mirrored other separatist impulses within lesbian-feminism, which faulted the larger Gay Liberation movement for, at times, being structured by masculinist forces and failing to challenge patriarchy. To this end, organizers articulated a need to "reclaim our history, the history of lesbians as a people, and to record it in a concrete form . . . for us and for our daughters, the lesbians of our future."[20] Likewise, organizers welcomed only lesbian-identified women to the event, asking straight women to share materials with organizers ahead of time rather than attend themselves. This exclusion ensured that the event was as much about consciousness raising and identity formation through history as it was an intellectual exercise in generating lesbian historical knowledge.[21]

As the passion for gay history grew within the Gay Academic Union, local gay and lesbian history projects continued to emerge across the country. In most instances, such endeavors came out of community researchers' own work, like that of Gregory Sprague and Allan Bérubé. Sprague, a Chicago-based graduate student in education at Loyola University of Chicago, got involved with the Gay Academic Union and began to organize community history endeavors in Chicago during the mid-1970s. Sprague's informal educational project, the Lavender University, led to the founding of the Chicago Gay History Project, which would eventually become the basis for the Gerber-Hart Library, the LGBT library and archive in Chicago. Bérubé, a college dropout turned antiwar activist, similarly pursued research interests in gay history and cofounded the San Francisco Gay and Lesbian History Project. Both Bérubé and Sprague exemplified the intellectual diversity of emerging community historians in the LGBT movement, as neither was formally trained in history yet both were deeply committed to community education and the development of historical organizations in service to the LGBT community. Similar efforts in Toronto led to the establishment of the Canadian Gay Archives just a few months before the founding of the GAU in the United States.[22] Canadian activists formed alliances with their American counterparts in the GAU and other smaller community projects, and from these cross-national partnerships emerged the Lesbian and Gay Researchers Network, a professional organization that fostered dialogue around the challenges to and methods for preserving LGBT history. The network later merged with the Committee on Lesbian and Gay History of the American Historical Association in 1982, a consolidation that echoed the shift in LGBT historical authorship away from community-based researchers and toward academic historians and professional archivists in the 1980s.

Memory Practices in the Queer Archive

For gays and lesbians beginning to work on historical projects, the very limited archival source base appeared as the first challenge. Although same-sex-loving experiences existed throughout history, the social repression of such had also silenced the archival record. Researchers looking for material on same-sex affection in mainstream repositories faced library catalogs that offered little to nothing under the headings of "gay" and "lesbian," and this lack of description and indexing required that researchers be creative in their work. Additionally, activists claimed a variety of kinds of sexual and emotional relationships as historical precedence, including casual erotic encounters, long-term affectionate relationships that may or may not have been erotic, and life partnerships that resembled contemporary gay and lesbian couples. Activists who began to work on collecting and describing LGBT materials entered a profession that usually did not acknowledge the topic at all. Both sides faced a need for new taxonomy that would acknowledge the historical presence of same-sex-loving people and practices.

Researchers working on gay and lesbian history topics in the 1970s relied heavily on one another. Networks often emerged from other Gay Liberation organizations, and this activism served to strengthen friendships and professional collaborations as activists moved deeper into the work of LGBT history. These networks also gave community scholars an opportunity to share resources and methods with one another as they researched and interpreted a new field of historical knowledge. Their collaboration served as another memory practice, as movement intellectuals who were generally unsupported by larger institutions sustained one another and worked in uncharted intellectual territory, oftentimes in geographic isolation. As scholars began to research same-sex topics, they found archival professionals who were often reluctant to acknowledge homosexual behaviors in their subjects' papers. This silencing led many researchers to share strategies with one another and inspired community archivists to develop professional tools to deal with their burgeoning queer archives. Likewise, as these community archives increasingly collaborated with one another, they honed professional methods for dealing with arrangement and description, influencing the larger archival profession as LGBT history became more mainstream.

Emerging LGBT historians found success in thinking broadly about possible sources, often beginning with their own contemporary and personal connection to the movement and working from there. Organizers of the Lesbian History Exploration sought out "research on known lesbians and lesbian communities of the past[;] personal testimony about the variety of ways that women have lived as lesbians . . . first-hand reports by women who have participated in the major events that have shaped the recent lesbian movement; historical fantasy; mythology; folklore; and re-creations of our lesbian past[;] stories about the lost women; women who should have been lesbians, women who were 'cured,' women who committed suicide."[23] Organizers of the event encouraged all participants to research a topic in lesbian history and present their findings at the gathering. Presenters were also urged to reproduce the materials they had to share with other participants for the sake of developing a collaborative lesbian researcher network and a source base for the community.

Early efforts at finding archival sources for same-sex-loving experiences in the past proved to be daunting. Yet one of the first researchers to undertake a sizeable gay history research topic, Jonathan Ned Katz, remembered no dearth of sources and faulted other mainstream institutional barriers that silenced love letters and buried other traces of queer history, a result of what one historian has called *archival power*.[24] Rumors proved to be a fruitful method for Katz, who received leads from other activists in the movement at parties or during informal chats about his work. Although often closeted themselves, queer librarians and archivists also proved quietly useful in the early days of Katz's research, as they would surreptitiously point him toward useful boxes.[25] Early scholars working on LGBT history topics shared information with one another on both methods and resources. Gregory Sprague corresponded with a variety of researchers regarding his projects to "hit [researcher's] pay dirt" as he mined what he could from traditional archives. Lesbian historian Judith Schwarz also corresponded with Katz, alerting him to archival items in the FBI files at the National Archives that documented numerous lesbians who had not yet been written about.[26] Suggestions and hints regarding how to locate sources were passed back and forth in letters between individual scholars doing research for books, slide shows, films, and community history courses. These letters illuminate the creative strategies necessary for LGBT historians working within an archive organized by forms of knowledge that did not recognize nor document gay and lesbian historical experiences.[27]

Usually working without formal institutional support, LGBT historians faced other obstacles, including limited access to academic repositories and financial support, as well as the general difficulty of sustaining energy for a project that may or may not come to fruition. Correspondence between Jonathan Ned Katz and other researchers such as John D'Emilio, Allan Bérubé, Madeline Davis, and Gregory Sprague reveal conversations about possible funding sources, publication strategies, source suggestions and interpretive debates, often couched in empathy for the difficulty of their work.[28] Katz also recalled his fear that the response to the publication of his first book, *Gay American History*, a compendium of historical sources relating to same-sex-loving experience, might generate further repression and that this volume might therefore be the only chance to get such material into publication.[29] Most of the correspondence between researchers was characterized by enthusiasm and a warm collegial tone. Researchers were often good friends with one another, and this network provided emotional support as well as pragmatic advice. In a postcard from 1980 meant to be more conversational than professional, D'Emilio reported to Katz that Bérubé's latest project was a slide show on gay men in San Francisco, enthusiastically stating that "my head spins, it's so exciting."[30] Letters that primarily sought advice on methods or sources almost always included warm encouragement and enthusiasm for the other's projects. These friendship networks brought much needed energy to the otherwise solitary work of gay and lesbian scholarship.[31]

One of the methods researchers employed in traditional archives was engaging with other topics of sexual difference. Indeed, Sprague spent much time searching through materials on vice districts and prostitution to locate materials on gay and lesbian history.[32] Like Katz, Sprague relied on rumor to generate research leads, and often such rumors led him to other topics of "deviance." In one instance from 1980, activist and community researcher James Wickliff advised Sprague on several local legends: a prostitute with a "very close woman friend;" a "very effeminate" Henry Holmes, the mass murderer who would go on to otherwise notorious status; and several vice districts that were known for, among other things, orgies.[33]

Individual memory served as an important source for other researchers as well. Several people wrote to Sprague after his articles on popular gay experience began to appear in *Gay Life* and the *Advocate*. These letters provided him with memories of gay subcultural life during the early part of the twentieth century. One author recalled his grandfather's involvement with the Society for Human Rights, the first U.S. homophile organization, which was founded by Henry Gerber in 1924, remarking, "for his troubles, grandpa and the other men spent some time in the Cook County Jail."[34] Another author recalled a year spent in study at the University of Chicago as especially opportunistic for meeting young men. In particular, he recalled the beach beyond Jackson Park as a favorite cruising spot, where on a bathroom wall one man had written, "my mother made me a queer," and another responded cheekily with "ask her to knit me one too."[35] Authors of these letters recalled a surprising amount of interracial spaces and early (pre-Stonewall) protests and boycotts against repressive businesses and police.[36] In addition to the recently developed importance and emphasis placed on the queer past by activists, it would seem, at least for some, a vital sense of predecessors was already part of community identity and sense of self.

Like their researcher counterparts, community archives also found a need for different archival memory practices to support and make accessible their rapidly growing collections. From the onset, Lesbian Herstory Archives collective members engaged in the task of making lesbian experience intelligible and accessible. To this end, they created new strategies for locating materials within mainstream archives and wrote finding aids for published materials housed elsewhere. Likewise, in April 1980, the Boston Area Lesbian and Gay History Project published *A Beginning Handbook for Researching Lesbian and Gay History in the Boston Area*. This guide advised researchers to employ a long, sometimes offensive, list of terms in card catalogs and indices, including *Amazon, Berdache, Convent, Flash in the Pan, Houseboy, Interior Decorating, Lesbos, Pederasty, Social Reform Movement, Spinster, Suffragist, Tribadism, Uranian*, and the ever-useful *Vice*. The handbook also republished a portion of the index from Jonathan Ned Katz's *Gay American History*, as well as etymological entries on *lesbian* and *gay*.[37] Similarly, the Circle of Lesbian Indexers produced a voluminous index of lesbian periodicals and a subject thesaurus "to foster in our community a sense of continuity with the lesbian past."[38] The index, a project of LHA collective members as well as author J. R. Roberts and historian Claire Potter, served as a guide for researchers working on lesbian topics. The index was divided into sections, including a file of authors and subject entries, book reviews, lesbian writings, poems, and reproduced visual art. The thirty-nine-page subject file offered an extensive annotated topical list, traversing topics as broad as *Back to the Land Movement, Feminist Wiccans, Conformity in the Lesbian Community, Plumbing Repair, Psychosurgery, Taxation*, and *Orange Juice Boycott*.[39] Among other indices, Deb Edel developed a bibliography to track the treatment of lesbians in psychology texts, a document that she topically divided into "friends, enemies, and wishy-washies."[40]

Before the distinction between academic work and community cultural activism began to solidify during the 1980s, collaboration between various community-based archival projects led to the publication of the *Lesbian/ Gay History Researchers Network Newsletter*. Each community-based organization took a turn at producing the newsletter, which featured essays, queries about research topics, announcements for slide shows, annotated bibliographies, professional training, and descriptions of affiliated collections. For example, in the second issue, researchers shared a guide to producing community oral history projects, as well as a guide to reading against the grain of FBI records and working with the Freedom of Information Act in the course of LGBT research.[41] These organizations served both academically trained historians and community-based activists at a point in the movement when the boundary between the two was not yet fully established.

As LGBT archivists worked to make historical documents of same-sex-loving experiences accessible, mainstream archives slowly began to respond to pressure to bring their materials out of the archival closet, as it were. Using venues like the Berkshire Conference of Women's Historians, lesbian historians and archivists in the late 1970s pressured women's repositories like the Schlesinger Library to use the label of "lesbian" on materials that contained same-sex-loving practices among women. In a similar manner, the lesbian and gay archival movement began to successfully pressure mainstream archives to collect the papers of gay and lesbian figures. Although acceptance into mainstream cultural organizations was viewed in some ways as a victory of the movement, this issue was always in tension with a desire to keep community assets under the purview of community organizations.[42]

The development of LGBT history provoked conversations within both community and academic history circles regarding the ethics and interpretive accuracy of applying the terms "gay" and "lesbian" to historical subjects who likely would not have used the terms themselves. By the late 1970s, community organizations like LHA were pressuring mainstream associations to uncloset their same-sex-loving subjects. Academic historians of sexuality began to debate the use of such terms, problematizing the use of contemporary categories of identity for the analysis of historical experiences. A few years later, such concerns made their way into academic history circles. In 1995, historian Leila Rupp argued that even using the category of sexual could be misleading, as it "still assumes that we know what is 'sexual' and that, however diverse, acts and relationships between people of the same sex share some fundamental similarity."[43] As scholarly historians debated the utility of analytic categories to be more inclusive and expansive, community historians and archivists fought with mainstream repositories to engage those very same categories to make available archival materials on same-sex-loving experiences.

Although community archival projects flourished during the 1970s and early 1980s, movement historians diverged over whether or not to keep the historical assets in the community or bring LGBT history into mainstream repositories. Just as Jonathan Ned Katz remembered that evidence of gay history was all around, often hidden by mainstream archivists who buried same-sex-loving experiences in collection description and cataloging, the *Gay Archivist* assured burgeoning queer historians that traces of the queer past were "simply everywhere," insisting that "gay people have always existed, and wherever there is recorded history, we may expect to find glimpses of them."⁴⁴ While frustration with mainstream archival practices led members of the Canadian Gay Archives, the organization that published the *Gay Archivist* newsletter, to argue for community-held repositories, others felt that keeping such historical materials out of mainstream institutions was a disservice to the history and the community.

Beyond the question of ownership of materials, LGBT archivists passionately debated one another over issues of access and collections control. Such conversations took place in a professional space that encompassed both self-trained community historians and professionally trained gay and lesbian archivists. Deborah Edel, an activist first and archivist second, lamented that some authors and artists in the community, although otherwise very supportive of LHA, deposited their own papers at a mainstream institution. Some of these women worried that their papers would receive a higher level of preservation care and were also desirous of the legitimacy bestowed by prestigious mainstream archives.⁴⁵ Another reason to entrust LGBT historical materials with mainstream institutions was articulated by Chicago GAU member Jim Monahan, who urged gay historians "to integrate the past into [mainstream] historical thinking."⁴⁶ Although Monahan recognized the importance of early archival activism in the hands of the community, he argued vehemently against keeping such materials in separatist organizations: "The only separation and faction this archival movement can tolerate is one that allocates tasks, and divides the labor required to bring the gay archives into, and thereby creating, the major research centers that hold them."⁴⁷ While Monahan advocated for sensitivity and security for LGBT historical materials, his main concern was the consolidation of gay materials into one or a few centrally located repositories located within academic libraries.

In response, Joan Nestle came out in favor of local and community control of historical materials. The occasion gave Nestle the opportunity to put forth a practice she termed *radical archiving*. Applied to the Lesbian Herstory Archives, *radical archiving* called for not only community ownership, but also for community responsibility for the archives:

> 1. All lesbian women must have access to the Archives; no academic, political or sexual credentials may be required for usage of the collection; race and class must be no barrier to the use or inclusion. 2. The Archives will collect the prints of all our lives, not just preserve the records of the famous or the published. Every woman who has had the courage to touch or desire another woman deserves to be remembered here. 3. The Archives shall be housed within the community, not on an academic campus which is by definition closed to many women, and shall be curated and maintained by lesbians. 4. The community should share in the work of the Archives. 5. The Archives shall be involved in the political struggles of all lesbians. 6. Archival skills shall be taught, one generation of lesbians to another, breaking the elitism of traditional archives. 7. Funding shall be sought from within the communities the archives serves [sic], not from the government or mainstream financial institutions.[48]

For Nestle, the practices connected with maintenance of the archives were woven into the daily fabric of the community, and as such were intertwined with the political struggles and other needs of the community. To this end, the lesbian community had an obligation to share in the work and financial well-being of the institution, and in return the community had a stake in a cultural organization that was open and available to all members as a cultural, historical, political, and social resource.[49] Although both Monahan and Nestle wanted LGBT history to serve the community, their significant disagreements illustrate the tension between using LGBT history for community-building and identity-making and the effort to gain mainstream acceptance through claiming a place in the national historical narrative. This tension was perhaps more keenly felt in the Gay Liberation movement than in the Black Freedom or Women's Liberation movements, due to the utter historical absence prior to this period.

Oral history projects also served to capture the diversity of the experiences within the community. In many ways, LGBT historians and archivists envisioned a democratization of historical authorship, and a key element of this movement promoted the use of oral history to document individual and collective historical experience. Guides for conducting oral histories trained nascent community historians in crafting an interview script that would acquire a rich snapshot of collective gay experience. Suggested questions probed personal background; early impressions of the queer community; coming out; same-sex meeting places; diversity of queer meeting places; sexual practices; friendship and relationships; queer humor; family-making practices; discrimination; institutional placements, including prisons, mental hospitals and the military; aging; and local history.[50]

Another important example of documenting LGBT collective memory was the Buffalo Oral History Project. Setting forth "to produce a comprehensive, written history of the lesbian community in Buffalo, New York," Avra Michelson, Liz Kennedy, and Madeline Davis began collecting oral histories in the spring of 1978. The project underscored the importance of oral history as a method that was "particularly valuable in documenting the lives of the invisible; one which allows the narrators to speak in their own voices of their lives, community, loves and struggles . . . [as] little research exists that documents the lives of 'common' lesbians who have left no written records."[51] Project founders considered their work a "political responsibility" and gave significant consideration to the ethics of representation, collaboration, and the return of project profits to the community. Davis, Kennedy, and Michelson also shared their methods for dealing with anonymity, publishing rights, archiving, and the parameters of consent forms. After three and a half years of oral history collecting, Kennedy and Davis began to write *Boots of Leather, Slippers of Gold: The History of a Lesbian Community*, a text that, once published, proved groundbreaking in the use of oral history method in history of sexuality literature.[52]

In addition to recording lived memory, LGBT archives sought to amass collections from community members. Organizations like LHA distributed guides to preserving one's own papers and collections, including conservation standards, annotation tips for correspondence, and organizational techniques.[53] Similarly, the San Francisco Lesbian and Gay History Project distributed a manual to show how "personal archives (letters, photographs and other artifacts), physician's case histories, institutional records (police, asylums, prisons, etc.), demographic statistics, residential patterns, and oral histories can be used to 'decode' the invisible history of gay people."[54] Grassroots projects such as these and other scattered local projects served not only to document and narrate a wide array of historical experiences but also to democratize the authorship of community history.

As in so many other facets of activism in the LGBT movement, a robust and passionate debate over archival ethics and practices flourished. While all archivists and historians sought to unearth tales of same-sex-loving practices from the past, there was a growing desire within the movement for all queer people to be visible. As Harvey Milk was calling for same-sex-loving individuals to come out in all aspects of their lives, LGBT archivists balanced a desire to preserve and tell the stories of the community with a need to respect wishes for privacy. When Joan Nestle issued a press release in 1982 to find lesbians who lived in New York City from the early to mid-twentieth century, she asked for materials and interviews spanning "anything that they are willing to share. Confidentiality assured."[55] Indeed, in most cases, archivists came down on the side respecting the privacy of their subjects, but this ethical position certainly was in tension with the larger movement's initiative to urge all queers out of the closet, a tension that never was fully resolved.

Throughout the 1970s and 1980s, grassroots and community history research projects served as an important cultural front for the goals of Gay Liberation. Countless projects blossomed on local, national, and transnational topics and took a wide array of forms: scholars hosted conferences devoted to the sexuality of Oscar Wilde and Walt Whitman's extended visit to Ontario; historians conducted oral histories of lesbians in New York City and in Cincinnati; and yet another project set out to document the lives of lesbian hobos. Activists developed archival collections in Toronto, North Carolina, Boston, and more; scholars put out research calls for sources on topics like lesbian pulp novels, lesbian and gay images in sci-fi literature, and leather subcultures.[56] In one particularly colorful example, the "Cincinnati Lesbian HYSTORICAL Society [emphasis in original]" put out a wide call in 1982 for anyone wishing to contribute their life story to the project, expressing a particular interest in "recording oral hystories."[57] Some of these projects failed to become fully realized. Yet their very proliferation illustrates the exciting frontier of LGBT history during the heyday of the Gay Liberation movement.

Community Education for LGBT Historians

LGBT activists who worked on the cultural front of the movement were passionate about sharing the collective past with other queer folk. These movement historians held dear the intimate connection between identity and history, and eagerly sought to return their research to the community. Out of this desire, LGBT historians developed community-based slide shows that were joyfully delivered and eagerly received. As improvised community centers filled to capacity with cheering crowds, young gays and lesbians coming of age during the 1970s and 1980s received an informal education in their own histories. Documentary films that attended to the historical experiences of same-sex-loving folks such as *Word is Out* and *Before Stonewall* also blossomed during this period, further generating interest in LGBT history. As queer historians reached out to the community through their educational efforts, they extended the larger movement goal of crafting a new political identity to the individual members of the movement.

LGBT historians eagerly embraced the community slide show format as a medium through which to share their research findings. These events gave scholars an opportunity to show visual materials like photographs, art, and book covers as they recounted LGBT historical narratives to highly enthusiastic audiences. John D'Emilio recalls a giddy euphoria sweeping over the audience as they watched images and listened to narration of a history they had long craved.[58] Scholars would often travel with their shows, booking a full tour of LGBT gatherings and relying upon local organizers to turn out a full house—a task that seemed to be anything but difficult in communities filled with gays and lesbians eager to learn more of a past they could claim as their own. Organizations like the Lesbian Herstory Archives also embraced the slide show format, in one instance sending "Archivette" Alexis Danzig out on a cross-country motorcycle tour to promote the collections and share the stories of lesbian history. The slide show format emerged rather organically for LHA. As archive volunteers sought out opportunities to connect with the community, they also found traveling with archival objects a challenging task.[59] Slides gave the presentation an exciting visual focus and were easily transported from one location to another. LHA representatives including Alexis Danzig, Deborah Edel, and Joan Nestle, traveled significant distances to present at Wake Forest University in Winston-Salem, North Carolina; in Toronto; Louisville, Kentucky; Santa Cruz, California; Washington, DC; and around New York City and upstate New York. Some slide show screenings, like the one at the Women's Studies Forum at SUNY Plattsburgh, complemented scholarly discussions, while women's bookstores organized others, with one slide show even functioning as a benefit for a local lesbian writers' group.[60]

One of the ways that LHA showcased the breadth of lesbian history was by the use of objects. One of their slide shows began with the *Ladder*, the first lesbian publication in the United States, and followed with other lesbian newsletters and publications, both historic and contemporary, after which came publications from international groups. The slide show showcased LHA's broad collecting scope through an impressively wide array of materials, including autobiographies, poetry, science fiction, handmade books, music, t-shirts, buttons, and boots. The show also offered a wide array of content, spanning themes as broad as lesbian mothers; male-authored works on lesbianism; third-world lesbian texts; conferences; photos of lesbian elders in New York City; a Daughters of Bilitis party in which a participant covered her face before the camera; and lesbian couples in literature, health, and sexuality.[61] For LHA, slide shows served not only to educate the lesbian community on its history, but also as a solicitation for donations of archival material.

Beyond LHA, many other community historians and activists in LGBT history projects utilized the communicative power of the slide show. On a given Friday or Saturday night during the mid-1970s to the mid-1980s, queers in towns across the country could take in a traveling slide show on an impressive array of same-sex-loving topics. Some were part of what would turn into scholarly research projects; some came out of the collective efforts of community history projects. Others were simply labors of love for a gay or lesbian individual who felt passionate enough about an LGBT historical topic to undertake research and produce a visual narrative. Some of the shows focused on simple historical inquiries bounded by space and time, such as Lesbians and Gay Men in Early San Francisco, 1849–1880; Our Boston Heritage; From the Gay and Lesbian Rights Movement to the Holocaust, 1860–1935; and 100 Years of the Lesbian in Biography. In other cases, slide show content reflected the growing transnationalism of the LGBT movement, covering topics as broad as African Women in Antiquity: Lesbian Themes among the Amazons; Mayan and Mexican Goddesses; and Gay Germany. Topics that echoed gynocentric themes flourished within the lesbian community, including The Goddess and the Witch; The Mother Goddess; Lesbian Erotica by Women Artists; and Yantras of Womenlove. Cultural history themes also proved quite popular, including What the Well-Dressed Dyke Will Wear—Dyke Fashion, 1900–Present; Gay Science Fiction; Lesbian Masquerades; Lesbian Pulp: Twilight Tales; Styles of Being Lesbian, 1890–1945; Lavender Letters: Lesbians in Literature; and *The Captive (1926)*. Still others underscored the importance of community to earlier generations, some examples of which were A Family of Friendship—Portraits of a Lesbian Friendship Group; Marching to a Different Drummer; From Boston Marriage to the Tell-All '70's; and The Heterodoxy Club of Greenwich Village.[62]

Film scholar Vito Russo took cues from his slide show peers in his own presentations. In community centers across the country, Russo screened film clips to illustrate his research for *The Celluloid Closet*, first a book (1981) and later a documentary film produced by Rob Epstein and Jeffrey Friedman with support from Russo. Russo's project traced changes in the treatment of gay and lesbian characters in American cinema. By screening such film segments, Russo brought his research into the community and used cinema to educate about the breadth of gay and lesbian experiences, causes, and identities: "Our movement has forgotten that our people are made up of drag queens, butch lesbians, angry mobs, s/m leather boys, vegetarians, AIDS activists, day-glo hippies, radical faeries, separatist lesbians, boy lovers, queer anarchists, witches, queer punks, pagans, and others."[63]

While slide shows certainly communicated a basic historical narrative to audiences, they also showcased complex scholarship. Narration often included quite nuanced historical points. For example, Gregory Sprague's introduction for his slide show *The Making of the Modern Homosexual* argued that "the cultural roots and antecedents of the post-Stonewall generation of gays can be traced back many decades before 1970. There is a continuity between those two worlds. This slide presentation will attempt to explore the historical transformation of urban gay subcultures into a national gay culture."[64] Sprague couched his scholarship within contemporary historiographical debates; this is perhaps most striking because his primary graduate training was not in history, but in education.[65] It is especially noteworthy that community historians brought such academic standards to bear on popular historical work. Most of these grassroots scholars, although devoted first and foremost to community education in the name of Gay Liberation, took their work quite seriously and gave audiences a carefully argued thesis rather than a simple congratulatory narrative. Occasionally, LGBT historians gave slide show presentations of material that would become monographs. Allan Bérubé presented his research on lesbian and gay soldiers in World War II via the slide show circuit before crafting his research into his highly praised book *Coming Out Under Fire*. Similarly, James Steakley, Eric Garber, and Vito Russo first presented research, which they would later publish, to community audiences.[66]

Although the gay and lesbian community enthusiastically embraced the production of slide shows, peer review was part of the process, as community historians often held themselves to the standards of academic intellectual production.[67] In a letter written to Sprague, visual artist and fellow slide show creator Judith Schwarz critiqued a proposed show entitled *Legacy of the Matriarchy.* Schwarz minced no words in her critique as she declared that she "failed to see how a goddess culture in a pre-technological culture can teach me how to deal with present society's treatment of women, especially lesbians, or even how I could deal with my sister lesbians in an atmosphere of 'peace and harmony.'"[68] Likewise, Eric Garber workshopped his *T'aint Nobody's Business* show with his peers at the San Francisco Lesbian and Gay History Project, where he received both support and constructive criticism. This discussion provided members of the group with the occasion to debate the political implications of a white scholar "speaking for" black gay experience.[69] Audience members and peers within the LGBT historian community also critiqued shoddy scholarship or inappropriately celebratory narratives, be the authors primarily academic or amateur historians. Although always enthusiastic for the experience, community members did not embrace slide shows uncritically but rather expected good scholarly practices from slide show authors.

LGBT historians who had some formal connection to the academy enjoyed research access and a kind of legitimacy that independent scholars did not have. Author and activist Marie Kuda presented over one hundred slide show lectures in a span of twenty-five years, yet her audience remained more of a popular one, and as an unaffiliated scholar she did not reap the benefits of academic affiliation. Active in the Gay Liberation movement in Chicago, Kuda researched and authored several slide shows and reference materials on the history of lesbian literature. She also organized conferences on the topic and wrote often for local and national gay and lesbian publications. Whether intentionally or not, her work found its audience on a much more grassroots level. Kuda utilized the slide show medium throughout the 1980s and 1990s to continue building awareness of gay and lesbian history, and she received several awards from local organizations for her educational and activist efforts. Yet her scope of influence remained largely outside of academic circles, possibly in part due to the fact that she confined her publishing efforts to bibliographic reference texts rather than interpretive works like Jonathan Ned Katz or Allan Bérubé.

The production of an LGBT past certainly produced a significant number of community and burgeoning academic historians, but the real impact of LGBT history was on the countless queer folks who couched their new political and often public identities in narratives of the past. After the publication of *Gay American History*, Katz recalled a profusion of correspondence from readers who were incredibly grateful for the new historical connections made to their own experiences.[70] Likewise, visitors to LHA often cultivated an intimate relationship between the personal and collective past, using archival documents for varied purposes from dealing with sexuality after mastectomy to using the space and materials to facilitate coming out to one's mother.[71] While community history projects undoubtedly provided an environment in which new political identities developed, they also offered a space of healing and grappling with the personal challenge of coming to terms with being lesbian or gay.

Into the Ivory Tower

From its beginnings in 1973, the GAU was a space for interdisciplinary collaboration and some of the movement's most significant intellectual production. The organizing members were a varied group, included academically trained historians John D'Emilio and Martin Duberman, literary scholar Karla Jay, and other young queer writers and teachers like Joan Nestle and Jonathan Ned Katz. Its membership thus spanned a potential divide between academics and community activists. By November of that year, the organization held its first conference with 325 gay men and lesbians in attendance.[72] Chapters quickly formed across the country, taking an organizational leadership role in both queer activism and academic legitimation. After much debate, members of the GAU settled on an agenda that straddled community and academy, collectively asserting "the interconnection between personal liberation and social change." Their statement of purpose articulated the link between the personal and the professional, as they sought "simultaneously to foster our self-awareness as individuals and, by applying our professional skills, to become the agency for a critical examination of the gay experience that will challenge those generalizations supporting the current oppression."[73] This initiative marked an important moment for the larger Gay Liberation movement—activists used the GAU to bring movement goals into the academy, a critical site of knowledge production about gay and lesbian experience.

As was common in many other grassroots organizations, contestation emerged over the purpose and direction of the GAU's mission. Although members agreed on the importance of equal gender representation, they disagreed over how to implement it, as well as over other issues like the inclusion of bisexuals. From the outset, the GAU attracted more gay men than lesbians, and women's roles within the organization became a conflicted issue. While many men felt strongly about the importance of dismantling patriarchy, others were less aware of masculine privilege within the Gay Liberation movement. Both men and women within the organization struggled to rectify this imbalance, first attempting to attract more women into membership, then striving for equal representation in leadership. Perhaps the most significant and fruitful outcome of this gender divide was the founding of the Lesbian Herstory Archives.[74]

As the Gay Academic Union flourished, its membership grew more diverse in terms of both member worldview and political goals. Many of its members embraced strong socialist values, including D'Emilio and Katz, yet as the organization grew, fewer members held radical viewpoints, and a more conservative group began to dominate the organization.[75] Union members began to debate the nature of the activism the organization should undertake. D'Emilio found the organization to offer a vibrant environment for debate, observing that "of course, we were academics. The verbal nitpicking for which we are famous at last served us well."[76] Yet rather than destabilizing the group, D'Emilio found that this contest led to a sense of "collective accomplishment."[77] But others felt that after a while the meetings started to lose track of the organization's founding purpose; Martin Duberman recalled feeling uncomfortable with how casually social the meetings had become, which he described as "excessive to the point of self-indulgence."[78]

Although the Gay Academic Union offered both social opportunity and scholarly support, the primary work of the organization focused on the legitimation of gay and lesbian scholars within the academy. This close connection to higher education was present for a few reasons. Many of its members came into the organization with a previous connection to universities and colleges, a relationship facilitated in part by the disproportionate percentage of highly educated white males involved in the organization's earliest days. For many of these activists, access to higher education came at the price of remaining in the closet, but they were also eager to change this by cultivating safe spaces for LGBT students, faculty, and staff. Participants of the organization's first conference recall that only a few members with academic appointments were actually out on their campuses, and certainly only if they had tenure.[79] Even in the cases where an academic might be out to colleagues and administration, ties to faculty members at other universities became a key form of support. Similarly academic members felt a need to organize within their individual disciplines. Historians within the GAU formed an informal committee of gay historians at the 1973 meeting of the American Historical Association (AHA) This group held sporadic meetings until 1976, when the committee fell apart due to a shift in GAU membership in which activists driven by a wider social justice moved out of the organization and the organization took a turn toward the conservative. In 1978, Gregory Sprague and Walter Williams organized the Committee on Homosexuality in History, which would shortly become the Committee on Lesbian and Gay History (CLGH).[80] CLGH did not gain official AHA recognition, however, until 1982, at which point the *Lesbian/Gay History Researchers Network Newsletter* was folded into the committee's publication. Not surprisingly, the emphasis on community-based archives and individual researchers rapidly shifted toward professional activities and disciplinary concerns at this point. In 1980, the *Lesbian/Gay History Researchers Network Newsletter* shared announcements about newly available research materials, including the *Gay Community News* on microfilm, popular books, memoirs, community newspaper articles, and pamphlets.[81] Other shifts toward the professionalization of history can be found as early as 1983, as the *Committee on Lesbian and Gay History Newsletter* featured a front page article recounting a discussion at the most recent AHA meeting in which presenter Harold Poor bemoaned that LGBT history tended to attract people interested in "rumors," a lament to which the panel's attendees nodded in agreement.[82] This is most striking in contrast to the eager embracing of rumor as the starting point for investigations for LGBT researchers only a decade earlier. In just under ten years, LGBT historical research had expanded from a frontier intellectual endeavor to a rapidly professionalizing practice, from casual conversation at parties and political meetings to the conference rooms of professional organizations.

Women working on lesbian history research also initially struggled for inclusion within women's history and women's studies professional circles. At the fourth meeting of the Berkshire Conference on the History of Women in 1978, a gathering of approximately two hundred of the conference's eleven hundred attendees, including a few gay men, convened as the lesbian caucus to address the systemic homophobia that prevented lesbian history from being integrated into women's history. Of the two hundred attendees, twelve lesbian historians, independent researchers, and archivists produced a memo to the program committee, blaming the conference planning group for a "proportionate lack of lesbian history content," in part by observing that the second conference in 1974 had featured two explicitly lesbian panels and that the third conference in 1976 had produced similar results. Caucus members were particularly frustrated that the 1978 conference engaged lesbian themes even less than earlier conference programs, a choice that seemed "to be, at best, a regression from the 2nd and 3rd conferences."[83] Using the rhetoric of feminist inclusion, the caucus argued the centrality of lesbian experience to women's history. This group, which remained an informal network after the conference, also provided a networking space for lesbian scholars and led to participants organizing several successful panels for the 1981 Berkshire Conference and the 1980 Women's Studies Association meeting.[84]

An Army of Historians Cannot Fail

The memory practices of a social movement like Gay Liberation are unintelligible in isolation. Memory, collective and individual, is a cultural production and, as such, reflects the larger context from which it comes. In this manner, the memory practices of Gay Liberation mirrored shifts in the larger movement. The early movement years were marked by a desire to connect all same-sex-loving people under a single unified, public political identity. During the early and mid-1970s, activists worked to lay a foundation for LGBT history, as they built collections and started to craft a master narrative of the community's history as an act of cultural self-determination. From these projects, they reached out to the larger community to offer up a new political identity to lesbian and gay individuals. Along the way, they conducted interventions into liberal institutions like the academy to redefine themselves and their pasts.

Shortly after publishing *Gay American History*, Jonathan Ned Katz reflected on how political consciousness and a desire for history were inextricable from one another:

> Only recently have lesbians and gay men begun to think of ourselves in time, as a long-oppressed and resistant social group. This new consciousness of ourselves arises from our recent political organization and activity. . . . Previously, deprived of our history, we were made

one-dimensional, diminished, trivialized. Without serious research into our history we made do with silly gossip. Learning our history gives us a deeper, more rounded, complex picture of ourselves. It tells us who we've been, so that we more clearly perceive who we are now, and who we could be in the future. [85]

For Katz and others, to seek a past went far beyond a recreational desire for history; rather, on-the-ground political work and cultural production reproduced one another. At the core of Katz's and others' sentiments was a desire to redefine their identity, to create a public, collective side that claimed full citizenship and celebrated difference. In this way, Gay Liberation activists were like their counterparts in the Women's Liberation and Black Freedom movements—all recognized the import of the cultural to such a goal. Katz's words are also illustrative of a striking phenomenon in the formation of identity. He began by talking of the newness of an LGBT historical identity, yet he also projected back in time a core, ahistorical gayness. Here Katz posited a coherent, stable, and timeless identity, a narrative that served to legitimate a contemporary political identity through the construction of a useable past.

LGBT history, borne out of private collections, rumors, living room conversations, letters exchanged between friends, and informal networks, changed remarkably during the 1970s and 1980s. Although LGBT history still has a strong connection to community organizations like archives and libraries, by 1990, historical authorship had transitioned from primarily being located in grassroots community projects and individual labors of love toward a highly professionalized academic endeavor. As LGBT studies became a legitimate area of research in the academy, the lines between community and scholarly history became more clearly drawn. Although community archives and individual scholars collaborated with one another, the majority of gay and lesbian scholarship centered on academic spaces and formally trained historians. Over time, the LGBT movement enjoyed much success in redefining same-sex relationships as normal loving human experiences, in significant part through the development of a political identity premised on the historical achievements and survival of same-sex-loving individuals and communities. As the movement shifted away from community educational efforts toward a larger social intervention, the terrain of LGBT history shifted also from community-based organizations toward larger liberal institutions.

Young girl dressed in tribal apparel at the Flagstaff powwow festival with parade performers in the background, 1963. Northern Arizona University, Cline Library, Marie Williams Collection, NAU.PH.2012.18.317.

CHAPTER 5

For the Sake of Cultural Survival
Red Power and Collective Memory

> Since our Indian culture is threatened by presumption of being absorbed by the American society, we believe we have the responsibility of preserving our precious heritage. We believe that the Indians must provide the adjustment and thus freely advance with dignity to a better life.
>
> —Statement of Purpose, American Indian Chicago Conference, 1961

On July 2, 1972, under a clear, cool summer sky in Flagstaff, Arizona, an audience primarily comprised of tourists waited with excitement for the Navajo-Yei-Be-Chai dancers to take the stage. Instead, a group of unidentified American Indian Movement activists took over the announcers' booth and flooded the stage just as the dancers began to move into the arena. The demonstrators encircled the dancers as they began their ritual movements, and off-site other activists cut the power to the public address system. The audience became aware of a scuffle in the announcers' booth, and an audience member yelled, "let him speak!" One of the protestors stepped forward in the booth, and in a projecting voice declared that "the Indian people should not have come to the Pow Wow and performed sacred ceremonies for money," suggesting instead that participants needed better housing, food, educational opportunities, health services, and jobs. After a number of activists were arrested, many remained, maintaining a protective circle around the dance.[1] For these activists and others mobilized by growing discussions of pan-tribal resistance, Native heritage was not an object to be commodified or to serve as amusement for white audiences, but rather a sacred practice that should be for tribal sustenance.

The Red Power movement, like other contemporary movements, deployed a variety of methods toward intertwining collective memory with political identities and movement initiatives. Place held particular significance for Native activists, and many political actions comingled historically symbolic locations with actions and demands for contemporary community needs. A significant portion of Red Power activism sought policy solutions, a distinction from other movements due to tribal nations' government-to-government relationships with the United States.[2] Additionally, the production of a politicized Pan-Indian identity remained a critical tactic, and much of the cultural activism involved strategies for producing and securing a Pan-Indian consciousness. The demand for self-determination and cultural autonomy in religion and other cultural practices proved a fundamental part of this work. Dominant U.S. culture had used American Indian culture and heritage in exploitative ways, and as such, part of the struggle sought to reclaim interpretive authority over cultural and historical narratives.

Many historians locate the emergence of the Red Power movement firmly within the context of other social movements that emerged during the 1960s and 1970s.[3] Indeed, it is useful to recognize the ways in which Red Power activists were inspired by and inspired other activists, especially those deploying the rhetoric of Black Power. Yet the intellectual foundations of American Indian activism are deeply anchored in indigenous activism that transpired in the several decades prior. Like the long Black Freedom movement, Native activists realized a variety of political and educational initiatives throughout the twentieth century, including the founding of the Society for American Indians in 1911, formation of multi-tribal organizations like the Alaskan Native Brotherhood and Sisterhood in 1912 and the Four Mothers Society circa 1895, the incorporation of the Native American Church in 1918, and the emergence of powwows in the same era. Although the Society for American Indians, the first Pan-Indian rights organization, only lasted about a decade, it is important to understand that the seeds of the Red Power movement were planted much earlier than the emergence of later, and better remembered, activist formations like the National Indian Youth Council in 1961 and the American Indian Movement (AIM) in 1968.[4]

This chapter, like others in this book, clusters heritage practices around three themes. First, a case study considers how one significant and long-running powwow served as a space of heritage negotiation between boosters in Flagstaff, Arizona, and Native communities who came together annually from 1929 to 1979. A second case study looks at the role that education played in the production of collective memory, especially as it manifested in tribal college curriculum and culture. Lastly, this chapter traces the use of memory in the American Indian Movement, with a particular focus on how activists used historically significant space in their occupations.

Heritage, Hegemony, Paternalism

To understand twentieth-century Native activism, one must recognize the nature of the relationship between American Indian nations and the federal government, an entanglement more complicated than the other movements studied here. The Indian Reorganization Act of 1934 (IRA), sometimes called the *Indian New Deal*, was an early federal attempt to shift away from centuries of paternalistic, at times genocidal, U.S. policy and toward the promotion of tribal self-governance. This well-intended effort, echoing other Progressive Era reform efforts, was an attempt to engage demands for sovereignty, but nonetheless codified the government's desire to treat all Native nations in the same manner.[5] In the 1950s, Congress began to espouse an entirely different approach, with a termination policy that would eliminate the legal standing of tribes and promote assimilation. This process would be realized, in significant part, through relocation programs that transplanted tribal populations from reservations into resettlement neighborhoods in various urban centers. Although termination and relocation were not bureaucratically linked, the processes worked together to create the conditions from which new Pan-Indian identities and activism would emerge. With the passage of the 1968 Indian Civil Rights Act, the federal government conceded assimilation as a failed project. As a result, much of the activism enumerated here contributed to the Indian Self-Determination and Assistance Act of 1975, a set of policies that increased the role of Native leadership in programs and initiatives.

From the 1860s to the 1970s, federal Indian boarding schools served as a fundamental link between U.S. government paternalism and the settler colonialist project of cultural extermination.[6] Some private, some facilitated by the Bureau of Indian Affairs (BIA), boarding schools removed Native youth from their tribal and familial contexts and sought to acculturate the next generation of Native communities in the ways of hegemonic American society, oftentimes through significant brutality and neglect.

Boarding school policy prohibited the use of tribal languages, and school leadership usually understood that part of their institutional mission was to eradicate the traditional cultural practices of Native communities. As such, boarding schools increasingly became a target of Native activism during the twentieth century, and the schools served as both a potent symbol of the need for self-determination and cultural autonomy and a touchstone for the cultural activism engaged in this chapter.

Arguably the most well-known manifestation of Native resistance in the twentieth century emerged in 1968 as the American Indian Movement (AIM). Building on the Pan-Indian consciousness that emerged in city centers during the earlier decades of urban relocation and community-building, movement leadership framed contemporary political struggles in the long history of Native/U.S. relations. Specifically, AIM activists sought "to halt America's longest war, which has continued for 483 years against the Native, sovereign, indigenous people; against our culture and our spiritual way of life; and against our Mother Earth."[7] In both outward-facing press releases and internal movement discourse, AIM activists framed their actions with a well-integrated sense of the interconnectedness of past, present, and future anticolonial resistance.

Education and Self-Determination

Indigenous activists had espoused sovereignty as a political goal and organizing principle for Native communities for much of the twentieth century. Although the founding of AIM in Minneapolis in July 1968 institutionalized Red Power, significant intellectual and activist underpinnings predated the organization's formation by a few decades.[8] The first long-lasting Pan-Indian political organization, the National Congress of American Indians (NCAI), was founded in 1944. Organized by boarding school graduates who had close ties to their individual tribes, early NCAI members had transformed the experience of being educated in multi-tribal environments into the basis for the Pan-Indian identities that would solidify in the following decades. Initially organized in response to BIA initiatives, one of NCAI's most significant outcomes was on the cultural level, namely the production and institutionalization of an early Pan-Indian identity and consciousness.[9] As the NCAI started to experience internal conflict by the late 1950s and early 1960s, the organization's central position within Native American activism shifted.

Out of the criticism for NCAI in 1961, the National Indian Youth Council (NIYC) emerged, heralding a new generation and approach to Pan-Indian activism, and arguing that "the future of Indian people will ultimately rest in the hands of the younger people, and Indian youth need be concerned with the position of the American Indian."[10] In contrast to NCAI members, NIYC activists were primarily recent college graduates from across the United States.[11] NIYC's younger activists embraced policy changes, but also foregrounded cultural concerns. This movement direction distinguished them from an earlier approach that worked more directly in partnership with the federal government.[12]

The American Indian Chicago Conference, a 1961 gathering in response to the destructive termination and relocation policies of the previous decade, brought a burgeoning group of young activists into collaboration with more established leadership. In the "Declaration of Indian Purpose" penned by D'Arcy McNickel and Tom Greenwood, delegates united under the principles of cultural sovereignty in the first point of the conference's working documents, declaring "we believe in the inherent right of all people to retain spiritual and cultural values, and that the exercise of these values is necessary to the normal development of any people."[13] Although the emergence of NIYC formally marked the rise of the Red Power movement, the self-determination groundwork laid by NCAI and other earlier activists served as fundamental bedrock to the subsequent activism of the 1960s and 1970s.

Despite a forward-looking vision that emphasized both youth leadership and the need to nurture a new kind of identity and political consciousness, the early Red Power movement nonetheless envisioned history as a fundamental tool of cultivating such. In the organization's founding documents, heritage was identified as central to realizing the new vision:

> We, the younger generation, at this time in the history of the American Indian, find it expedient to band together on a national scale in meeting the challenges facing the Indian people. . . . [W]e recognize the future of Indian people will ultimately rest in the hands of the younger people, and . . . we further recognize the inherent strength of the American Indian heritage, and believing in a greater Indian America.[14]

Indeed, activists like Clyde Warrior contrasted the development of new Native identities against the "selling out" of heritage, linking a reverence for customs and traditions to political activism.[15] Although the platform of the movement was sparked in part by dissatisfaction with the earlier generation's vision, activists also connected their own work to the legacy of the proceeding generations who resisted assimilation and U.S. hegemony.

The development of the Red Power movement, especially as manifested in organizations like NIYC, was deeply informed by other contemporary social movements. Although efforts toward self-determination had marked Native activism for the entire history of tribal interactions with the federal government, this demand especially took on new urgency and cultural intelligibility alongside the Black Power movement. Red Power activists recognized such commonalities, "when for instance, the blacks began to demand equal opportunity and civil rights," youth organizer Tony Machukay recalled that he too "began to figure out what the hell it was I really wanted as an Indian. When they shouted and cheered 'Black is Beautiful' I asked myself disconcertingly 'What about brown? What about that color?'"[16] For Machukay, this recognition provided not only political motivation but also personal transformation, as he "not only found some answers about myself, but also attained a sense of individual order, personal stability, well-being, continuous inquiry of the self, and a thirst for knowledge."[17] Indeed, other American Indian scholars argue that community education served as a vital approach for Red Power activists, an understanding of activism that complicates an earlier prioritizing of direct action tactics within the movement itself, as well as the resulting historical literature on the era.[18] Although this sentiment echoes so precisely that of many of the Black Power activists' reflections on their activism and educational work, at least one historian has argued that the distinguishing feature of the Red Power movement was its embracing of the ideas and values of an earlier generation of American Indian activism.[19]

Powwow: The Rise of Pan-Indianism as a Strategy of Cultural Survival

The history of powwows is a complex one and echoes larger themes in twentieth-century American Indian history, namely the resistance to both assimilation and the colonial gaze. One scholar of Native American history and culture has called powwows "one of the most powerful expressions of identity in the contemporary Indian world."[20] Yet beyond providing cohesion to tribal communities, powwows often were public events, attracting a white spectator crowd looking for an "authentic" encounter with the

Native other.²¹ As a result, Native articulations of heritage navigate both a communal sense of the shared past and a hegemonic, stereotypical narrative created by settler colonial culture. Indian hobbyists, or white devotees of Native spectatorship, often sought an image of the noble savage that was frozen in time and deeply primitive.²² Native dancers, on the other hand, used such spaces to cultivate and sustain Indian culture while also engaging in stereotype mimicry for economic survival. Thus, powwow gatherings were a contested space, cultivating group and individual identity and simultaneously providing white audiences with a screen on which to project their racialized ideas of the American Indian.

The rise of powwows in the post-World War II United States is noteworthy as an expression of a new Pan-Indian consciousness, but it is also a culmination of decades of resistance to policy that sought to eradicate dancing traditions. The first significant suppression of dancing culture came in the late 1880s, as the Ghost Dance ritual, a new religious practice embraced across tribal lines, emerged.²³ In 1890, the Wounded Knee Massacre emerged out of, in part, policy-makers and BIA officials' fear of the practice, and the ensuing slaughter of over two hundred Lakota people reflected the growing federal discomfort with Native cultural expression. BIA staff often sought to control tribal dances, and during the 1920s, some agents created "The Secret Dance File," a collection of reports on dancing traditions gathered under the leadership of BIA director Charles Burke, intended to help staff recognize and suppress cultural expression.²⁴ These documents denounced dancing practices as amoral and identified them as barriers to the assimilation envisioned by Burke's administration.²⁵ Despite this repression, powwow traditions emerged, echoing many different tribal war dances and even the Wild West shows of the late nineteenth and early twentieth centuries.²⁶

By the early twentieth century, white Americans expressed increasing interest in Native culture, when a new crop of youth organizations embraced naturalist activities that often included lore about Native populations. Organizations like the Boy Scouts and Campfire Girls appropriated Native crafts, dress, and dance as part of their curriculum.²⁷ Dances increasingly appeared in local fairs across the west, and one particularly well-institutionalized example was the fifty-year powwow that took place in Flagstaff, Arizona.

In 1929, a group of Flagstaff city boosters seized upon regional tribal cultures as both a tool for economic development and an attempt at cultural inclusion. That year, Elks club members Fred W. Moore, Kenneth L. Webber, and M. J. Pilkington took over the city's floundering Fourth of July celebration and incorporated Native dances into the festival's entertainment roster. They continued the tradition throughout the Depression, when the events barely broke even, and during the postwar years, the events proved increasingly popular. In the early 1930s, the boosters institutionalized the event, incorporating as Pow-Wow, Inc., seeking "to further, promote, manage, direct and hold, in the City of Flagstaff, Coconino County, Arizona, and elsewhere, Indian fairs and cultural exhibitions and displays of every kind and description for the purpose of educating the public in regard to the cultural developments and achievements of the Indians of the Southwest."[28] Although the organizers portended to be motivated by altruistic visions of education and cultural exchange, their own financial interests and desires to build up the city of Flagstaff must be kept central to this story. Regardless, by the end of the decade, an impressive number of Native folks were travelling to take part in the celebration; planners expected as many as twelve thousand in 1939. Most Native attendees did not dance or sell crafts, motivated instead by community and cross-tribal exchange. That same year, the event boasted that it hosted numerous tribes from southwest states, including Apache, Havasupai, Hopi, Hualapai, Navajo, Mojave, Piute, and Santo Domingo representatives. Many traveled hundreds of miles, coming from Colorado, California, and Montana.[29]

Although the event was envisioned to support a cross-cultural exchange, it is important to recognize that this event was organized and facilitated by white Americans, with little Native input in the organization and daily affairs. Increasingly, tribes began to participate in the festival as formal representatives of their respective nations. Likewise, Native communities increasingly took part in the planning and execution of festival activities. Yet still, by the mid-1970s, the twenty-six-member board of directors included only seven Native representatives, and as such, the Flagstaff powwow must be understood as an event that, at least in some respects, nurtured spectatorship and fueled objectification of Native participants for white Americans.[30]

By the late 1930s, event planners organized a residential space for Native participants, inviting them to camp in the Coconino National Forest. The powwow's 1939 brochure details the "Indian Village" that organized there, inviting white participants to visit the space and purchase handiwork from

Native residents, calling the opportunity to buy authentic crafts a "golden opportunity."[31] In fact, the village was billed as an attraction itself; the brochure alerted white spectators that the social dances held there were free to watch and even join in.[32] Organizers' paternalism and support for the federal government's history of removal was laid bare by the souvenir program that touted that "Not since the old days when the army rounded them up tribe by tribe have so many Indians gathered in one group as will be seen at the Pow-Wow Celebration."[33]

The festival certainly provided white Americans with numerous opportunities to produce racialized views of Native Americans. In one early piece of promotional literature, organizers offered up the region as "the lands of romance: the Indian Reservations, lakes, forests, mountains, Painted Desert, cliff dwellings," and so on.[34] Here, like in so many other mainstream representations of American Indians, tribal communities were melded, in the white mind, seamlessly with the landscape itself, rendering them as part of the natural world, objects that could be managed by dominant society. In contrast, the experience for Native participants was of a dynamic gathering with members from the same and other nations, a venue for the celebration (rather than the eradication) of their cultural traditions, and an opportunity to make money.

The festival often walked a delicate line between exploitation and cultural conservation. Planners imagined themselves giving Native participants a level of ownership over the powwow, even if through an amnesia of the white organizational history of the event: "It is the Indians' own celebration, their own get-together to dance, chant, compete in rodeo contests, trade and chat with old friends. But the whites have just as much fun watching the Indians cut loose at this, their own, annual fun fest."[35] Given that the festival drew large gatherings of Natives who did not participate in the marketplace or the dancing, Indians likely did define the gatherings on their own terms, beyond the intention of white Flagstaff organizers. Throughout the introduction to the festival, language choices place the agency of the powwow in the hands of tribal dancers. Yet the organization itself was run by white Flagstaff residents, offering a nonprofit structure that was "organized for one purpose only, to *assist* [emphasis is mine] the Indians in staging their Celebration."[36]

At turns, the descriptions in festival materials reinforced dominant views of Indian dancers and camp community as primitive, backward, and irrational. A section of the 1958 program brochure from the festival called "Superstitions and Taboos" depicts traditions that expressed fear of the dead, blinding powers of mothers-in-law, avoidance of traveling in darkness, and terror of cameras.[37] Other years' descriptions simultaneously attempted to debunk the stereotype of an uncivilized Native person while also reinforcing it by suggesting that we all have a savage within:

> Now, to awaken the "savage" within us doesn't mean that we will immediately seize a tomahawk and go on the warpath. At [sic] a matter of fact, most "savages" are much more peaceful, much less aggressive than highly civilized peoples. The true savage is very apt to accept the stranger as a brother unless some of the tribal taboos and rules are violated by the newcomer. The true savage is very probably less "savage" than a modern day representative of a totalitarian power. No "savage" anywhere ever did the things the Germans did in Buchenwald. No "savage" anywhere at any time did the sort of things the Kremlin orders done today to gain political goals.[38]

In fact, this description reflects more about Cold War U.S. diplomatic affairs than any true illustration of Native culture, using Nazi Germany and the Cold War-era U.S.S.R. as contrasting examples.

Although festival organizers' interests were served by cultivating an orientalist gaze, they also possessed a notable amount of concern for the interests of Native participants. The 1939 program prohibited spectators from recording any performances without explicit permission. Organizers' own financial interests certainly benefitted from this provision, but the disclaimer also offered a channel through which to secure permission for recording, provided that "such requests are from bona fide institutions and if the Indians concerned are compensated."[39] Such protective measures continued into the 1950s, when programs admonished white visitors to "enjoy walking through the camp, but before you take any pictures, be sure and secure permission from the Indians. If you treat them with proper respect, and friendliness, you will find they quickly respond."[40] Although the souvenir programs failed to document how Native participants perceived these issues, it is likely that the performers asserted the rights to their own images at some point in the festival's history.

By the 1950s, powwow festival leadership made efforts to contextualize each of the dances within the traditional cosmologies for the Apache, Oglala Sioux, Cochiti, Hopi, Zuni, Cheyenne, Jemez, and Sac & Fox nations. Scripts written for powwow announcers provided tribal background as they called the dances. For example, spectators learned that the Apache's Crown Dance was "in preparation for the deer hunting;" that the Cochiti Parrot Dance was "one of the most moving, because it is one of the most ancient, and history . . . ties this to the Mexican Aztecs;" that kids were standing in for the clown figures in the Hopi Happy Dance, because "clowns are very sacred priests in Pueblo ceremonies, and cannot be brought to outside events;" and that the Cheyenne Rabbit Dance was an opportunity to challenge stereotypes of the serious Native figure, as it was "one of those gay social occasions—a get acquainted affair where everybody dresses up and shows off."[41] By the early 1950s, event organizers began soliciting dance descriptions from the nations themselves, and it is worth noting that the tribes took advantage of this to manage the interpretation of their dances, as "the Apache want us to know that no real crown dance is held outside of the reservation," alerting white spectators that they were granted access only to the non-sacred parts of the dance.[42] Although the festival records do not reveal what led to these inclusions, it is very likely that the Native participants brought this knowledge, perhaps even demanded it, to the negotiation of the performance requirements.

Despite the increase in Native agency over the shape of festival activities by the 1960s and 1970s, the tone of the descriptions of the Indian Village had much more fully developed objectification as a part of the festival experience. In 1972, the Indian Village description introduced the spectacle on a more human level, but through a remarkably more exotic lens. Visitors were introduced to the encampment as "the site of trading stands, family reunions, and fun," reminding readers that "Indians are like people everywhere."[43] The guide goes on to instruct white visitors in a proper etiquette that reveals an ahistorical objectification: "For the white man, the encampment offers an unparalleled opportunity to see first hand how the Indian has blended the old ways with the new. . . . The white visitor is welcome in the encampment and he can look at anything or anyone he wants—he can even stare. But the favor will be returned in kind, because, frankly, the Indian is just as curious about the white man—his ways, his styles, his outlook on life—as the white man is about the Indian."[44] In this view, Native communities are constructed as a culturally isolated, pre-contact stereotype. Many historians have argued that their scholarship works against the idea that, by the twentieth century, Native Americans had all but disappeared, if not corporeally, then at least culturally.[45] In this instance, Native populations were configured as present but frozen in time, depoliticized from the context of the rising Red Power movement and rendered a curious premodern other.

More broadly, heritage tourism offered a complicated cultural production during the 1970s. The Bureau of Indian Affairs played a part in this, as they created materials to promote heritage tourism, materials that tried to engage white audiences with stereotypical views while also gesturing toward what a culturally sensitive engagement might look like. Throughout the 1970s, the BIA produced a series of calendars that highlighted Pan-Indian heritage. The 1975 version offered that "indian [sic] hospitality is well known, and the public is frequently invited," but also cautioned that "indian [sic] land is owned by Indians. If you attend an event on it, you are a guest of the Indians."[46] The publication also assured possible tourists that a portion of the cost of the calendar went toward a Native American educational fund for college scholarships. This invitation for white Americans to engage tribal communities reflected the anticolonialist activism of twentieth-century Native communities.

Powwow events, like the Flagstaff festival, held a complicated place within the growing American leisure culture of the twentieth century. Such events served as both a space where racialized views of Native Americans were produced and reinforced, but they also provided spaces for the nurturing of Pan-Indian identity and culture. By capitalizing on the fascination and exotic lure perpetuated by dominant society, they reinforced ideas of Native communities as primitive and subordinated. But they also challenged the idea that warfare and other policies had eradicated Native cultural expression and gave dancers the opportunity to craft a new sense of self that transcended the bounds of individual nations while also celebrating Indianness. Although the AIM protests described at the beginning of this chapter sought to reclaim Native dancing culture from white boosters and spectators, their own political consciousness was built, in part, on the changing definition of community nurtured by powwow culture.

Self-Determination, Identity, and Educational Autonomy

The desire for political autonomy and complete nationhood had been a guiding principle in Indian activism throughout the history of U.S./Native relations, but had accelerated and formalized in the twentieth century. One can see the logic of self-governance and community control from the earliest threads of early-twentieth-century Pan-Indian activism, and the principle itself became codified under BIA director John Collier through the Indian Reorganization Act of 1934, which restored Native control over mineral and land rights and sought to strengthen reservation life for Native nations. Activists argued that "Indians must help the BIA to correct its impression that Indian educational services are a privilege. Education is a right and an entitlement that was granted by the United States government to the nations in exchange for the real estate on which it stands. The battle continues."[47] To this end, educational activism sought to rectify centuries of cultural damage wrought by boarding schools through the promotion of a multicultural curriculum, active engagement with tribal languages, school calendars that honored holidays significant to Native populations while disregarding U.S. dates, fieldwork that cultivated Pan-Indian consciousness by bringing students into other tribal contexts, school space designed by Native architects, and a history curriculum that was organized, in part, around the political narrative of U.S./Native conflict.[48] From the preschool through postsecondary years, Native educators envisioned learning experiences that fulfilled the cultural, spiritual, and political needs of their students.

The first tribal college, Navajo Community College (later called Diné College) in Tsaile, Arizona, was formed in 1968, and by early 1969 offered classes and an Associate of Arts degree.[49] The 1970s saw the model spread to other reservations, and tribal colleges continued to grow through the end of the twentieth century. By 1995, there were twenty-eight tribally controlled colleges and three federally chartered Native colleges.[50] After the opening of Navajo Community College, other tribal colleges and universities (TCUs) shortly followed, including United Tribes Technical College in North Dakota (1969), Cankdeska Cikana Community College in North Dakota (1970), Sinte Gleska University in South Dakota (1970), D-Q Community College in California (1971), Oglala Dakota College in South Dakota (1971), Turtle Mountain Community College in North Dakota (1972), Nebraska Indian Community College in Nebraska (1973), Sitting Bull College in North Dakota (1973), and Blackfeet Community College in Montana (1974). By the twenty-first century, there were over thirty such institutions granting degrees across tribally held lands located in the United States.

TCUs were founded to address a decades-long desire for American Indians "to achieve participation in and control over their educational systems."[51] Although the ideological underpinnings for TCUs could be linked to early- and mid-twentieth-century conversations and organizational work, serious efforts emerged in the mid-1960s toward institutionalized tribal control over education at the primary, secondary, and postsecondary levels.

For NIYC members and other Red Power activists, one of the major strategies for cultivating a greater awareness of Native heritage was in the development of tribal colleges.[52] These community-controlled institutions were envisioned as both an alternative to mainstream colleges and universities, which had embraced curriculum that was either silent on Native issues or represented Native culture, experience, and history in a woefully incorrect manner. As a correction to this, the plan for tribal colleges sought to shift control of Native education back to the tribal communities as well as incorporate Native culture into all aspects of postsecondary learning.

Educational activists envisioned that the colleges would conserve individual tribal traditions, but also nurture Pan-Indian consciousness and movement-building. Planners sought to "do more than merely 'preserve' tribes . . . [but also] be the means for educating large numbers of Indians in an environment suitable for the development of self-confidence, both individual and collective."[53] Native education activists, like their contemporaries in other movements, recognized the importance of identity development in both creating stable individuals and an empowered community. In fact, tribal colleges were categorically charged with the task of assisting "students [with] their [college] orientation by developing a pride in the Native American heritage."[54] From their first encounter with tribal institutions, students would receive messages that directly contradicted the messages about Native culture, history, and identity that they had received from dominant society.

Beyond the production of identity, movement leaders looked to tribal colleges as a space to cultivate the next generation of tribal leadership, both as a general preparatory experience that built character and leadership skills, and also as professional development for specific fields. Planners asserted that it was very important to have "strong programs in Native American history, anthropology, religion, [and] folklore" to facilitate the general development of students.[55] Part of the reason these fields were underscored was their significance to cultural heritage, but they were also seen as opportunities to rewrite dominant narratives about Native culture, as "some of these fields have been dominated by an Anglo-American point of view, often to the detriment of the Indian community."[56]

Navajo Community College

As significant as the emergence of Navajo Community College (NCC) was in 1968, the idea long predated it.[57] Early-twentieth-century Native American activists discussed the idea of an Indian college when organizers of the Society for American Indians contemplated remedies to the damage wrought by boarding schools. The idea continued to appear throughout the twentieth century, at times envisioned as a revamping of a BIA boarding school, at other instances as a new institution. Regardless, the idea only gained serious traction in Native activist circles in the 1960s.[58]

NCC did not emerge in a vacuum, but rather echoed the decades of activism on Native educational autonomy. Patricia Locke, a Native educational activist and theorist who wrote extensively on decolonizing schools, envisioned heritage being woven throughout curriculum tailored for Native students. This vision was perhaps most viscerally imagined for St. Michael's School, located on a Navajo reservation in Arkansas, where the school building intentionally lacked running water, requiring students to carry all necessary water, a practice aimed at connecting them with the labor of their ancestors.[59] In addition to traditional arts comprising the core of the curriculum, space was also considered vital to educating Native youth. In a proposal for Native primary schools, planners envisioned that the buildings be "placed in the center of the community and designed by Indian architects who will incorporate cosmological concepts in the structure itself, including maleness and femaleness of structures, sacred colors, direction of entrances, and spatial preferences [as] an integral part of the learning environment."[60]

NCC's first brochure framed the initiative as an important step toward political self-government, recognizing its status as the first college to be located on a reservation, the first to be controlled by an Indian Board of Regents, and the first to be developed for the sole purpose of fulfilling the educational needs of young Native Americans.[61] The brochure also educated its readers on the importance "that these educational systems be directed and controlled by the society it is intended to serve."[62] In fact, activists would settle for no less that complete control over the tribal college.

NCC was an endeavor in creating an educational environment that cultivated tradition, but also reformed it for the contemporary needs of the Red Power movement. Rather than seeking to transmit Native traditions in a static manner, administrators recognized that education needed to be relevant to immediate needs within the community by observing that within the Navajo community "in between the spectrum of both the traditional and progressive Indian lies the majority of the Navajo, the moderate Indian, who has embraced a portion of the Indianness and white man's way of life. Establishing a college which could accommodate the Traditional, Moderate, and Progressive Indian has been and still is a challenge of this institution."[63] Yet this balance was not envisioned from the founding of NCC; rather, it emerged from debates that included the perspective of young Indians. In 1969, students responded to the heavy emphasis on history and culture within the curriculum. "Teaching us Navaho history, religion, and culture is good, but [not] trying to convert us back to real traditional Navahos, to the extreme. We can learn the old Navaho ways, but not stuff it down the students throat in terms of helping them find their identity. Our culture (which is slowly fading away into the past) is hard to regain. No matter what we do to regain our culture we can never be like our true traditional grandfathers. For this is a different generation with a different environment."[64] It is clear that the students' concerns impacted administrators, as just a few years later the accreditation report directly engages this matter.[65] Ultimately, although the preservation of traditional culture was fundamental to the project of tribal colleges, like other social movement contemporaries, a younger generation of activists ensured that these initiatives were constantly in touch with contemporary political struggles.

From its inception, Navajo heritage was envisioned as a critical piece of education and institutional culture at NCC. The school's initial brochure boasted that it was the first such college entirely under tribal leadership. School leadership tied their initiative to the overall well-being of the tribe as they recognized that "for any community or society to grow and prosper" self-determination in education was fundamental. Furthermore, it was "absolutely necessary for every individual to respect and understand his culture and his heritage," and this knowledge was intimately tied to the future of the tribe.⁶⁶ Here the tension between the pan-tribal impulses of the larger Red Power movement and the desire of some activists to focus their efforts within tribal bounds emerges most clearly. For many NCC leaders, the preservation of Navajo traditions superseded the development of pan-tribal movement-building.

NCC organizers were mindful that their new college emerged as part of a national and even international push for cultural ownership over education and the transmission of heritage. As students staged sit-in protests to establish black studies programs on campuses across the country and women were also beginning to demand courses that addressed gender issues, administrators contextualized NCC within the larger milieu of both radical educational reform and the larger social movements that gave birth to such. Navajo tribal chairman Raymond Nakai identified that recent activism: "This past decade has called to our attention the very real fact that we cannot ignore the minorities in our land—whether they are housed in ghettos, in the cities, or reside on reservations. The minorities, regardless of race, color, creed, and their convictions, are praying, pleading, and protesting to make their hopes and dreams known."⁶⁷

Curricular goals also echoed the causal relationship between autonomous tribal education and the production of new political, heritage-based identities for Native youth. This correlation could be seen most clearly in the objectives for the Native studies major, which sought to inculcate students with "respect [for] Navajo history, culture, and language," pride in being both Navajo and Indian, a commitment to working toward "Indian unity and cooperation," and engagement with "sacred and historical places important to Navajo culture."⁶⁸ Curriculum planners also saw the major as providing a significant foundation for the entire curriculum at the college, as it would prepare students with a fundamental knowledge of their history, culture, and the contemporary issues facing the tribe.⁶⁹

One of the most important issues addressed by TCUs was the instruction of Native language. Two major factors had led to a generation of Navajo youth who had little, if any, literacy in their tribal language: the assimilationist curriculum of the late-nineteenth and early-twentieth-century boarding schools and the termination and relocation programs of the mid-twentieth century. Built by Christian missionaries, social reformers, and one enthusiastically assimilationist army officer, Richard Henry Pratt, in the late nineteenth century, boarding schools plucked Native children out of their tribal communities and placed them in residential institutions far removed from their families and nations. In the name of civilization, school leadership sheared the hair of Native students, enforced English as the only language used, and prohibited students from wearing all cultural objects and apparel. By the 1890s, the BIA had embraced the model, opening several schools across the western and midwestern states. The cultural violence perpetrated by the boarding schools would come to haunt the educational self-determination struggles in the mid- to late twentieth century. The mid-twentieth-century BIA policies designed to terminate Native tribal structures and relocate Native Americans to urban centers furthered this process. Termination sought to close tribal rolls, liquidate assets, and make a final payment to all tribal members. Relocation programs gave incentives and promised new opportunities to Indians willing to move to cities, inflicting further damage on Native languages and cultural traditions.[70]

Like other movement educational initiatives, the curriculum at NCC somewhat mirrored that of mainstream colleges, but it was also constructed to serve the larger needs of the political movement. Historical and cultural narratives served both as instructional examples and as models for the kind of leadership needed by the Red Power movement:

> The history, tradition and culture of our Indian heritage are full of the tales of brave, proud men who led our people in peace and in war. Today, we face a new kind of battlefield, the battlefield of the dominant culture. Many of our reservations, our pueblos, our Indian communities are desperately in need of positive change. On every front we face crises, including education, housing, health care and economy. We worry that our culture will be lost, our young people will join the mainstream, our identity disappear.[71]

Tribal colleges were, at least on the surface, entirely in line with U.S. federal policy. By the early 1970s, policy-makers had rhetorically embraced the value of self-determination in Native education. The Department of the Interior issued a statement regarding NCC, congratulating the college on the progress it was making, in 1972. The letter called the college "a vital facility for the translation into action of President Nixon's policy" that prioritized "Indian acts and Indian decisions."[72] This sentiment would be translated into action when the BIA announced a few months later that it would pay the tuition for eligible Indians.[73]

U.S. national holidays like the 1976 bicentennial provided an interesting opportunity for the school. While acknowledging the complexity of engaging with the origin narrative of settler colonialism, Navajo Community College's presidential newsletter laid claim to having a part in that narrative:

> Indians are very much a part of this nation's history.... WE were Americans for thousands of years before Europeans came to our land and eventually built a United States in it. The most distinctive things about America are Indian—from the agricultural and medical contributions of our ancestors, to the fact that we have no peasants in America. Without Indian corn, tobacco, potatoes, beans, tomatoes, chocolate, cotton, and rubber, more than half of the US agricultural income would not exist.[74]

Although tribal college leadership devoted significant energy toward decolonizing Native collective memory, they also recognized that there was power in connecting the narrative to commemoration in mainstream culture. By resisting historical erasure in the national narrative, activists generated pride based on their role in larger historical forces such as agricultural development and the cultivation of foodways.

NCC administrators and advisors chose college faculty with care. Although the school opened with a mixture of Native and Anglo teaching staff, the vision of an all-Native faculty drove administrators to draw new faculty from nontraditional backgrounds and dismiss Anglo instructors whenever possible. In 1971, four Anglo instructors were terminated, an act that leadership touted as providing "another step toward the college's goal of Indian control over Indian education."[75] One way to realize the goal of Navajo instruction was to recognize skills and experience in lieu of traditional academic credentials. Instructor Mike Mitchell was one example of such an organic intellectual; he first worked at the college as a janitor, but as administrators became familiar with his rich knowledge of cultural heritage gleaned through a decade of self-study of Navajo dances and ceremonies, he became valued by the Navajo studies faculty, first as a guest lecturer, then as an instructor of record in history and heritage classes.[76] By employing Mitchell and others, NCC administration emphasized the importance of the transmission of heritage and rejected the dominant standards of historical knowledge production and education.

Another important NCC initiative tapped into the repatriation movement that claimed community control over cultural resources.[77] Museums from the northeastern portion of the United States began returning cultural artifacts to Indian nations at this time, and NCC leadership took this opportunity to develop a cultural center.[78] Administrators envisioned a space that both reflected and protected Navajo cultural resources, calling "for a multi-story building with a sanctuary in the center modeled after the Navajo legends' description of Changing Woman's home, built to the sun with walls of turquoise, abalone shell, white shell, and jet. The culture center will also contain a 'living' Navajo museum, a museum for arts and crafts from all Indian nations and classrooms and offices for the Navajo Studies and Arts and Crafts programs."[79] Material culture thus became an important teaching resource even as mainstream museums increasingly returned culturally significant objects to their communities of origin.[80]

In addition to language instruction, NCC administrators sought to incorporate traditional knowledge into the Native studies curriculum. To that end, they secured a $28,000 grant from the Weatherhead Foundation in New York City to collect oral histories from tribal elders and incorporate the findings into the curriculum.[81] Navajo studies and the larger curriculum both provided the Navajo nation with autonomy and community control over their children's education and served as an important correction for the twentieth-century disruption in heritage transmission, a result of both urbanization and early BIA education policy.

Despite its hopeful and auspicious beginnings, NCC soon encountered criticism from within and outside the institution. On the occasion of the school's dedication in 1974, an anonymous student shared his dissatisfaction with its leadership in a memo distributed to college personnel and visitors, charging the institution with top-down decision-making and a disregard for student council input.[82] Outsiders who wished to see the college succeed also found failure in unrealized potential. Peter A. Janssen, education editor for *Time* magazine, cited low graduation rates as an indicator and also faulted financial aid packages for skewing perspectives, as most students got more in tuition, room and board, and spending money than many Native families earned all year, promoting a lack of desire to graduate from the college and leave behind the financial aid.[83] In the same article, an unnamed faculty member also charged an absentee rate over 25 percent as a sign of the college's failure to cultivate a serious educational environment.[84]

Despite this criticism, NCC continued to operate. In 1997, the administration changed the school's name to Diné College, reflecting a growing preference for the name that came from their own language. In 1998, the school granted its first four-year degree. The success of the tribal colleges reflects the continued significance of heritage-based education for Native communities long beyond the acme of the Red Power movement.

The American Indian Movement: Space, Performance, and Collective Memory

> I am tired of talk that comes to nothing. It makes my heart sick when I remember all the good words and all the broken promises. There has been too much talking by men who had no right to talk. Too many misinterpretations have been made; too many misunderstandings have come up between the white men about the Indians. . . . Let me be a free man, free to travel, free to stop, free to work, free to trade where I choose, free to choose my own teachers, free to follow the religion of my fathers, free to think and talk and act for myself—and I will obey every law or submit to the penalty.
>
> —Chief Joseph

AIM activists chose the words and memory of Chief Joseph to lead off the Longest Walk Manifesto, one of the documents produced by the American Indian Movement.[85] In the quotation, the tribal leader expressed his frustration and disenchantment as the Nez Perce nation was forcibly removed from the Wallowa Valley in Oregon to a reservation in Idaho in 1877. Grounded in past struggles with the federal government, the manifesto articulated AIM's political demands within the context of Pan-Indian history. AIM, perhaps more than any other mid-century social movement, deeply intertwined the collective past with the demands for changes in federal policy and cultural autonomy. Throughout several actions involving the takeover of symbolic space, AIM cultivated a collective memory that was Pan-Indian and celebrated the long struggle for self-determination in Native American history.[86]

In July 1968, a group of about two hundred American Indians gathered for a meeting in Minneapolis, Minnesota, to discuss community issues, a meeting which resulted in the formation of the American Indian Movement (AIM). Established activists Clyde Bellecourt, Dennis Banks, Eddie Benton Banai, and George Mitchell identified urban Indian needs such as housing, education, economic independence, and legal autonomy. AIM spread across the United States, and local actions began to draw national membership support. Many of the organization's first notable actions included the tactical occupation of historic spaces, including participation in the Alcatraz Island occupation near San Francisco (1969–1971), Wounded Knee in South Dakota (1973), Fort Lawton in Seattle (1970), Ellis Island in New York City (1970), and the Bureau of Indian Affairs offices in Washington, DC (1972).[87] Although each of these actions demanded tangible outcomes for Native communities, the symbolic and cultural importance of these occupations called for recognition and inserted AIM into a historical narrative grounded in place. Additionally, activists envisioned such strategies as acts "to liberate ourselves for the sake of cultural survival."[88] Given the continual focus on the material needs of the community, it is noteworthy that activists also held such cultural survival as central to the movement.

The first of these occupations transpired on Alcatraz, a small piece of land in the San Francisco Bay. Under U.S. jurisdiction, the island had served as a Civil War fortress, a federal penitentiary, a lighthouse, and a bird sanctuary.[89] On November 20, 1969, several dozen Native American activists claimed possession of the island, seeking to "create a meaningful use for our Great Spirit's Land."[90] Although the occupation consisted of a rotating set of inhabitants, the group issued a proclamation that clearly outlined a vision for repurposing the island to serve the goals of community education and political uplift based in the growing Pan-Indian identity. Among the institutions envisioned by occupiers was a Center for Native American Studies, a spiritual center, an ecological center, and an educational center that was part vocational, part cultural preservationist in nature.[91] Leadership in the occupation contextualized the action as an "attempt to better the lives of all Indian people."[92] Activists also envisioned a museum to make an intervention in the cultural and historical narratives that demeaned Native culture. This cultural center was intended to interpret the "noble and tragic events of Indian history, including the broken treaties, the documentary of the Trail of Tears, the Massacre of Wounded Knee, as well as the victory over Yellow-Hair Custer and his army."[93] This document set the tone for all subsequent occupations and undergirded the movement with a political purpose squarely built on past injustices. The Alcatraz occupation continued until June 1971, ending only after the population at the island became increasingly drug-oriented and the U.S. government cut off electrical and water services to the island.

Although the occupation emerged most directly from the work of Indians of All Tribes, a San Francisco-based pan-Indian group, Red Power activism had been growing in the region for more than a decade. In 1955, the Intertribal Friendship House opened on Telegraph Avenue. Sponsored by the American Friends Service Committee, the house first served as a recreational space, then began incorporating a variety of services for recently transplanted Native communities who had been resettled by the BIA's relocation policy. The organization moved in 1960 to a location on 9th Street, then to Oakland in 1965. By 1969, the board of directors was entirely comprised of Native leadership, and in 1971, they launched a full social work program.[94] During the 1970s, the organization took on explicit heritage work, developing an oral history program documenting Native experiences during relocation and an educational slide show for center visitors, partnering with Oakland Museum and Oakland Public Schools on educational programming, and conducting in-service training for educators who desired to enhance their Native cultural literacy.[95] In October 1969, the center burned down, leaving a vast cultural and social hole in the community that would shortly thereafter be filled by the Alcatraz occupation.

The significance of the Alcatraz occupation was manifold. Taking place on historically symbolic land, it was a performance of collective memory linked to space, and as such became a construction of place.[96] As a somewhat isolated environment adjacent to and easily accessible by urban populations, the island provided a space that was intelligible as a Native reservation by virtue of its lack of running water and heat, a painful comparison made here by occupation leadership:

> 1. It is isolated from modern facilities, and without adequate means of transportation. 2. It has no fresh running water. 3. It has inadequate sanitation facilities. 4. There are no oil or mineral rights. 5. There is no industry and so unemployment is very great. 6. There are no health-care facilities. 7. The soil is rocky and non-productive, and the land does not support game. 8. There are no educational facilities. 9. The population has always exceeded the land base. 10. The population has always been held as prisoners and kept dependent upon others.[97]

Activists also found this a desirable space due to its proximity to the Golden Gate Bridge, a symbolic location that greeted international ships, where visitors could "be reminded of the true history of this nation."[98]

AIM continued to use the tactic of spatial occupation to build political momentum, make demands of the BIA that were rooted in historical injustices, and nurture a Pan-Indian identity. By claiming that the Fort Laramie Treaty of 1868 had deleterious effects not only for the Lakota Sioux nations but for all Native Americans, AIM ingrained in individual activists a sense of the Pan-Indian struggle. First in 1970, then again in 1971, AIM activists occupied Mount Rushmore to demand that the U.S. government honor the terms of the treaty, including the payment for land taken by white settlers.[99] In the space of Mt. Rushmore, AIM symbolically engaged one of the most impressive symbols of U.S. government. This national memorial space again became significant to the organization in 1975 as part of the "Bicentennial Year of Mourning."[100] For this action, AIM strove "to 'blow out the bicentennial candle' during 1976," a goal that the group kicked off with a four-mile march between Keystone, South Dakota and the federal memorial. Activists felt that the carvings desecrated the Paha Sapa, a space held to be a highly sacred center that was used for communication with the gods.[101] AIM's action was envisioned to "start a year of mourning" and included a "ceremony honoring Indian war dead;" the group also called upon Native Americans and non-Natives alike to hold peaceful vigils at FBI buildings.[102]

AIM again produced an intentional mingling of space and collective memory during the summer of 1972 when activists made plans for "The Trail of Broken Treaties," a mobile protest in which activists traveled across North America from the west coast to Washington, DC. Out of this action came a twenty-point position paper that demanded retribution for broken treaties and a new treaty review process, the abolition of the BIA, and increased self-determination in Native political affairs, as well as restitution in the form of social services like education, healthcare, housing, and economic opportunity programs.[103] The culmination of the march was the takeover of the BIA building in Washington, DC, an occupation that lasted six days and involved AIM seizing records from the agency that leadership found "incriminating." AIM leader Russell Means enthusiastically declared, "we have accomplished one of the major objectives of coming to Washington D.C.," to demonstrate the history of corruption and injustice committed on behalf of the federal government in Native policy.[104] This tactic not only used archival documents in the pursuit of contemporary legal justice, a strategy employed repeatedly by AIM throughout the 1970s, but also took the historical tools of dominant society to seek restorative justice for communities who relied less on documents than other sources for heritage.

The contest for religious freedom and unrestricted cultural expression was another significant issue for AIM activists. One of the key provisions demanded by the Trail of Broken Treaties Position Paper was a change in policy toward Native religious practices. Point 18 insisted:

> Congress shall proclaim its insistence that the religious freedom and cultural integrity of Indian people shall be respected and protected throughout the United States, and provide that Indian religion and culture, even in regenerating or renaissance or developing stages, or when manifested in the personal character and treatment of one's own body, shall not be interfered with, disrespected, or denied. (No Indian shall be forced to cut their hair by any institution or public agency or official, including military authorities or prison regulation, for example.) It should be an insistence by Congress that implies strict penalty for its violation.[105]

This language laid the groundwork for the ensuing struggle over religious and cultural autonomy that would crystalize in the late 1970s with legal defenses of the Native American Church, a claim that was supported primarily through the logic of heritage entitlement and religious freedom.

Probably the most famous AIM occupation was that of Wounded Knee. Began on February 27, 1973, over two hundred members of the Oglala Sioux tribe, buttressed by AIM members, occupied the town of Wounded Knee on the Pine Ridge Indian reservation in South Dakota to protest corrupt tribal leadership, U.S. failure to honor treaties, and the murders of two Indian men, Wesley Bad Heart Bull and Raymond Yellow Thunder. The location provided two opportunities for AIM to make an intervention into contemporary politics through narratives of the past: the first was to demonstrate how the history of the BIA had generated corrupt tribal leadership, and the second was to inhabit a symbolic place that echoed the history of treaty failure and federal repression of religion and culture through the Wounded Knee Massacre of 1890.[106] During the start of the 1973 occupation, AIM activist Carter Camp outlined the movement's demands:

1) The Senate committee headed by Ted Kennedy launch an immediate investigation of the BIA and the Department of the Interior for their handling of the Oglala Sioux nation.
2) Senator William Fulbright should investigate the 371 treaties between the federal government and the Indians to show how the government has failed to live up to the terms of its treaties.

3) The Pine Ridge Reservation tribal constitution be suspended and the Oglala Sioux be allowed to elect their own officials.[107]

These demands melded the interests of the Oglala nation and the larger Pan-Indian movement and reflect the matured AIM strategies, inhabiting historically significant spaces and using narratives of the past to support tribe-specific demands in the present.

As the encampment began to plan for the future, leadership was restructured and social organization closely mirrored the traditional ways of Native nations, including communal living, equal distribution of clothing and food, and the establishment of medical aid and building provisions. Occupants distributed labor equally and set up a provisional government that was, interestingly enough, modeled on the Provisional Revolutionary Government of South Vietnam.[108] In this, movement leadership cultivated awareness of tradition for a younger generation of activists, some of whom may have never lived on a reservation or perhaps even outside of urban communities.

Although spirituality had been a focus in other encampments, Wounded Knee leadership especially emphasized the significance of traditional religious practices to the success of their nation-building efforts. Indeed, "spiritual strength" was a critical front "in the work to overcome the U.S. government."[109] Leonard Crow Dog served as the spiritual leader of AIM, which identified the significance of embracing traditional Native spiritual practices in the context of sustaining social movements. Within the fledgling community, "people are given time to meditate, pray, and question the way of living. . . . [T]he Indian people, Black people, Chicano people as well as national minorities have gone through a cultural awareness awakening. Inside Wounded Knee the fighting spirit is guided by a spiritual way of life that appeals to all enslaved people to join together and become free *by any means necessary* [emphasis is mine]"[110] Although historians often see continuity across social movements in this era, it is important to recognize the ways in which activists themselves were drawing connections to contemporary struggles for liberation, a gesture clearly made here by using the words of Malcolm X within AIM internal literature.

The significance of these occupations to Native identity was varied. One contemporary anthropologist noted that while many of the federal policy decisions realized during the twentieth century had led to a deterioration of Native identity, "the Occupation, the court trials [related to the occupation], and the Sun Dance [a ritual of renewal that was used as part of the protest to reference Sioux cultural traditions] are arenas wherein Indian manhood and achievement can be displayed."[11] It is also notable that this scholar identified the gendered components of the production of identity, as few social scientists in the 1970s actively used an analysis of gender in their work. Still another Native scholar applauded the centrality of ritual to AIM's interventions, identifying the importance of intergenerational connections through "the strong ceremonial life and the presence of medicine men in the Wounded Knee compound[, which] diffused a great deal of the criticism that would have been forthcoming from members of other Indian nations."[112]

The use of historically symbolic space proved a powerful tactic in the cultivation of collective memory within AIM. The occupation strategy first expressed at Alcatraz drew public attention to the history of federal displacement policies, creating an explanation for the contemporary struggles of American Indians. The Longest Walk, a 1978 five-month protest march from San Francisco to Washington, laid a kind of claim to vast swaths of land that had been once "occupied" entirely by Native populations, and the subsequent takeover of the BIA building in Washington, DC, implicated the federal agency in the long history of exploitation and repression. The occupation on the Pine Ridge reservation served as a demand for political autonomy and introduced the demands of AIM to white Americans. Other more short-lived occupations at Fort Lawton in Seattle and on Ellis Island in New York City brought awareness of Native American history to their respective surrounding communities. And equally significant, these actions gave a new generation of Native activists a personal connection to narratives of the past.

Conclusion

The Red Power movement's memory practices both paralleled and departed from other identity-based movements in several ways. Like the Black Power movement, self-determination was at the forefront of Red Power activism, even if the historical and legal structures surrounding this matter looked very different for each movement. Similar to other movements, the sharing and building of cultural memory, especially through the development of tribal colleges, served as both narrative and process in support of nationalist efforts. Like efforts in the Women's Liberation and Gay Liberation movements, American Indian efforts to redefine indigeneity sought to shift one's internal sense of self toward the collective, particularly the Pan-Indian. While a negotiation existed between the essentializing stereotypes of mainstream history and the movement's political interest in cultivating a strong sense of Pan-Indian identity, Red Power activists transformed the traditional narrative of social and cultural pathology into one of resistance, resilience, and adaptation.

A tension lingered within the Red Power movement's cultural heritage strategies between maintaining and preserving individual tribal customs and identities and generating a Pan-Indian consciousness. This somewhat contradictory work explains the simultaneous reservation-based cultural preservation like fish-ins alongside urban Native activism like AIM occupations and rhetoric that promoted a singularity of Native activism. Likewise, Red Power renegotiated the long legacy of the policy relationship with the federal government. For example, the trauma wrought by boarding school education fueled many formal and informal educational initiatives within the movement.

The collective memory practices of Red Power supported the more overtly political actions of the movement and operated on several fronts. Across forty years of the Flagstaff powwow festival, participants claimed cultural self-definition, Pan-Indian community-building, and economic benefit from an event premised on hegemonic exploitation and white authority. Educational activism like the development of tribal colleges served as a direct initiative toward self-determination, which built on decades, if not centuries, of struggle. AIM's symbolic work of place-based interventions was a direct response to centuries of treaty violations, the production of poverty within the reservation system, and the cultural warfare of termination. Through a variety of collective memory practices, Red Power activists transformed the legacy of assimilation, termination, and urbanization into reclamation of culture, identity, and hope for the future.

Conclusion
From Foot Soldiers to Citizen Historians

> We have lost control of our cultural institutions. Liberalism long ago captured the arts, the press, the entertainment industry, the universities, the schools, the libraries, the foundations, etc. This was no accident.
>
> —Rush Limbaugh

In 1992, the Maryland Historical Society in Baltimore handed the keys to their artifact storage room to Fred Wilson, a young visual artist of African, European, and American Indian decent, allowing him free rein in creating an exhibit. Using only items in the collection, Wilson's *Mining the Museum* employed historical artifacts in radically different contexts, a curation that teased out racial narratives embedded in seemingly neutral objects and disrobed the social role of museum collections. Wilson presented his work as an intervention in the museum itself, a place where "multiple meanings are lost and the complexity of the object and of those who remembered them is lost with it." Wilson cautioned that, "museum people are mistaken when they believe museums collect 'things.' They collect memories, meanings, emotions, and experiences."[1] His institutional intervention was an act of reclamation that exposed latent taxonomical meanings and hidden histories within the museum's collections and interpretations. It was a memory practice that would have made the activists considered within this book proud.

In the late 1980s and into the early 1990s, the political climate in the United States was erupting in what came to be known as the culture wars. By the end of the 1970s, identity-based movements had mostly dissipated, their activist and social justice energy diffusing into myriad other efforts at both the policy and the grassroots levels. As this reform energy moved from the margins toward the center of American society, the focus of cultural activism shifted from internal identity construction and separatist nation-building toward a demand for mainstream cultural and educational institutions to accurately reflect the diversity of American identities and experiences.[2] As a result, activists concerned with identity-based history work began to focus on representation in mainstream museums and state and national curricular standards.

Although debates over history education flourished throughout the twentieth century, in the late 1980s conservatives began to attack both public school curriculum and cultural organizations for embracing multiculturalism and critically interrogating the historical production of whiteness, masculinity, and compulsory heterosexuality.[3] This backlash was a clear response to the political and cultural advancement made by women, people of color, and sexual minorities in the decades prior. Although what became known as the "curriculum wars" provided instructive examples of the contours of the conservative backlash of this era, perhaps the most significant impact of the memory practices of the 1960s and 1970s can be seen in national and mainstream museums. While it is important to interrogate this conservative backlash, we must also recognize the changes in the cultural sector and museum professions that influenced the more pluralistic and inclusive narratives, as well as recognize the influence of earlier social movements on those professional changes. Focusing here on the shifts that emerged within museums, we can see the tendrils of identity-based ownership of history that branched out from social movement collective memory work. The impacts of this collective memory work and the professional response to it were: 1) the proliferation of new museum exhibits and programming on traditionally underrepresented history topics; 2) the demand (if not always a successful one) for identity-based national museums; 3) new museum approaches that strove for inclusivity, multiculturalism, and dialogue; and 4) the resultant backlash from the newly formed conservative religious right.

By the early 1980s, mainstream cultural institutions were beginning to mount exhibits on black and women's history and increase their holdings in art created by black, women, and queer artists. One of the most significant examples of the multiculturalist turn in mainstream cultural organizations, *Mining the Museum* provided a model for critical curation from the perspective of a historically marginalized subjectivity. Fred Wilson's work directly challenged longstanding recurrent themes in U.S. history, from westward expansion to the benevolence of slavery. In the first exhibit room, Wilson placed drug store Indian statues facing photographs produced by the Maryland Commission on Indian Affairs against a map of Maryland. The map overlaid contemporary hunting and gun clubs with historical Native tribal territories. In another section, video featuring a dark-skinned narrator was projected through a torn canvas depicting the face of a white man, an installation that evoked the inner struggles of racial passing as the voice whisperingly reminded, "nobody knows that I am inside of you."[4] Provocative juxtapositions like a Ku Klux Klan hood nestled in a nineteenth-century baby carriage startled viewers into engaging with the enduring legacy of racism.[5] In a section entitled "African-Americans Who Resisted Slavery," a painting depicting the uprising at Harper's Ferry and pikes used in the struggle contrasted with the domestic idyll of a child's dollhouse showing black domestic labor, as the names of black abolitionists projected across the scene.[6] Throughout the exhibit, traditional narrative labels were abandoned in favor of loose associations. As a result, time and space flowed freely as visitors were left with impressionistic ideas about race, violence, exploitation, and memory, while also encountering many of the themes taken up by Black Power activists nearly two decades earlier.

Beyond expanding content to include black history in a mainstream museum, *Mining the Museum* marked a significant shift in exhibition practices within professional museum circles, exemplifying a larger change in mainstream cultural institutions that was just beginning to foment. The efforts of movement activists to institutionalize their community history within grassroots organizations, the academy, museums and archives, and curriculum standards inspired, and at times pressured, cultural institutions to redefine their constituent base. The political, intellectual, rhetorical, and cultural impact of the social movements of the earlier decades generated a crisis in museum authority, and Wilson's work was a perfect example of recent shifts in cultural authority, a shift applauded by many, but also reviled by some.

In 1988, the Smithsonian National Museum of American History opened their first major exhibit on black history with *Field to Factory: Afro-American Migration, 1915–1940*. Historian and curator Spencer Crew transformed a 1985 public radio piece into a visual format, telling the stories of the Great Migration. Widely praised for tackling important and overdue content, *Ebony Magazine* declared that *Field to Factory* was "such an important part of America's social and demographic history from a Black perspective."[7] The exhibit, which was based on oral histories, led visitors through a series of rooms intended to invoke the journey northward. While *Field to Factory* took fewer risks than Wilson's juxtaposed symbols of white supremacy and white childhood, it nonetheless marked an important moment with the arrival of black history on the National Mall.[8]

Gender also increasingly became a category of analysis for mainstream history museums, even if it didn't provoke such significant interventions as African American history. For example, an exhibit produced by the New York Historical Society in 1982, entitled *The Female Touch: The Ladies' Periodical as a Reflection of an Age*, explored the ways in which late-nineteenth-century women navigated a public world that was relatively hostile toward their participation.[9] Here a major cultural institution sought to be more inclusive in the stories told and gave in to cultural pressure to represent the history of women as more than an accent to traditional narratives. Other early exhibits devoted to women's history included the 1964 opening of the First Ladies exhibit at the Smithsonian National Museum of American History and 1984's *Black Women: Achievement against the Odds* at the Anacostia Neighborhood Museum, both revealing the ways museums were responding to the larger political demands of the women's movement.[10]

The history of queer Americans was less easily integrated into mainstream institutions, but inroads were made with the New York Public Library's *Becoming Visible: The Legacy of Stonewall* in 1994.[11] The exhibit, developed to commemorate the twenty-fifth anniversary of the Stonewall Riots, proved to be a litmus test for questions of funding, as the National Endowment for the Humanities (NEH) refused to back it, a cautious decision that was likely fueled by the NEA funding controversies regarding queer artists whose work provoked another conservative backlash.[12] Major museums like the Chicago History Museum (CHM) and the Minnesota Historical Society began to undertake major interpretive projects and programming related to LGBT historical experience, but these did not appear until the late 2000s and early 2010s, with the 2011 opening of CHM's *Out in Chicago* as the first major exhibit on LGBT experience in a mainstream history museum. Around this time, historic house museums like Chicago's Jane Addams Hull House Museum also began to experiment with interpreting same-sex-loving experiences through methods such as exhibit labeling that promoted dialogue about identity and history. Such inclusive

CONCLUSION 161

exhibitions, while not yet fully embraced by national museums and taking a significantly longer time to emerge than other identity-based exhibits, nonetheless demonstrated that the cultural activism of the earlier generation had successfully, if slowly, shifted mainstream representations toward a pluralistic ideal that was nearly unimaginable thirty years prior.

Arguably, the most visible outcome of 1960s and 1970s activism on the institutional landscape of the 1980s and 1990s was the development of the identity-based Smithsonian museums. During the late 1960s, Smithsonian administrators embarked on a few projects meant to bring African Americans and American Indians more meaningfully into the national museum fold, including the development of the Anacostia Community Museum (interpreting black history in a Washington, DC, neighborhood) and the Smithsonian Folklife Festival, a multicultural celebration that showcases living cultural traditions, including American Indian exhibits.[13] While each identity group generally held these initiatives as positive experiences, archaic and at times even offensive representations within the larger Smithsonian venues remained. After legislative introduction in 1989 and many years' worth of work to bring it to fruition, the National Museum of the American Indian opened its doors in 2004. Spanning an even more remarkably long period of development, black history activists first voiced a desire for a national memorial in DC in 1915, and after decades of efforts and varied plans to recognize the contributions of black Americans to U.S. history, the National Museum of African American History and Culture finally opened its doors in 2016. Efforts at establishing a national women's history museum date back to the 1990s, and in 2013 Congress finally directed a commission to study the possibility of making it a federal entity. In 2016, a bill was introduced to commission a study on developing the Smithsonian Asian Pacific American Center into a full-fledged museum. Efforts to establish an American Latino Museum led to the introduction of a bill, also in 2016, but it remains to be seen if and when such museums are incorporated into the Smithsonian complex in the future. Other national identity-based museums emerged in the 1990s and 2000s, but none carry the cultural heft of the National Mall museums.[4]

If we compare the memory practices of social movements in the 1960s and 1970s to museological shifts in the 1990s, we can see some of the impact of identity-based claims on the past. Red Power had perhaps one of the most immediately significant impacts on cultural policy. After fifteen years of lobbying efforts, in 1990 Congress passed the Native American Graves Protection and Repatriation Act (NAGPRA), legislation that provided for the return of unlawfully obtained human remains and cultural artifacts to Native American tribes. In concert with NAGPRA, the passage of the National Museum of the American Indian Act provided for the establishment of a stand-alone Smithsonian institution that would facilitate the repatriation of objects held by museums. Repatriation required that human remains, culturally significant objects, and sacred objects be returned to the tribe, clan, or village from whence they came. Although the museum had a contentious relationship with various activists and groups, this was the first identity-based institution to secure cultural space on the National Mall.[15] This victory fueled the concurrent demands for other identity-based Smithsonian outposts, enriching the mainstream public history institutions toward inclusion and a fuller representation of American experience. The slow shift in cultural authority seen in the history of the Flagstaff powwow festival and the reclamation of historically significant spaces by American Indian Movement activists prefigures this policy change, as Native Americans reclaimed their heritage away from the forces of settler colonialism and white cultural appropriation.

The idea for the National Museum of African American History and Culture had circulated much earlier, yet organized efforts to realize a national museum devoted to African American experience and history grew significantly more forceful in the late 1980s and early 1990s.[16] After much continuing debate over the interpretive scope and the rationale of a separate institution, the National Museum of African American History and Culture was endorsed by Congress in 2003 and voted into existence by the Smithsonian Board of Regents in 2006. In 2016, the museum opened to positive reviews from popular and scholarly sources alike. Criticisms emerged from the traditional voices of culture warriors like Senator Jesse Helms who "warned that approving an African-American museum would only open floodgates to demands by other groups," an outcome that was perhaps likely, although not lamented by those committed to liberal values.[17]

The drive to establish a national women's history museum has had a much more fraught path. After several years of pressure, in 1997 Congress voted to restore the location of a 1920 statue depicting women's rights advocates Elizabeth Cady Stanton, Susan B. Anthony, and Lucretia Mott from a basement "crypt" to the Capitol Rotunda. *The Woman Movement,* or the *Sisters of the Crypt* as the piece had come to be known due to its exhibit location, had been commissioned by the National Women's Party to mark the passage of the Nineteenth Amendment and was promptly hidden from view after the dedication ceremony.[18] In 1995, feminists Joan Meacham and Karen Staser used the occasion of the seventy-fifth anniversary of the Nineteenth Amendment to call for a more prominent place of display for the statue. The sculpture was not only a site of struggle for the historical interpretation of gender, however, but also of race. As the campaign to move the piece into the rotunda brought attention and conversation to the artwork, the National Political Congress of Black Women began to push to add activist Sojourner Truth, an African American woman, to the sculpture, asserting that the struggle for women's right to vote would be incomplete without Truth's inclusion.[19] Efforts to place the statue in the rotunda succeeded, and Congress also conceded to placing a bust of Truth in the Capitol.

Reflecting the contestation over fixing women's place in the national historical canon, efforts to establish a national museum devoted to women's history have proven elusive. The women who worked to restore the suffragist memorial sculpture to the Capitol Rotunda extended their efforts toward building a museum on the National Mall. After nearly two decades, the museum has yet to secure the funding and political will to do so, though the appointment of the Congressional Commission on an American Museum of Women's History in 2014 to study the viability of the project was a step forward. Some have blamed mismanagement of the National Women's History Museum fundraising campaign for the inability of the project to get off the ground.[20] The museum also has experienced significant controversy over its leadership, with two successive presidents who seemed indifferent to historical scholarship and the input of historians of women. In 2014, the museum made news by summarily dismissing their Scholarly Advisory Council shortly after council members raised concerns about an online project that was "riddled with historical errors and inaccuracies."[21] Although women's experiences have been significantly integrated into other mainstream museums, many feel that there remains a significant lack in "America's Front Yard" as long as a national museum dedicated to women's history remains an unrealized vision.[22] This desire to have an institutionalized space within the federal museum system without concern for historical accuracy or complexity is an example of the limits of identity politics in public history. The current leadership of the National Women's History Museum desires to uncritically celebrate the achievements of women, an approach to collective memory that leaves no room for critical engagement, diverse representation across race, sexuality, and other categories of privilege, and also fails to integrate women into the national narrative by favoring the "add-women-and-stir" method critiqued by scholars of women's history for several decades.[23]

Somewhat similarly, the LGBT community has yet to realize a mainstream national museum. Although the holdings at San Francisco's GLBT Historical Society are rich and national in collecting scope, the "queer Smithsonian" lacks the state-sanctioned validation enjoyed by the National Mall institutions. Time will tell if LGBT groups will seek their own federally sanctioned national museum, but if the other identity-based museums indicate anything, it's that such an endeavor requires a mixture of political will, legislative savvy, and extensive negotiation between stakeholders and professionals.

Another significant outcome of the memory practices of the 1960s and 1970s emerged within museum professional practices. The 1990s ushered in a growing commitment by museum professionals to broaden representation and to create democratic spaces for civic dialogue, one charge among a "dizzying list of new social purposes" taken on by history museums in the last several decades.[24] Having been generally influenced by the demands from social movements of the 1960s and 1970s and particularly inspired by the cultural interventions made by activists like those examined in this book, curators, administrators, and museum educators began to reimagine their role less as authorities and more as facilitators. Two groundbreaking conferences sponsored by the Smithsonian International Center in 1988 and 1990 resulted in the publication of two highly influential edited volumes, *Exhibiting Cultures* and *Museums and Communities*.[25] Ivan Karp and Stephen D. Levine, editors of *Exhibiting Cultures*, echoed the language of earlier collective memory activists, arguing that debates over cultural representation "resolve themselves into claims about what a nation is or ought to be as well as how citizens should relate to one another."[26] Shortly after, the American Association of Museums released a report entitled *Excellence and Equity: Education and the Public Dimension of Museums*, a document that called for museums to reimagine themselves as in service to their communities broadly as educational institutions and pluralistic sites of debate.²⁷ In the ensuing decades, history museum professional culture deeply embraced the shift from temple to forum, still serving as a space for the reverent contemplation of material culture, but also deeply embracing the role of promoting dialogue about contemporary issues and the interpretation of the past.²⁸

Democratizing work also transpired in other cultural sectors. The passage of NAGPRA, as mentioned earlier, further urged cultural institutions to be accountable to their communities and to view themselves more as stewards than authorities. Similarly, a new generation of social historians serving on the curriculum committee at Colonial Williamsburg in 1977 initiated a major revision in the interpretive scope of the site itself, toward "a 'laboratory' in which to examine social relationships rather than 'as a storehouse of moral precepts.'"²⁹ This example illustrates one way that museum leadership began to envision their cultural role as one that promoted dialogue rather than simply transmitted knowledge.

Academic conversations also echoed concern with the power of cultural representation, with the expansion of Michael Frisch's concept of *shared authority* being one of the most widely influential ideas to emerge.³⁰ Although Frisch introduced the concept as both an ethical practice and unintended outcome of the process of the oral history interview, the framework gained rapid popularity in museum studies and the new field of public history, providing cultural workers a method for engaging communities and exploring multiple meanings in interpretation. From this angle, it seemed that the cultural activism of earlier social movements had won a major victory by pressuring mainstream institutions to rethink their representational choices and methods. This practice both validated the existence of community memory and gave museum professionals a method for engaging communities directly. Without the groundwork laid by social movement activists a generation earlier, such a practice would have been unthinkable.

But the advances made toward more pluralistic and democratic cultural representations were not without backlash. As professional debate over cultural authority and ownership flourished in museum circles in the early and mid-1990s, a conservative response emerged against museum exhibits that employed pluralistic inclusion and shared interpretive authority. In an essay on the recent democratic impulses in the museum world, one conservative periodical expressed anxiety over "would-be radical reformers . . . working within the state-dominated museum to subvert the 'perpetuation' of the supposed 'ideology' of the state" and cited *Mining the Museum* as an example of this trend.[31] Conservative pundit Rush Limbaugh's 1993 book *See I Told You So* served as the conservative's battle cry to the culture wars, and conservatives heeded the call, rallying around several projects and exhibits that emerged in museums and educational institutions during the 1990s. The book was enormously influential, boasting the second biggest early sales of a hardcover book in publishing history.[32]

At the heart of the conservative reaction was a romanticized defense of American experience and power relations before the inclusionary pressures that came out of the social movements of the 1960s and 1970s. Several museum exhibits came under fire during this time, including exhibits produced by Smithsonian museums. As the official national museums, the location of these debates reflects how much impact marginalized communities had made regarding the preservation and interpretation of their histories. In 1992, *The West as America,* an art exhibit mounted by the National Museum of American Art that critically engaged with westward expansion, was lambasted as an example of what the conservative right identified as the despicable outcome of identity politics and the denial of American greatness.[33] Another well-documented example in 1994 was the controversy over the National Air and Space Museum's exhibit, *The Crossroads: The End of World War II, the Atomic Bomb and the Cold War.* The exhibit commemorated the bombing of Hiroshima for the fiftieth anniversary of the event and featured the fuselage of the *Enola Gay*, the plane that dropped the atomic bomb on Japan during World War II. After plans for the exhibit became public, controversy erupted in several communities, including Air Force and veterans' groups, scholarly historians, and Japanese Americans.[34] Remarkably, after many months of negotiations with the various interest groups, museum staff cancelled the full exhibit, opting instead to exhibit only the fuselage in a neutrally decontextualized manner. Later that same year, Lynne Cheney, a former head of the National Endowment for the Humanities, sparked an angry outpouring toward the new National Standards for U.S. History, designed to provide guidance in developing precollegiate history curriculum. In decrying the standards, Cheney faulted organizations that represented African Americans and Native Americans, as well as "an academic establishment that revels in the kind of politicized history" Cheney found so abhorrent.³⁵ In still other theaters of the culture wars, conservatives decried National Endowment for the Humanities (NEH) and the National Endowment for the Arts (NEA) funding for visual and performance art exhibits, as well as museums and other cultural organizations. Conservatives also wielded private funds in an attempt to restore the national narrative to a hagiographic celebration of a select few, as evidenced by the 2002 controversy over Catherine Reynolds' $38 million gift to the National Museum of American History. The gift was intended to create a Hall of Achievement, profiling successful Americans, but came with the stipulation that Reynolds would name two-thirds of the committee to determine who would be included as "prominent Americans."³⁶ Although author Timothy Luke points out that these cultural struggles are "simply the most recent flare-ups in conflicts that never end," we would be mistaken not to recognize the direct connection between the collective memory work of social movement activists and the subsequent conservative backlash on the interpretation of national history.³⁷

Although most of the activists who sought to use history in movement-building in the 1960s and 1970s had ambitious goals for their work, few of them would have imagined their impact within the hallowed halls of museums across the country. Even if a black nationalist state or queer communist revolution or liberated lumpenproletariat or dismantled patriarchy did not emerge from their efforts, the impact of contributing to a radically different kind of cultural production and process of representation is significant. The foundations of public history and the museum professions did advance via the ideas of well-meaning liberals who sought change from within, but the impact of the activists of the 1960s and 1970s must be included in that change. Indeed, Rush Limbaugh's horror over shifts in cultural institutional authority surely was a victorious outcome on its own for the civil rights marchers, the black nationalists, the angry feminists, the joyous queers, and the unwavering indigenous activists invoked here.

The Legacy of Collective Memory Practices of the 1960s and 1970s

Although most of the collective memory projects of the Civil Rights, Black Power, Women's Liberation, Gay Liberation, and Red Power movements were relatively small, they performed critical internal work on the consciousness of African American, women, LGBT, and Native American communities. Clio's foot soldiers, thus, instilled in activists and community members an inextricable sense of a shared history, along with a transformed sense of themselves as political and social agents. Beyond this, they developed strategies for building collective memory that existed apart from, and oftentimes in contradiction to, established national history. They built institutions to support their collective memory work, and then many made inroads into mainstream institutions, demanding representation and ownership of their heritage.

Significantly, they developed new narratives and cultural memory forms that functioned as a useable past. The Black Freedom movement, through the work of Civil Rights and Black Power activists, crafted collective memory that laid claims to both full U.S. citizenship and Pan-African heritage. Relying on a longstanding tradition of education as racial uplift, activists created parallel institutions for both children and adults to rectify the wrongs of more than a century of separate and unequal learning. They used history to claim civic entitlement as well as to undergird a new political identity for Afrocentric communities and institutions. Women's Liberation activists used personal relationships and intimate, communal forms of expression to develop a narrative of shared historical experiences and struggles. They drew inspiration from past movements and used history to claim women's rightful place in civic life, both historically and in contemporary political, social, and cultural milieus. Gay Liberation activists articulated a collective past in tandem with the development of a public political identity. They used history to demonstrate presence, unearthing predecessors where none had been visible before. Native Americans reclaimed authority over their historical narratives and practices, and constructed Pan-Indian traditions that served Native communities as they increasingly left reservation life and created new homes in urban centers. They used historically significant spaces to frame movement demands, educated themselves, and built new sovereign educational organizations to sustain tradition throughout future generations. Although their efforts led to various degrees of acceptance in mainstream venues, for all these movements, memory was a means by which to empower, mobilize, inspire, and validate.

Comparative history must attend to both difference and similarities. As cultural formations that emerged in the middle of the twentieth century, all of the collective memory efforts considered here have a shared relationship to political, social, and cultural themes that recur in U.S. history.

Twentieth-century liberal thought established shared values and attitudes that underpin all these activities, namely that all human beings ought to enjoy the same liberties from and responsibilities to the larger society, that human history ought to move forward in time toward an ideal of freedom and self-determination, and that identity is a salient organizing principle. By necessity, each movement attended to historically determined political and cultural issues. These intersections and points of departure can be seen in both the kinds of narratives told and the forms of the memory practices deployed.[38]

Not surprisingly, narratives generated by activists are fairly consistent within each individual movement, while still reflecting slight differences in the respective identity's political goals. Within Civil Rights, most narratives celebrated black achievement and resiliency. Under Highlander's leadership, the citizenship schools tended to focus on the history of black civic participation, framing it within the cultural traditions of songs of resistance to enslavement. Under the leadership of the Southern Christian Leadership Conference, curriculum planners expanded the stories of political resistance during slavery, embedding a demand for full citizenship within the materials. Examples from the Black Power movement are the most distinct from each other, but the organizations represented here also vary significantly in terms of visions for a just future. The Nation of Islam promoted stories of racial superiority during its early years, then shifted toward an Afrocentric celebration of values and traditions. Malcolm X Liberation University continued this celebration, expanding further into training students in life skills that echoed these values while also celebrating the cultural achievements of the African past. The Black Panthers took a notably different narrative direction, emphasizing commonalities in different identity groups' experiences with white supremacy and economic oppression. A key difference in narrative between the Nation of Islam and the Black Panthers was the celebration of Afro-blackness on the part of the Nation, in contrast to the Marxist critique of race espoused by Black Panther Party activists. Differences aside, these stories celebrated blackness while also refuting centuries of cultural representations of racial inferiority.

Women's Liberation and Gay Liberation groups deployed narratives that generally demonstrated historical presence and contributions to larger society. The Women's Herstory Library sought to document that women were simply present and in possession of agency in the public sphere. The

Summer Institute for Women's History enhanced this idea to emphasize women's participation in political life, and the Helaine Victoria Press similarly produced narratives of social and political impact on nineteenth- and twentieth-century life. Likewise, but more ambitiously, Judy Chicago's art installation *The Dinner Party* took on the task of reframing the entirety of human history around women's contributions. LGBT activists worked across projects to first demonstrate historical presence and create identity pride by reclaiming historic figures as "gay" or "lesbian," then telling a more inclusive social history of hidden communities and shared resistance, and lastly focusing on integrating LGBT experience into the larger national narrative. While, in some respects, all of these movements used history-making as a means of undoing trauma, the process of claiming LGBT history was distinctive from other movements, since the very notion that same-sex-loving individuals and communities existed was a radical revision of dominant historiography.

Red Power narratives echo elements of the other movements, while also celebrating resilience and additionally revealing the depths of cultural and social violence brought on by the forces of federal policy and settler colonialism. Acknowledging dance and craft as a kind of narrative, the Flagstaff powwow festival provided a tale of cultural survival and adaptation. Tribal colleges also supported such work, expanding outward to connect tradition to articulated values and worldviews. The American Indian Movement's tactical use of space constructed a spatial narrative, laying claim to historical lands and embedding tribal stories into protest and performance.

In all cases, narrative production first served internal movement purposes, then secondarily performed rhetorical work in the larger political and cultural milieu. In some instances, activists produced stories of celebration that were overly romantic toward their subjects, creating heroic narratives that they failed to interrogate critically. While this is an entirely understandable outcome of identity-based history, it limited the effectiveness of such narratives in larger historical discourse, and even ran the risk of providing fodder for the dismissal of such cultural work.

Identity-based history-making also had limits in breadth of topics and richness of contextualization.[39] Occasionally movement historians placed a great deal of hope on the outcome of their work, with aspirations that weren't always met. The vision that history would foment a socialist revolution or heal the psychic wounds of internalized homophobia was perhaps a great deal to pin on the past. Utopian thinking that cut across the movements produced grand visions for the impact of collective memory work. Although we have no way of assessing the actual impact of a postcard narrative as it travelled across the country, the hopes that social change might be sparked by 4x6 images might have been overly idealistic.

Activists at times were guilty of transhistorical thinking, superimposing contemporary identities on historic people and places. When claiming nineteenth-century figures as "gay" or "lesbian," for instance, Gay Liberation historians imposed an identity on these figures that would not have been intelligible to either their contemporaries or themselves. Hindsight reveals the ahistorical nature of such uses of collective memory. While we might be entirely sympathetic to the rhetorical power of claiming historical figures as predecessors to contemporary experiences and struggles, we must also acknowledge that such behavior reveals the political goals of the activists as much as it reveals a necessarily accurate representation of the past. The inability of these projects to transcend the ideological perspectives of their movements both reflects the power of the useable past and reveals the limits of identity politics in service of the creation of historical knowledge.

Another limit to identity-based history-making, at least in its early years, was the singularity of identity. Although there are scattered examples of white activists in Women's Liberation and Gay Liberation thinking critically about race, I encountered limited instances of activists of color authoring history projects that reflect intersectional identities. Black lesbian Mabel Hampton was central to the work of the Lesbian Herstory Archives, interpreting the experiences of black lesbians in New York City. Likewise, women of color ensured that *The Dinner Party* reflected at least a portion of the full spectrum of womanhood. But the limited engagement with multiple identities echoes the early singularity present in both the Women's Liberation and Gay Liberation movements, and foretells the intersectional work that needed to emerge in the 1980s and 1990s.

Looking comparatively at these initiatives, different forms of memory practices also reflect the respective cultural needs of each movement. Civil Rights activists preferred educational efforts that would strengthen the movement's goals of establishing full citizenship and cultivating respectability. As one historian has noted, the hopes that integrated education could lead to racial equality "if not precisely dead, were mostly moribund."[40] Black Power activists focused their energies on separatist endeavors that took control of educational process and granted community knowledge and authority in both adult and K-12 education. That the Black Freedom movement shifted from narratives of inclusion toward narratives of separatism echoed differing political visions within the movement.[41] Women's Liberation efforts sought to challenge women's internalized narratives about gender via forms that allowed for personal reflection, such as consciousness-raising discussions, postcards, and visual art. Collective memory activists here too served the movement's particular needs by creating texts that began with internal identity work and moved toward a claiming of public space. This engagement with publicness happened at both the representational and embodied levels, demonstrating women's impact on the public sphere throughout history while also putting such images themselves into public venues and circulation. Gay Liberation advocates sought to document historical presence through the establishment of source repositories and the development of research culture. They strove to cultivate community as well, through the theater and entertainment of traveling slide shows. Their work required the identification and documentation of queer bodies and experiences, and as a result, much of their early work was focused on claiming historically significant figures as same-sex-loving. In contrast, Red Power movement members sought both cultural and political self-determination through the reclaiming of cultural expressions. In addition, they also sought to undo the damage of relocation and termination by building colleges at the tribal level. Thus, Red Power narratives focused on cultural survival intermingled with political resistance. Additionally, Red Power collective memory work celebrated respective tribal traditions while also nurturing Pan-Indian consciousness, echoing the primary goals of the larger movement.

This cultural work manifested in an array of different forms. The reclamation or re-articulation of identity in the face of decades or centuries of negative stereotypes was central to all efforts. Identity production is perhaps best exemplified through efforts like the freedom and liberation schools' use of historical re-creation as a teaching tool, *The Dinner Party*'s use of female genitalia imagery and traditional arts forms, and the negotiation of cultural authority at the Flagstaff powwow festival. As some movements needed to establish a source base, the development of the Women's Herstory Library and the various LGBT archives founded by movement activists reflect another key aspect of institutionalization of community-authored history. Similarly, the preservation of cultural traditions undertaken by tribal college leadership and the Carawans' work with music documentation and preservation sought to actively conserve cultural traditions that were at risk of disappearance. Additionally, activists formulated myriad ways of weaving in community history throughout other quotidian movement activities by means of calendars, postcards, the occupation of historically symbolic space, and newspaper articles.

Educational initiatives that explicitly sought to teach movement members about their pasts took a wide variety of forms, including K-12 education, higher education initiatives, and varied forms of adult education. The Black Panthers, Nation of Islam, and Southern Christian Leadership Conference took on primary and secondary education as an act of cultural and political separatism; after decades of substandard education under Jim Crow, the concentration of educational reform within the Black Freedom movement is unsurprising. Separatist higher educational initiatives like Malcolm X Liberation University and the tribal colleges sought to grant college access to their young people while providing them with educations that were relevant and useful to the goals of the movements, through the integration of traditional subjects with culturally specific forms of knowledge. Other interventions into mainstream higher education included research and professionalization initiatives like the Gay Academic Union and movement leadership education through the Summer Institute for Women's History. Adult educational initiatives took the widest array of forms, spanning efforts like LGBT slide shows, Red Power symbolic occupations, prison coursework, voter literacy drives, and postcard narratives. Although highly varied, the unifying theme across all these projects was education that was relevant to social justice reformers and the production of new political identities.

The long-lasting impact of this wide array of collective memory work is significant. New narratives emerged out of the research efforts of activists whom we would now call *citizen historians*. Advocates who were concerned about the archival record collected and preserved documents and artifacts, creating new collections and institutions to serve as caretakers of the past. By insisting on articulating their own histories, social movement activists laid groundwork for more democratic, evidence-based, and culturally sensitive history-making. And they proved beyond a doubt that the useable past is indeed relevant, meaningful, and transformative.

Notes

Introduction

1. Jocelyn Cohen, interviewed by Lara Kelland, May 18, 2011, San Francisco, CA, interview in possession of the author.
2. Denise Meringolo, *Museums, Monuments, and National Parks: Toward a New Genealogy of Public History* (Amherst: University of Massachusetts Press, 2012).
3. Sandra E. Adickes, *The Legacy of a Freedom School* (London: Palgrave Macmillan, 2005); John M. Glen, *Highlander: No Ordinary School*, 2nd ed. (Knoxville: University of Tennessee Press, 1996).
4. Bruce Watson, *Freedom Summer: The Savage Season of 1964 that Made Mississippi Burn and Made America a Democracy* (New York: Penguin Books, 2011); "Freedom School Curriculum," San Francisco Freedom School, 2004, http://www.educationanddemocracy.org/ED_FSC.html.
5. Edward E. Curtis IV, *Black Muslim Religion in the Nation of Islam, 1960–1975* (Chapel Hill: University of North Carolina Press, 2012); *Islam in Black America: Identity, Liberation, and Difference in African-American Islamic Thought* (Albany: State University of New York Press, 2002). For Black Panther efforts to build liberation schools, see Peniel E. Joseph, *Waiting 'Til the Midnight Hour: A Narrative History of Black Power in America*, reprint ed. (New York: Holt Paperbacks, 2007); Joshua Bloom and Waldo E. Martin Jr., *Black against Empire: The History and Politics of the Black Panther Party* (Berkeley: University of California Press, 2014).
6. For more background on cultural and educational activism in these movements, see Julie L. Davis, *Survival Schools: The American Indian Movement and Community Education in the Twin Cities* (Minneapolis: University of Minnesota Press, 2013); Jim Downs, *Stand by Me: The Forgotten History of Gay Liberation* (New York: Basic Books, 2016); Stephanie Gilmore, *Feminist Coalitions: Historical Perspectives on Second-Wave Feminism in the United States* (Urbana: University of Illinois Press, 2008); Lillian Faderman, *The Gay Revolution: The Story of the Struggle* (New York: Simon & Schuster, 2015); Jane Gerhard, Claire Potter, and Renee Romano, *The Dinner Party: Judy Chicago and the Power of Popular Feminism, 1970–2007* (Athens: University of Georgia Press, 2013); Paul Chaat Smith and Robert Allen Warrior, *Like a Hurricane: The Indian Movement from Alcatraz to Wounded Knee* (New York: The New Press, 1997).

7. "What is Public History," National Council of Public History, 2017, http://ncph.org/what-is-public-history/about-the-field/.
8. Much fine recent scholarship has addressed similar populist history-making. See, especially, Tammy S. Gordon and Harold Skramstad, *Private History in Public: Exhibition and the Settings of Everyday Life* (Lanham MD: AltaMira Press, 2010), ch. 3. Benjamin Filene offers the term "outsider history-maker" to frame individuals' engagement with the past beyond the scope of cultural or educational organizations. See Benjamin Filene, "Passionate Histories: 'Outsider' History-Makers and What They Teach Us," *The Public Historian* 34, no. 1 (February 2012): 11–33. The digital turn has also ushered in an enthusiasm for crowdsourcing, leading even the otherwise conventional U.S. National Archives to recruit "citizen archivists." See "Citizen Archivist Dashboard," National Archives, 2017, https://www.archives.gov/citizen-archivist/.
9. Benedict Anderson, *Imagined Communities: Reflections on the Origin of the Spread of Nationalism* (London: Verso, 1983).
10. Edward Said, *Orientalism* (New York: Vintage, 1979).
11. Dipesh Chakrabarty, *Provincializing Europe: Postcolonial Thought and Historical Difference* (Princeton: Princeton University Press, 2000), 237–55.
12. Michel-Rolph Trouillot, *Silencing the Past: Power and the Production of History* (Boston: Beacon, 1995), 57.
13. Andrea A. Burns, *From Storefront to Monument: Tracing the Public History of the Black Museum Movement* (Amherst: University of Massachusetts Press, 2013); Gordon and Skramstad, *Private History in Public*; James Green, *Taking History to Heart: The Power of the Past in Building Social Movements* (Amherst: University of Massachusetts Press, 2000); Trouillot, *Silencing the Past*.
14. Maurice Halbwachs, *On Collective Memory* (Chicago: University of Chicago Press, 1992); Alison Landsberg, *Prosthetic Memory: The Transformation of American Remembrance in the Age of Mass Culture* (New York: Columbia University Press, 2004); George Lipsitz, *Time Passages: Collective Memory and American Popular Culture* (Minneapolis: University of Minnesota Press, 2001); Eviatar Zerubavel, *Time Maps: Collective Memory and the Social Shape of the Past* (Chicago: University of Chicago Press, 2004).
15. Iwona Irwin-Zarecka, *Frames of Remembrance: The Dynamics of Collective Memory* (New Brunswick, NJ: Transaction Publishers, 2007), 4.
16. Other scholars of history and ethnography have used the notion of *practices* as a way to engage how communities and individuals employ activities and methods in the production of group identities. For the theoretical basis for using practices as an analytic tool, see Michel de Certeau, *The Practice of Everyday Life* (Berkeley: University of California Press, 1988). For more on the turn toward practices and how they are productive of social identities, see Karin Knorr Cetina, Theodore R. Schatzki, and Eike von Savigny, eds., *The Practice Turn in Contemporary Theory* (New York: Routledge, 2001). For an ethnographic use of the concept deployed in a comparative context, see Annemarie Mol, *The Body Multiple: Ontology in Medical Practice* (Durham, NC: Duke University Press, 2002).

Chapter 1: In a Long Line of Protest

1. Jacqueline Goggin, *Carter G. Woodson: A Life in Black History* (Baton Rouge: Louisiana State University Press, 1993); Pero Gaglo Dagbovie, *The Early Black History Movement, Carter G. Woodson, and Lorenzo Johnston Green* (Urbana: University of Illinois Press, 2007); Janet Sims-Woods, *Dorothy Porter Wesley at Howard University: Building a Legacy of Black History* (Charleston, SC: The History Press, 2014); Elinor Des Verney

Sinnette, *Arthur Alfonzo Schomburg: Black Bibliophile and Collector* (Detroit: Wayne State University Press, 1989).
2. For more on late-nineteenth- and early-twentieth-century forms of African American memory practices, see W. Fitzhugh Brundage, *The Southern Past: A Clash of Race and Memory* (Cambridge, MA: Belknap Press, 2008); Genevieve Fabre and Robert O'Meally, eds., *History and Memory in African-American Culture* (New York: Oxford University Press, 1994); Alessandra Lorini, *Rituals of Race: American Public Culture and the Search for Racial Democracy* (Charlottesville: University of Virginia Press, 1999).
3. Although black communities had possessed rich collective memory before this era, especially through the media of jazz music, the early black arts movement, and black scholarship, the mid-twentieth-century movement for racial equality used collective memory to bolster the goals of democratic education, enfranchisement, and social parity.
4. For more on the use of social justice rhetoric in the citizenship schools, see Stephen A. Schneider, *You Can't Lock Up an Idea: Rhetorical Education at the Highlander Folk School* (Columbia: University of South Carolina Press, 2014).
5. James D. Anderson, *The Education of Blacks in the South, 1860–1935* (Chapel Hill: University of North Carolina Press, 1988), 33–77.
6. William Edward Burghardt Du Bois, "The Training of Negros for Social Power," in *Du Bois on Education*, ed. Eugene F. Provenzo (Lanham, MD: Rowman & Littlefield, 2002).
7. William Edward Burghardt Du Bois, "The Talented Tenth," in *Du Bois on Education*, ed. Provenzo.
8. Adalaine Holton, "Decolonizing History: Arthur Schomberg's Afrodiasporic Archive," *Journal of African American History* 92, no. 2 (Spring 2007): 222–23.
9. Jeffrey C. Steward and Fath Davis Ruffins, "A Faithful Witness: Afro-American Public History in Historical Perspective, 1828–1984," in *Presenting the Past: Essays on History and the Public*, ed. Susan Porter Benson, Steven Brier, and Roy Rozensweig (Amherst: University of Massachusetts Press, 1986), 307–38.
10. Mitch Kachun, *Festival of Freedom: Memory and Meaning in African American Emancipation Celebrations, 1808–1915* (Amherst: University of Massachusetts Press, 2003).
11. David Whisnant, *All That is Native and Fine: The Politics of Culture in an American Region* (Chapel Hill: University of North Carolina Press, 1983).
12. Georgia Commission on Education, Untitled Broadside, 1957, Digital Library of Georgia, http://dlg.galileo.usg.edu/highlander/efhf003 php.
13. Highlander Folk School, *21st Annual Report*, 1953, Highlander Research and Education Center Archives, New Market, TN.
14. John M. Glen, *Highlander: No Ordinary School* (Lexington: University of Kentucky Press, 1988), 187.
15. Glen, *Highlander*, 200–203.
16. Septima Clark and Cynthia Brown, *Ready from Within: Septima Clark and the Civil Rights Movement* (Navarro, CA: Wild Trees Press, 1986), 30.
17. Septima Clark to Myles Horton, June 21, 1954, Highlander Research and Education Center Archives, 9:12, Wisconsin Historical Society, Madison, WI.
18. Unpublished History of the Extension Programs on Johns Island and Charleston, Septima Clark Papers, 3:5, Avery Research Center, College of Charleston, Charleston, SC.
19. Stephen Schneider, "The Sea Islands Citizenship Schools: Literacy, Community Organization, and the Civil Rights Movement," *College English* 70, no. 2 (2007): 144–67.
20. Aimee Horton, *The Highlander Folk School: A History of its Major Programs, 1932–1961* (Brooklyn: Carlson, 1989), 218.
21. Schneider, "Sea Islands Citizenship Schools:" 144–67.
22. Glen, *Highlander: No Ordinary School.*

23. Myles Horton and Paulo Freire, *We Make the Road by Walking: Conversations on Education and Social Change* (Philadelphia: Temple University Press, 1990).
24. Clark and Brown, *Ready from Within*, 53.
25. Ibid.
26. Ibid.
27. Horton, *Highlander Folk School*.
28. Citizenship Schools Book, Clark Papers, 7:10.
29. James MacGregor Burns, *Government by the People* (New York: Prentice Hall, 1952); Hattie Mabel Anderson and Joseph Hill, *My Country and Yours* (Austin, TX: Steck Company, 1944); Report on Educational Materials Purchased for Citizenship Schools, Highlander Research and Education Center Archives, 38:2.
30. Notes on Constitutional Amendments, c. 1960, Clark Papers, 7:10.
31. For more on the role of music in the movement, see Reiland Rabaka, *Civil Rights Music: The Soundtracks of the Civil Rights Movement* (Lanham, MD: Lexington Books, 2016).
32. Guy Carawan, *We Shall Overcome! Songs of the Southern Freedom Movement* (New York: Oak, 1963), 5.
33. Bernice Robinson, Report on Sing for Freedom Workshop, August 27-September 3, 1960, Highlander Research and Education Center Archives, 64:16.
34. "Throw Me Anywhere Lord," adapted by Bessie Smith, in *Sing for Freedom: The Story of the Civil Rights Movement through Its Songs*, comp. Guy Carawan and Candie Carawan (Mongomery, AL: New South, 2007), 187.
35. "We Are Soldiers," anonymous adaptation, in Carawan, *We Shall Overcome!*, 12–13.
36. "Spiritual Singing in the South Carolina Sea Islands," n.d. (c. 1960), Clark Papers, 7:24.
37. Ibid.
38. "King Jesus is A-Listening to Hear That Freedom Cry," *Sing for Freedom*, 25, August 1960, Clark Papers, 7:24.
39. "John Brown's Body," *Sing for Freedom*, 34, August 1960, Clark Papers, 7:24.
40. "Report on the Conference for Southern Community Cultural Revival," October 1965, Highlander Research and Education Center Archives, 65:2.
41. Guy Carawan and Candie Carawan, *Ain't You Got a Right to the Tree of Life? The People of Johns Island, South Carolina, Their Faces, Their Words, and Their Songs* (New York: Simon and Schuster, 1967), 10–11.
42. Alan Lomax, "Report from the 'Sing for Freedom' Workshop," 1965, Highlander Research and Education Center Archives, 65:1.
43. Josh Dunson, "Slave Songs at the 'Sing for Freedom,'" *Highlander Research and Education Center Archives*, 64:17.
44. For more on early-twentieth-century efforts to preserve and document American folk music, see Benjamin Filene, *Romancing the Folk: Public Memory and American Roots Music* (Chapel Hill: University of North Carolina Press, 2000).
45. "Folk Music Workshop at Highlander Center," *Southern Patriot: The Newsletter of the Southern Conference Educational Fund*, October 1965, Highlander Research and Education Center Archives, 65:2.
46. Ibid.
47. "Report on the Conference for Southern Community Cultural Revival," October 1965, Highlander Research and Education Center Archives, 65:2.
48. Ibid., 3.
49. Ibid.
50. Jeanne Theoharis and Komozi Woodard, *Groundwork: Local Black Freedom Movements in America* (New York: New York University Press, 2005), 117.
51. Southern Christian Leadership Conference, *Citizenship School Workbook*, 2, Reference Files: "Citizenship Schools," Highlander Research and Education Center Archives.

52. Although many teachers in the South during Jim Crow certainly taught a white supremacist narrative of the past, some black teachers in black public schools were able to teach black history.
53. Southern Christian Leadership Conference, *Citizenship School Workbook*, 2, Reference Files: "Citizenship Schools," Highlander Research and Education Center Archives.
54. Ibid.
55. Southern Christian Leadership Conference, *Citizenship School Workbook*, 22, Reference Files: "Citizenship Schools," Highlander Research and Education Center Archives.
56. Ibid.
57. Ibid.
58. Septima Clark, "Success of SCLC Citizenship School Seen in 50,000 New Registered Voters," *Southern Christian Leadership Conference Newsletter*, September 1963: 11.
59. Southern Christian Leadership Conference, Application Form for Teacher Training, Highlander Research and Education Center Archives, 38:13; Southern Christian Leadership Conference, Citizenship Education Program, Highlander Research and Education Center Archives, 5:1.
60. Southern Christian Leadership Conference, Application Form for Teacher Training, Highlander Research and Education Center Archives 38:13.
61. Required readings included J. W. Schulte Nordholt, *The People that Walk in Darkness* (London: Burke, 1960); V. O. Key, *Southern Politics in State and Nation* (New York: Knopf, 1949); Howard Fast, *Freedom Road* (New York: Duell, Sloan, and Pearce, 1944).
62. Southern Christian Leadership Conference, SCOPE Brochure, c. 1965, Highlander Research and Education Center Archives, Record Group MH-RG2-I-10, "Citizenship School: SCLC."
63. Reprint of Benjamin Mack, "Lesson to Citizenship Education Staff," *North and South: Southern Christian Leadership Staff News*, March 1967: 2, Bernice Robinson Papers, 4:2 Avery Research Center, College of Charleston, Charleston, SC.
64. Marian Wright Edelman, *Lanterns: A Memoir of Mentors* (Boston: Beacon, 1999), 126.
65. Raymond Arsenault, *Freedom Riders: 1961 and the Struggle for Racial Justice* (Oxford: Oxford University Press, 2006), 451.
66. Southern Nonviolent Coordinating Committee, "SNCC's Educational Program," 1, Highlander Research and Education Center Archives 9:12.
67. Ibid.
68. Charles Cobb, "Prospectus for a Summer Freedom School Program in Mississippi," December 1963, Student Nonviolent Coordinating Committee Papers, 1959–1972, 40, http://www.educationanddemocracy.org/FSCpdf/CurrTextOnlyAll.pdf.
69. Southern Nonviolent Coordinating Committee, "SNCC's Educational Program," Highlander Research and Education Center Archives 9:12.
70. For more on the life and work of Staughton Lynd, see Carl Mirra, *The Admirable Radical: Staughton Lynd and Cold War Dissent, 1945–1970* (Kent, OH: Kent State University Press, 2010).
71. It is worthwhile to note that while the Harlem Branch housed the Schomburg Collection, the premiere holdings documenting black history and culture, the collection positioned itself as more of a cultural uplift organization than a space for activist education. Charles M. Payne, *I've Got the Light of Freedom: The Organizing Tradition and the Mississippi Freedom Struggle* (Berkeley: University of California Press, 1995), 182.
72. Clayborne Carson, *In Struggle: SNCC and the Black Awakening of the 1960s* (Cambridge: Harvard University Press, 1981), 109.
73. Sandra Adickes, *Legacy of a Freedom School* (New York: Palgrave Macmillan, 2005), 39.
74. "Guide to Negro History," Mississippi Freedom School Curriculum, Student Nonviolent Coordinating Committee Papers, 1959–1972, 10, http://www.educationanddemocracy.org/FSCpdf/CurrTextOnlyAll.pdf.

75. Ibid., 212.
76. Ibid., 216–18.
77. Ibid., 213.
78. Ibid., 226.
79. Ibid., 214.
80. Ibid., 220.
81. Ibid.
82. Ibid., 106.
83. Ibid., 234.
84. Ibid., 246.
85. Barbara Bennett Peterson, "Otis A. Pease (1925–2010): In Memorium." *Pacific Historical Review* 80, no. 2: 332–34.
86. "Guide to Negro History," Mississippi Freedom School Curriculum, Student Nonviolent Coordinating Committee Papers, 1959–1972, 250, http://www.educationanddemocracy.org/FSCpdf/CurrTextOnlyAll.pdf.
87. Ibid., 18–19.
88. Adickes, *Legacy of a Freedom School*, 68.
89. Elizabeth S. Martinez, *Letters from Mississippi* (Brookline, MA: Zephyr Press, 2007), 106.
90. John F. McClymer, *Mississippi Freedom Summer* (Belmont, CA: Thomson/Wadsworth Press, 2004) 199.
91. Adickes, *Legacy of a Freedom School*, 75.
92. "Guide to Negro History," Mississippi Freedom School Curriculum, Student Nonviolent Coordinating Committee Papers, 1959–1972, 332-33, http://www.educationanddemocracy.org/FSCpdf/CurrTextOnlyAll.pdf.
93. Ibid., 284.
94. Ibid., 277.
95. Ibid.
96. Graphic from *Student Voice*, Student Nonviolent Coordinating Committee, February 18, 1964, 4, http://cdm15932.contentdm.oclc.org/cdm/ref/collection/p15932coll2/id/50279.
97. Quintin Horare and Geoffrey Nowell-Smith, *Selections from the Prison Notebooks of Antonio Gramsci* (London: Electric, 2001), 131–47.
98. Similarly, Leon Fink uses the term *movement intellectual* in a manner similar to Gramsci's *organic intellectual*, emphasizing knowledge and direction emerging from popular experience and grassroots leadership. Leon Fink, *Progressive Intellectuals and the Dilemmas of Democratic Commitment* (Cambridge: Harvard University Press, 1997).
99. Septima Clark, "Beyond Chaos: A New History for a New Generation," c. 1975, Clark Papers, 3:27.

Chapter 2: Knowledge of Self

1. Many historians have complicated a distinct periodization between the Civil Rights and Black Power movements, and I follow their interpretive lead. For more on the use of the long Black Freedom movement, see Peniel E. Joseph, *Neighborhood Rebels: Black Power at the Local Level* (New York: Palgrave Macmillan, 2009), 10–15. See also, Jacquelyn Dowd Hall, "The Long Civil Rights Movement and the Political Uses of the Past," *Journal of American History* 91, no. 4 (March 2005): 1233–63; Sundiata Keita Cha-Jua and Clarence Lang, "The 'Long Movement' as Vampire: Temporal and Spatial Fallacies in Recent Black Freedom Studies," *Journal of African American History* 92, no. 2 (2007): 265–88.

2. There had been numerous figures and debates within black intellectual circles regarding the interpretation of the black American past, and these conversations served as backdrop to the efforts made by social movements in this chapter. For more on early Pan-African intellectual history, see Wilson Jeremiah Moses, *The Golden Age of Black Nationalism, 1850–1925* (Hamden, CT: Archon Books, 1978); William L. Van Deburg, *Modern Black Nationalism: From Marcus Garvey to Louis Farrakhan* (New York: New York University Press, 1997).
3. Conference Report, July 22, 1967, Cleveland Sellers Papers, 12:8, Avery Institute, College of Charleston, Charleston, SC.
4. For more on the cultural impact of Afrocentrism, see Algernon Austin, *Achieving Blackness: Race, Black Nationalism, and Afrocentrism in the Twentieth Century* (New York: New York University Press, 2006); Wilson Jeremiah Moses, *Afrotopia: The Roots of African American Popular History* (New York: Cambridge University Press, 1998).
5. There has been much recent literature on the Black Power movement. For more, see Devin Fergus, *Liberalism, Black Power, and the Making of American Politics, 1965–1980* (Athens: University of Georgia Press, 2009); Joseph, *Neighborhood Rebels*; Peniel E. Joseph, *Waiting 'Til the Midnight Hour: A Narrative History of Black Power in America* (New York: Holt Paperbacks, 2007); Jeffrey O. G. Ogbar, *Black Power: Radical Politics and African American Identity* (Baltimore: Johns Hopkins University Press, 2005); Timothy B. Tyson, *Radio Free Dixie: Robert F. Williams and the Roots of Black Power* (Chapel Hill: University of North Carolina Press, 2001).
6. For more on the foundations and significance of Marcus Garvey and Garveyism, see Colin Grant, *Negro with a Hat: The Rise and Fall of Marcus Garvey* (New York: Oxford University Press, 2010); Mary G. Rolinson, *Grassroots Garveyism: The Universal Negro Improvement Association in the Rural South, 1920–1927* (Chapel Hill: University of North Carolina Press, 2007); Thomas J. Sugrue, *Sweet Land of Liberty: The Forgotten Struggle for Civil Rights in the North* (New York: Random House, 2009).
7. The development of community-based museums was another cultural endeavor central to Black Power activism. For more, see Andrea Burns, *From Storefront to Monument: Tracing the Public History of the Black Museum Movement* (Amherst: University of Massachusetts Press, 2013).
8. Martha Lee, *The Nation of Islam: An American Millenarian Movement* (Syracuse: Syracuse University Press, 1996), 21–25.
9. Elijah Muhammad, *Message to the Blackman in America* (Chicago: Muhammad Mosque of Islam, No. 2, 1965), 31.
10. "Truth about 'Negro' History," *Muhammad Speaks*, March 1962, 18
11. Elijah Muhammad, *Message to the Blackman in America* (Chicago: Muhammad Mosque of Islam, No. 2, 1965), 34.
12. Claude Andrew Clegg, *An Original Man: The Life and Times of Elijah Muhammad* (New York: St. Martin's, 1998), 42–50; Edward E. Curtis, *Black Muslim Religion in the Nation of Islam, 1960–1975* (Chapel Hill: University of North Carolina Press, 2006), 67–94.
13. Elijah Muhammad, Untitled Speech, Philadelphia Arena, Oct. 7, 1962, published in *Muhammad Speaks*, October 31, 1962.
14. Muhammad, *Message to the Blackman in America*, 34.
15. "Education University of Islam," *Time*, April 30, 1934, 45.
16. Ibid.
17. Clifton E. Marsh, *From Black Muslims to Muslims: The Transition from Separatism to Islam, 1930–1980* (Metuchen, NJ: Scarecrow Press, 1984), 60–61.
18. "Muslim Women in History," *Muhammad Speaks*, July 1962, 26.
19. Curtis, *Black Muslim Religion in the Nation of Islam*, 85.

20. "Muslims Welcome Probe: Call Charges 'Ridiculous,'" *Chicago Daily Defender*, May 14, 1962, 1.
21. "Senator Gottschalk Meets the Muslims," *Muhammad Speaks*, July 1962, 8.
22. Ibid.
23. "Vows to Continue Fight Against Muslim School," *Chicago Daily Defender*, May 22, 1962, 3.
24. "Teacher Bargaining Bill Dies in Senate," *Chicago Tribune*, June 28, 1963, 2.
25. "Islam Grads Move into Top Colleges," *Muhammad Speaks*, September 27, 1963, 18.
26. "University of Islam Rescues a 'Dropout,'" *Muhammad Speaks*, June 19, 1964, 21.
27. "The Facts about Race Poison in Textbooks," *Muhammad Speaks*, July 1962, 27.
28. Ibid.
29. "Blast Civil War 'History' Books Slur on Negro's Role," *Muhammad Speaks*, February 14, 1964, 23. John Hope Franklin was in some ways an ideal figure of liberal historical authorship; he viewed his task as a highly regarded academic historian "to weave into the fabric of American history enough of the presence of blacks so that the story of the United States could be told adequately and fairly." John Hope Franklin, "Speech the 50th Anniversary of the Publication of *From Slavery to Freedom*," quoted in "Pioneering Historian John Hope Franklin Dies," *Washington Post*, March 26, 2009.
30. "Student Enrollment, Rules of Islam," Malcolm X Collection: Papers, 11:4, Schomberg Center for Research in Black Culture, New York, NY.
31. Memo, March 15, 1975, *Nation of Islam Collection*, 11:9, Schomberg Center for Research in Black Culture.
32. Herbert Berg, *Elijah Muhammad and Islam* (New York: New York University Press, 2009), 130.
33. University of Islam lesson packets, *Malcolm X Collection*, 11:4.
34. "Boston's Freedom Schools," *Muhammad Speaks*, December 20, 1963, 9.
35. "New Negro History Society," *Muhammad Speaks*, April 29, 1963, 20.
36. "Demonstrators Fight for Negro History in Schools," *Muhammad Speaks*, August 3, 1963, 19.
37. Muhammad, *Message to the Blackman in America*, 35.
38. Although other leaders like W. E. B. Du Bois, Carter Woodson, and Marcus Garvey had invoked elements of an African past in their efforts to build a black nation, none before had so explicitly linked a personal sense of heritage to a black separatist political agenda.
39. Malcolm X, *Autobiography of Malcolm X*, published in *The Civil Rights Reader: American Literature from Jim Crow to Reconciliation* (Athens, GA: University of Georgia, 2009), 193.
40. Manning Marable, *Malcolm X: A Life of Reinvention* (New York: Viking Press, 2011), 116.
41. Ibid., 7.
42. Malcolm X, *Malcolm X on Afro-American History* (New York: Grove Press, 1965), 14–15.
43. Ibid., 18–19.
44. Ibid., 30.
45. Malcolm X, *Autobiography*, 178.
46. Ibid.
47. For background on the rapid growth of black studies, see Fabio Rojas, *From Black Power to Black Studies: How a Radical Social Movement Became an Academic Discipline* (Baltimore: Johns Hopkins University Press, 2007).
48. Although HBCUs usually had all black administrations, many originated or experienced indirect control from white elites. In contrast, MXLU was formed as a conscious act of separatism, imagined as creating citizens for a new Afrocentric culture and a self-determining separatist nation. See James D. Anderson, *The Education of Blacks in the South, 1860–1935* (Chapel Hill: University of North Carolina Press, 1988).
49. Fergus, *Liberalism, Black Power, and the Making of American Politics*, 38.
50. "Proposal for Malcolm X Liberation University," Spring 1970, 3, Sellers Papers, 12:3.

51. Ibid., 6.
52. Gregg L Michel, *Struggle for a Better South: The Southern Student Organizing Committee, 1964–1969* (New York: Palgrave Macmillan, 2004), 83.
53. Keith Lowe for the Southern Student Organizing Committee, "Towards a Black University," c. 1967, inside cover, Sellers Papers, 11:6.
54. Ibid., 3.
55. Memo from the Foundation for Community Development to Faculty at Neighboring Universities, April 10, 1969, *Sellers Papers*, 12:3.
56. Conference Program, May 2–4, 1969, *Sellers Papers*, 12:3.
57. "Proposal for Malcolm X Liberation University," June 5, 1969, Sellers Papers, 12:3.
58. Conference Program, May 2–4, 1969, Sellers Papers, 12:3.
59. Ibid.
60. Ibid.
61. "Controversial School Comes of Age," *Greensboro Record*, undated, found in Sellers Papers, 12:9
62. For a thorough analysis of black community support of MXLU, see Fergus, *Liberalism, Black Power, and the Making of American Politics*, 74–75.
63. "Tell No Lies, Claim No Easy Victories," *Black World/Negro Digest*, October 1974, 18–22.
64. Rojas, *From Black Power to Black Studies*.
65. Pero Gaglo Dagbovie, *African American History Reconsidered* (Urbana: University of Illinois Press, 2010), 4.
66. For more on the rise and fall of the Black Panther Party, see Joshua Bloom and Waldo E. Martin Jr., *Black against Empire: The History and Politics of the Black Panther Party* (Berkeley: University of California Press, 2016); Robin D. G. Kelley, *Freedom Dreams: The Black Radical Imagination* (Boston: Beacon Press, 2003); Donna Jean Murch, *Living for the City: Migration, Education, and the Rise of the Black Panther Party in Oakland, California* (Chapel Hill: University of North Carolina Press, 2010).
67. Speakers Kit, "History of the Black Panther Party," Dr. Huey P. Newton Foundation, Inc. Collection, Series 2, 12:6, Stanford University, Palo Alto, CA.
68. Ibid.
69. Ibid.
70. "What You Are, Speak So Loud I Hardly Hear Anything You Say," *Black Panther*, November 8, 1969, 6.
71. David Walker (1796–1830) was a black abolitionist who wrote "An Appeal to the Coloured Citizens of the World," a condemnation of slavery and a critical engagement with predominant conceptions of race. Henry Highland Garnet (1815–1832) was a black minister and anti-slavery activist best known for his 1843 speech entitled "Call to Rebellion," in which he encouraged enslaved folks to rise up against their owners. "The Roots of the Party," *Black Panther*, May 25, 1969, 4.
72. For more on the development of black studies on U.S. university campuses, see Martha Biondi, *The Black Revolution on Campus* (Berkeley: University of California Press, 2014); Ibram X. Kendi, *The Black Campus Movement. Black Students and the Racial Reconstitution of Higher Education, 1965–1972* (New York: Palgrave Macmillan, 2012); Rojas, *From Black Power to Black Studies*.
73. Syllabi for black studies program, Newton Collection, 2:56:6.
74. John Hope Franklin, *From Slavery to Freedom: A History of American Negroes* (New York: Alfred A. Knopf, 1956); John Hope Franklin, *Reconstruction* (Chicago, University of Chicago Press, 1961); Kenneth M. Stampp, *The Peculiar Institution: Slavery in the Ante-Bellum South*. (New York: Alfred A. Knopf, 1956); C. Vann Woodward, *Origins of the New South, 1877–1913* (Baton Rouge: Louisiana State University Press, 1951).
75. "Liberation Schools," *Black Panther*, July 5, 1969; Jean-Jacques Rousseau, *Emile: or, On Education* (New York: Basic Books, 1979); John Dewey, *The School and Society; and, The Child and the Curriculum* (Chicago: University of Chicago Press, 1990).

76. Published in every issue of *Black Panther*.
77. "The Youth Make the Revolution," *Black Panther*, Aug 2, 1969.
78. *Oakland Community Learning Center News*, April/May 1979, 4, Newton Collection, 2:16:4.
79. "Experiments with Education Guide Ex-Panthers' Work," *Oakland Tribune*, October 8, 2006.
80. Murch, *Living for the City*, 180. Murch argues that the liberation schools took cues from the burgeoning black studies movement, which started at San Francisco State University in 1968.
81. Interview with Erika Huggins for *The Black Commentator* in June 2008, as transcribed at http://www.blackcommentator.com/285/285_iss_oakland_community_school_pinkney.html.
82. Stokely Carmichael and Charles V. Hamilton, *Black Power: The Politics of Liberation in America* (New York: Vintage Books, 1967).
83. "Interview with Ericka Huggins," in *Black Women in America*, ed. Darlene Clark Hine, 2nd ed. (Brooklyn, NY: Carlson Publishing, 1993), 222.
84. "Bobby Seale Dedicates New Youth Institute and Son of Man Temple to Community," *Black Panther*, October 23, 1973, 3.
85. Brochure, 1977, Newton Collection, 2:16:4.
86. "OCS Director Ericka Huggins Highlights Chicago Alternative Schools Conference," *Black Panther*, June 19, 1976, 14.
87. Ericka Huggins, interviewed by Lara Kelland, May 20, 2011, San Francisco, CA, interview in possession of the author.
88. Ericka Huggins, interviewed by Lara Kelland.
89. Murch, *Living for the City*, 182–83.
90. Flyer, n.d., Newton Collection, 2:16:4.
91. Newsletter, February-March 1980, Newton Collection, 2:16:2.
92. Social Science Curriculum, n.d., Newton Collection, 2:17:6.
93. Teacher's Manual, n.d., Newton Collection, 2:16:15.
94. Ibid.
95. Social Science Curriculum, n.d., Newton Collection, 2:17:6.
96. Curriculum Design Notebooks, n.d., Newton Collection, 2:17:3–6.
97. Ibid.
98. "Proposal for Malcolm X Liberation University," June 5, 1969, Sellers Papers, 12:3.
99. "Black Power" speech, October 1966, as transcribed at http://www.encyclopedia.com/doc/1G2-3401804839.html.
100. Charles M. Payne and Carol Sills Strickland, eds., *Teach Freedom: Education for Liberation in the African-American Tradition* (New York: Teachers College, 2008).
101. Ericka Huggins has suggested the term "Black Liberation movement" instead of the "Black Power movement," to underscore the interconnectedness of Black Panther activism with Women's Liberation and Gay Liberation movements. For reasons of clarity and to connect these three examples, I have chosen to keep "Black Power." Ericka Huggins, interviewed by Lara Kelland.

Chapter 3: A History of One's Own

1. Ruth Rosen, *The World Split Open: How the Modern Women's Movement Changed America* (New York: Penguin, 2000), 266.
2. Julie Des Jardins, *Women and the Historical Enterprise in America: Gender, Race, and the Politics of Memory, 1880–1945* (Chapel Hill: University of North Carolina Press, 2003), 43.
3. Letter to members of the World Center for Women's Archives, reprinted in Anne Relph, "The World Center for Women's Archives, 1935–1940," *Signs* 4, no. 3 (1979): 602.

4. Letter from the World Center for Women's Archives, November 25, 1940, Mary Ritter Beard Collection, 2:23, Sophia Smith Collection, Smith College, Northampton, MA. See also, Mary Ritter Beard and Ann J. Lane, *Making Women's History: The Essential Mary Ritter Beard* (New York: Feminist Press at the City University of New York, 1977); Nancy F. Cott, *A Woman Making History: Mary Ritter Beard through Her Letters* (New Haven: Yale University Press, 1991); Anke Voss-Hubbard, "'No Document—No History': Mary Ritter Beard and the Early History of Women's Archives," *American Archivist* 58, no. 1 (1995): 16–30, http://www.jstor.org/stable/40293886.
5. For more on the establishment of the Sophia Smith Collection and the Arthur and Elizabeth Schlesinger Library, see Suzanne Hildenbrand, *Women's Collections: Libraries, Archives, and Consciousness* (New York: Haworth Press, 1986); "'Never Another Season of Silence': Laying the Foundation of the Sophia Smith Collection, 1942-1965," in *Revealing Women's Life Stories: Papers from the 50th Anniversary Celebration of the Sophia Smith Collection, Smith College, Northampton, Massachusetts, September 1992* (Northampton, MA: Smith College, 1995).
6. For more on the role of consciousness raising in the development of the Women's Liberation movement, see Lisa Maria Hogeland, *Feminism and Its Fictions: The Consciousness-Raising Novel and the Women's Liberation Movement* (Philadelphia: University of Pennsylvania Press, 1998); Anita Shreve, *Women Together, Women Alone: The Legacy of the Consciousness-Raising Movement* (New York: Ballantine Books, 1990).
7. Alix Kates Shulman, "Sex and Power: Sexual Bases of Radical Feminism," *Signs* 5, no. 4 (1980): 593, http://www.jstor.org/stable/3173832.
8. The language of "rap sessions" was borrowed from Black Power organizing strategies.
9. Claudia Dreifus, *Women's Fate: Raps from a Feminist Consciousness-Raising Group* (New York: Bantam Books, 1973), 5-6.
10. Kathie Sarachild, "Consciousness Raising: A Radical Weapon," in *Redstockings, Feminist Revolution* (New York: Random House, 1979), 144.
11. Alice Echols, *Daring to Be Bad: Radical Feminism in America, 1967–1975* (Minneapolis: University of Minnesota Press, 1989), 85.
12. Shreve, *Women Together, Women Alone*, 5–15.
13. Echols, *Daring to Be Bad*, 53.
14. "Guidelines to Feminist Consciousness Raising," NOW Records, 209:72, Schlesinger Library, Radcliffe Institute, Harvard University, Cambridge, MA.
15. Kathie Sarachild, "The Power of History," in *Redstockings, Feminist Revolution*, 17.
16. Laura dropped her last name and took "X" as a rejection of patriarchal naming traditions, but also as homage to Nation of Islam naming practices.
17. "Women's History Research Center Library," 1971, Boston NOW Collection, 19:690, Schlesinger Library, Radcliffe Institute, Harvard University.
18. Introduction to "Women's Songbook," Boston NOW Collection, 19:690.
19. Ibid.
20. Laura X and Women's History Research Center, Collections Subject Guide, January 28, 1970, 3:13, Women's History Research Center Collection, Schlesinger Library.
21. Although an earlier generation of feminists had formed collections like the Sophia Smith Collection and the Schlesinger Archives, these projects were linked to academic institutions. During its short tenure, the Women's History Research Center provided an archival space that was committed to its public, namely the newly politicized feminists organizing under the banner of Women's Liberation.
22. Laura X, "Grow Your Own . . . Women's History Research Center," *School Library Journal* 19 (January 1973): 39–42.
23. Requests for Information, 1973, Women's History Research Center Records, 16:9-11.
24. Ibid.
25. "Women's History Research Center Library," 1971, Boston NOW Collection, 19:690.
26. Introduction to "Women's Songbook," Boston NOW Collection, 19:690.

27. Laura X, "Grow Your Own . . . :" 41.
28. Judy Chicago, *The Dinner Party: A Symbol of Our Heritage*, 1st ed. (Garden City, NY: Anchor Press/Doubleday, 1979), 33.
29. Jane Gerhard, Claire Potter, and Renee Romano, *The Dinner Party: Judy Chicago and the Power of Popular Feminism, 1970–2007* (Athens: University of Georgia Press, 2013); Amelia Jones, ed., *Sexual Politics: Judy Chicago's Dinner Party in Feminist Art History* (Los Angeles: UCLA at the Armand Hammer Museum of Art and Cultural Center in association with University of California Press, Berkeley, 1996); Gail Levin, *Becoming Judy Chicago: A Biography of the Artist* (New York: Crown, 2007).
30. Judy Chicago, *The Dinner Party Bibliography: Our Heritage Is Our Power* (Santa Monica, CA: Through the Flower, 1979), 4.
31. Undated Researcher Notes, Judy Chicago Papers, 17:12, Schlesinger Library.
32. Research Files, Chicago Papers, Boxes 37–39.
33. Chicago, *Dinner Party Bibliography*, 4.
34. For a useful definition of cultural feminism and its universal views of womanhood, see Echols, *Daring to Be Bad*, 243–47.
35. Archival documents do not reveal whether or not this consciousness toward race and ethnicity came from Chicago herself or if volunteer feminists of color insisted on an inclusive history.
36. Visitor letter, June 9, 1979, Chicago Papers, 24:23.
37. Visitor letter, July 31, 1979, Chicago Papers, 24:27.
38. Visitor letter, October 2, 1979, Chicago Papers, 24:22.
39. Chicago Papers, 24:7; 22:27; 20:22.
40. Letter from students in William Monter's course, Chicago Papers, 24:1.
41. Letter from Lynn Firth, n.d., Chicago Papers, 24:3.
42. Draft of "Revelations of the Goddess," 1–2, Chicago Papers, 15:1.
43. Ibid., 5.
44. Ibid., 16–17.
45. Jocelyn Cohen, interviewed by Lara Kelland, May 18, 2011, San Francisco, CA, interview in possession of the author.
46. Closure Press Releases, 1983, Helaine Victoria Press Records, box 6, Sophia Smith Collection.
47. Jocelyn Cohen, interviewed by Lara Kelland.
48. Ibid.
49. Research Files, Helaine Victoria Press Records, 17.
50. Jocelyn Cohen, interviewed by Lara Kelland.
51. Helaine Victoria Enterprises Catalog, 1975, 1–4, Helaine Victoria Press Records, 12.
52. "Views from Our Friends and Customers," Catalog, n.d., back cover, Helaine Victoria Press Records, 12.
53. Letter to Friends and Customers," Helaine Victoria Press Records, 12.
54. Postcards, Helaine Victoria Press Records, 17.
55. Jocelyn Cohen, interviewed by Lara Kelland.
56. Ibid.
57. "Highlights from the History of Helaine Victoria Press," Helaine Victoria Press Catalog, 1979–1980, 3, Helaine Victoria Press Records, 12.
58. "Views from Our Friends and Customers," Catalog, n.d., back cover, Helaine Victoria Press Records, 12.
59. Ibid.
60. For more on the formation of women's studies as a discipline within academe, see Alice E. Ginsberg, *The Evolution of American Women's Studies: Reflections on Triumphs, Controversies, and Change* (New York: Palgrave Macmillan, 2012); Robyn Wiegman,

ed., *Women's Studies on Its Own: A Next Wave Reader in Institutional Change* (Durham, NC: Duke University Press, 2002).

61. Welcome Letter from the Institute on Women's History, May 4, 1979, Women's Action Alliance Records, 101:4, Sophia Smith Collection.
62. "Report from the 1979 Institute on Women's History for the Leadership of National Women's Organizations," 3, Women's Action Alliance Records, 102:2.
63. Welcome Letter from the Institute on Women's History, May 4, 1979, Women's Action Alliance Records, 101:4.
64. Ibid.
65. "Report from the 1979 Institute on Women's History for the Leadership of National Women's Organizations," 3–4, Women's Action Alliance Records, 102:2.
66. "Basic Books in the History of American Women," Women's Action Alliance Records, 101:2.
67. "Report from the 1979 Institute on Women's History for the Leadership of National Women's Organizations," 5, Women's Action Alliance Records, 102:2.
68. Ibid., 18.
69. The term *lavender menace* was first used at a NOW meeting by Friedan to silence lesbians who were demanding that the movement address the issues of same-sex-loving women.
70. "Report from the 1979 Institute on Women's History for the Leadership of National Women's Organizations," 8–9, Women's Action Alliance Records, 102:2.
71. In my Gay Liberation chapter, I discuss the efforts of the women's caucus to include scholarship on lesbians within the Berkshire Conference of Women Historians and the National Women's Studies Association.
72. Excerpts, letter from an anonymous institute participant, Fall 1979, in "Report from the 1979 Institute on Women's History for the Leadership of National Women's Organizations," 7, Women's Action Alliance Records, 102:2.
73. Ibid.
74. "Report from the 1979 Institute on Women's History for the Leadership of National Women's Organizations," 14–16, Women's Action Alliance Records, 102:2; Letter sent out with National Women's History Week Packet, Loretta Ross Papers, 21 28, Sophia Smith Collection; Molly Murphy MacGregor, NWHP Oral History Project, http://smatters.users.sonic.net/wordpress/wp-content/uploads/2014/10/nwhp-oral-history-transcript.pdf.
75. "Report from the 1979 Institute on Women's History for the Leadership of National Women's Organizations," 14–16, Women's Action Alliance Records, 102:2.
76. "National Women's History Week Packet," Loretta Ross Papers, 21:28.
77. Speech by Gerda Lerner given at the Smithsonian Awards Breakfast for Institute Participants, as printed in "Report from the 1979 Institute on Women's History for the Leadership of National Women's Organizations," 14, Women's Action Alliance Records, 102:2.
78. The founding of the Association for the Study of African American Life and History in 1915 and the *Journal of Negro History* in 1916, as well as the establishment of the Schomburg Center for Research in Black Culture, indirectly provided an intellectual foundation for the development of community collective memory. Although the founding of the Berkshire Conference of Women Historians provided scholars with an opportunity to network and socialize with one another, the organization did not make the promotion of women's history a major goal until the founding of the "Big Berks" conference in 1973. Journals devoted to women's studies and women's history were also founded in the 1970s and 1980s. Additionally, although the Sophia Smith and Schlesinger Collections were actively serving as institutional bedrock for academic women's history,

geographic isolation combined with the institutional barriers of being associated with Radcliffe College and Smith College left many women's liberation activists seeking more grassroots archives and projects.
79. Barbara Smith and Beverly Smith, "I Am Not Meant to Be Alone and without You Who Understand: Letters from Black Feminists, 1972-1978," *Conditions* 4 (Winter 1978): 62–77.
80. Early historians of women paved the way for such intellectual production, including Julia Cherry Spruill, Mary Sumner Benson, and others.
81. Jocelyn Cohen, interviewed by Lara Kelland.

Chapter 4: Scripted to Win

1. I use LGBT and queer as umbrella terms when the explicit focus of activists is unclear or inclusive. When activists are particularly focusing on gay men or lesbians, I use the more precise identity category.
2. Jonathan Ned Katz, "Why Gay History?", *Body Politic* 55 (August 1979): 19–20.
3. "Sappho of Lesbos," *Ladder*, December 1, 1958, 12.
4. For more on such "proprietary claims on the past," see Charles E. Morris III, "My Old Kentucky Homo: Lincoln and the Politics of Queer Public Memory," in *Framing Public Memory*, ed. Kendall R Phillips (Tuscaloosa: University of Alabama, 2004), 98.
5. Ron Anderson, "Gay History," *Gay Life*, June 24, 1977, 3.
6. The meeting brought together faculty, graduate students, and other public intellectuals, including Jonathan Ned Katz, Joan Nestle, John D'Emilio, Wayne Dines, and Martin Duberman, among others.
7. Rachel F. Corbman, "A Geneology of the Lesbian Herstory Archives, 1974–2014," *Journal of Contemporary Archival Studies* 1, no. 1 (2014).
8. Deb Edel, "Building Cultural Memories: The Work of the Lesbian Herstory Archives," in *Our Right to Love: A Lesbian Resource Book, ed.* Ginny Vida (New York: Prentice Hall, 1978), 270–72.
9. *Fem* is a spelling used by some mid-century lesbians, invoking a sexual identity that also embraced a working-class identity.
10. Joan Nestle, interviewed by Lara Kelland, March 25, 2011, New York, NY, interview in possession of the author.
11. "Gay History Meeting at Jonathan Ned Katz's Apt. in Greenwich Village, January 28, 1978," Jonathan Ned Katz Papers, box 41, Manuscripts and Archives Division, Humanities and Social Sciences Library, New York Public Library, New York, NY.
12. As lesbian separatism diminished in favor within the movement in the 1980s, LHA began to relax the policy. During the 1970s, a few gay male researchers who had proven themselves feminist allies through their activism were occasionally allowed to conduct research at the archives, including John D'Emilio and Jonathan Ned Katz. Although most of the lesbians involved in the archives had some amount of separatist tendencies, most cultivated alliances with gay men who were sensitive to gender issues within the Gay Liberation movement. When the archives opened a new building in Brooklyn in 1990, cis-male researchers with a clearly defined research query began to be admitted.
13. Deb Edel, interviewed by Lara Kelland, March 23, 2011, New York, NY, interview in possession of the author; and Joan Nestle, interviewed by Lara Kelland.
14. Deb Edel, "Building Cultural Memories," 270.
15. Barbara J. Love and Nancy F. Cott, eds., *Feminists Who Changed America, 1963–1975* (Urbana: University of Illinois, 2006), s.v. "Nancy L. Toder."
16. "Lesbian History Exploration Invitational Packet," November 1, 1974, 3, Lesbian History Exploration Collection, box 1, Lesbian Herstory Archives, Brooklyn, NY.

17. Jan Oxenberg, as quoted in Transcript of Lesbian History Collective Meeting Notes, May 13, 1974, "Lesbian History Exploration Invitational Packet," November 1, 1974, 6, Lesbian History Exploration Collection, box 1.
18. Jo Hyacinthe, as quoted in Transcript of Lesbian History Collective Meeting Notes, May 13, 1974, "Lesbian History Exploration Invitational Packet," November 1, 1974, 5, Lesbian History Exploration Collection, box 1.
19. "Lesbian History Exploration Invitational Packet," November 1, 1974, 1, Lesbian History Exploration Collection, box 1.
20. Ibid.
21. Ibid., 3.
22. Rich Bebout, "Stashing the Evidence," *Body Politic* 55 (August 1979): 21–22.
23. "Lesbian History Exploration Invitational Packet," November 1, 1974, 1, Lesbian History Exploration Collection, box 1.
24. Such abuses of archival power can be found in Michel-Rolph Trouillot, *Silencing the Past: Power and the Production of History* (Boston: Beacon, 1995), 55–57.
25. Jonathan Ned Katz, interviewed by Lara Kelland, March 23, 2011, New York, NY, interview in possession of the author.
26. Letter from Judith Schwarz to Jonathan Ned Katz, October 28, 1997, Katz Papers, box 9.
27. See Correspondence Files, Gregory Sprague Papers, Chicago History Museum, Chicago, IL; Correspondence Files, Katz Papers.
28. Katz Papers, box 1.
29. Jonathan Ned Katz, interviewed by Lara Kelland.
30. Postcard, March 31, 1980, Katz Papers, box 1, folder: "John D'Emilio."
31. John D'Emilio, interviewed by Lara Kelland, March 16 2011, New York, NY, interview in possession of the author.
32. Research folders recording research at Chicago History Museum, Newberry Library, Northwestern University, University of Chicago, and University of Illinois at Chicago, Sprague Papers, 7:5-9.
33. Letter, September 2, 1980, Sprague Papers, 11:3.
34. Letter from Patrick Townson to Gregory Sprague, May 15, 1981, Sprague Papers, 11:3
35. Letter from Edouardo Roditi to Gregory Sprague, November 11, 1983, Sprague Papers, 3:2.
36. Later academic scholarship on same-sex relations in Chicago's south side would build on this knowledge. See Kevin Mumford, *Interzones: Black/White Sex Districts in Chicago and New York in the Early Twentieth Century* (New York: Columbia University, 1997).
37. Chris Czernik, comp., "A Beginning Handbook for Researching Lesbian and Gay History in the Boston Area," April 1980, Topical Files: "History," Lesbian Herstory Archives.
38. "Mission Statement from the Circle of Lesbian Indexers," San Francisco Lesbian and Gay History Project Records, 1:10, GLBT Historical Society, San Francisco, CA.
39. The orange juice boycott was a protest sparked by Anita Bryant's spearheading of the "Save Our Children" campaign to repeal a gay rights ordinance in Dade County, Florida, in 1977. As orange juice was a major commercial produce from the area, organizers hoped to put economic and public relations pressure on the constituents of Dade County. "The Lesbian Periodicals Index and Thesaurus of Subjects," 3rd ed. September 1981, Circle of Lesbian Indexers Collection, folder 1, Lesbian Herstory Archives; "Preserving Our Words and Pictures," transcript of interview with Joan Nestle and Deborah Edel by Beth Hodge, c. 1980, Topical Files: "Publicity," Lesbian Herstory Archives.
40. "Gay History Meeting at Jonathan Ned Katz's Apt. in Greenwich Village, January 28, 1978, Katz Papers, box 41.

41. *Lesbian/Gay History Researchers Network Newsletter*, Summer 1980, March 1981, Topical Files: "History Projects," Lesbian Herstory Archives.
42. Deb Edel, interviewed by Lara Kelland.
43. Leila J. Rupp, *A Desired Past: A Short History of Same-Sex Love in America* (Chicago: University of Chicago, 1999), 9.
44. Jonathan Ned Katz, interviewed by Lara Kelland; "Problems with Research of Gay History," *Gay Archivist* 1 (May 1977): 2.
45. Deb Edel, interviewed by Lara Kelland.
46. Jim Monahan, "Considerations in the Organization of Gay Archives," *Gay Insurgent* 5 (1978): 9.
47. Ibid.
48. Maxine Wolfe, "The Lesbian Herstory Archives: A Passionate and Political Act," Maxine Wolfe Papers, box 1, folder: "1995," Lesbian Herstory Archives.
49. Transcript of an interview with Joan Nestle, "Radical Archiving: A Lesbian Feminist Perspective," *Gay Insurgent* 5 (1978): 10.
50. "Suggested Questions for Doing Gay Oral History Tapes," SAGE New York Oral History Project, Topical Files: "Oral History Guide," Lesbian Herstory Archives.
51. Press Release of the Buffalo Oral History Project, as distributed at the National Women's Studies Association Conference, June 1, 1979, Topical Files: "History Projects," Lesbian Herstory Archives.
52. Elizabeth Lapovsky Kennedy and Madeline D. Davis, *Boots of Leather, Slippers of Gold: The History of a Lesbian Community* (New York: Routledge, 1993).
53. "Preserving Your Individual and Community Herstory," March 4, 1986, Topical Files: "History," Lesbian Herstory Archives.
54. "Handbook of Gay Historical Research," Project Proposal, 1979, San Francisco Lesbian and Gay History Project Records, 1:1, GLBT Historical Society.
55. Joan Nestle, Press Release, December 1982, Topical Files: "History Projects," Lesbian Herstory Archives.
56. Flyers for various slide shows, Topical Files: "History Projects," Lesbian Herstory Archives.
57. "Cincinnati Lesbian HYSTORICAL Society Needs You!", flyer, 1982, Topical Files: "History Projects" Lesbian Herstory Archives.
58. John D'Emilio, interviewed by Lara Kelland.
59. Joan Nestle, interviewed by Lara Kelland.
60. Flyers for various slide shows, Topical Files: "History Projects," Lesbian Herstory Archives.
61. Ibid.
62. Fliers for various slide shows, Topical Files: "History Projects" and "Slide Shows," Lesbian Herstory Archives.
63. Flyer for "The Celluloid Closet" slide show, 1989, Vito Russo Papers, 20:1, Manuscripts and Archives Division, Humanities and Social Sciences Library, New York Public Library.
64. Flyer for "The Making of the Modern Homosexual" slide show, c. 1980, Sprague Papers, 12:17.
65. Sprague explained his own work as being in conversation with the works of Michel Foucault, Kenneth Plummer, and Jeffrey Weeks. "Proposal for AHA Paper," n.d., Sprague Papers, 12:17.
66. Allan Bérubé, *Coming Out under Fire* (New York: Free Press, 2000); Eric Garber, *Uranian Worlds: A Reader's Guide to Alternative Sexuality in Science Fiction and Fantasy* (Boston: G. K. Hall, 1983); Vito Russo, *The Celluloid Closet: Homosexuality in the Movies* (New York: Harper & Row, 1981); James D. Steakley, *The Homosexual Emancipation Movement in Germany* (New York: Arno Press, 1975).

67. The San Francisco Gay and Lesbian History Project, which would later become the Gay, Lesbian, Bisexual, and Transgender Historical Society, was founded in 1979, and by 1980, members work-shopped slide shows, as their peers offered feedback for improving the content and presentation. Audio recordings of slide show workshops, San Francisco Lesbian and Gay History Project Records, box 2.
68. Letter from Judith Schwarz to Gregory Sprague, August 18, 1982, Sprague Papers, 3:1.
69. "Eric Presents 'T'aint Nobody's Business,'" cassette tape, January 27, 1981. San Francisco Lesbian and Gay History Project Records, box 2.
70. Jonathan Ned Katz, interviewed by Lara Kelland.
71. Joan Nestle, interviewed by Lara Kelland.
72. "The Gay Academic Unmasks," *Chronicle of Higher Education* 8, no. 2 (February 25, 1974): 20.
73. "Gay Academic Union Statement of Purpose," http://www.rainbowhistory.org/gau.htm.
74. Karla Jay, interviewed by Lara Kelland, March 26, 2011, New York, NY, interview in possession of the author; Joan Nestle, interviewed by Lara Kelland; Jonathan Ned Katz, interviewed by Lara Kelland; John D'Emilio, interviewed by Lara Kelland.
75. Ibid.
76. John D'Emilio, *Making Trouble: Essays on Gay History, Politics, and the University* (New York: Routledge, 1992), 122.
77. Ibid.
78. Martin Duberman, *Left Out: The Politics of Exclusion. Essays, 1964–1999* (Basic Books: New York, 1999), 280.
79. John D'Emilio, interviewed by Lara Kelland.
80. *Committee on Lesbian and Gay History Newsletter*, Fall 1980, 3, from the personal papers of John D'Emilio.
81. *Lesbian/Gay History Researchers Network Newsletter*, Fall 1980, 3, Sprague Papers, 26:20.
82. *Committee on Lesbian and Gay History Newsletter*, Summer 1983, Sprague Papers, 22:10.
83. The Lesbian Caucus of the '78 Berkshire Conference. "Memo to the Program Committee of the Berkshire Conference on the History of Women," November 13, 1978, Topical Files: "History Conferences," Lesbian Herstory Archives.
84. "The Lesbian Caucus News," Topical Files: "History Projects," Lesbian Herstory Archives.
85. Katz, "Why Gay History?", 19.

Chapter 5: For the Sake of Cultural Survival

1. "Aim Leaders Threaten More Protests," *Arizona Daily Sun*, July 3, 1972, 1.
2. Although the Civil Rights movement also worked on the policy level, the interdependent relationship between the Bureau of Indian Affairs and tribal governments meant that Red Power activists had a particularly strong focus on policy work.
3. For more on the development and activities of the Red Power movement, see Julie L. Davis, *Survival Schools: The American Indian Movement and Community Education in the Twin Cities* (Minneapolis: University of Minnesota Press, 2013); Frederick Hoxie, *This Indian Country: American Indian Activists and the Place They Made* (New York: Penguin Books, 2013); Troy R. Johnson, Joane Nagel, and Duane Champagne, eds., *American Indian Activism: Alcatraz to the Longest Walk* (Urbana: University of Illinois Press, 1997); Gregory D. Smithers and Brooke N. Newman, *Native Diasporas: Indigenous Identities and Settler Colonialism in the Americas* (Lincoln: University of Nebraska Press, 2014).
4. For more on the development of Pan-Indian activism in the early and mid-twentieth century, see Daniel M. Cobb, *Native Activism in Cold War America: The Struggle for*

Sovereignty (Lawrence: University Press of Kansas, 2008); Thomas W. Cowger, *The National Congress of American Indians: The Founding Years* (Lincoln: University of Nebraska Press, 1999).
5. For more on the history of the principle of sovereignty, see Vine Deloria and Clifford M. Lytle, *The Nations Within: The Past and Future of American Indian Sovereignty* (New York: Pantheon Books, 1984).
6. For more on Indian boarding schools, see David Wallace Adams, *Education for Extinction: American Indians and the Boarding School Experience, 1875–1928* (Lawrence: University Press of Kansas, 1995); Margaret Archuleta, Brenda J. Child, K. Tsianina Lomawaima, and Heard Museum, *Away from Home: American Indian Boarding School Experiences, 1879–2000* (Phoenix: Heard Museum, 2000); Amelia V. Katanski, *Learning to Write "Indian": The Boarding-School Experience and American Indian Literature* (Norman: University of Oklahoma Press, 2005). For more on settler colonial theory within the context of American Indian activism, see Walter L. Hixson, *American Settler Colonialism: A History.* (New York: Palgrave Macmillan, 2013).
7. AIM Bicentennial Commission, 3, Roger A. Finzel American Indian Movement Papers, 1:2, University of New Mexico Center for Southwest Research, Albuquerque, NM.
8. For more on the long Red Power movement, see Cobb, *Native Activism in Cold War America.*
9. Cowger, *The National Congress of American Indians.*
10. National Indian Youth Council, *Articles of Incorporation,* 1962, National Indian Youth Council Records (hereafter NIYC Records), 1, University of New Mexico Center for Southwest Research.
11. David E. Wilkins, *American Indian Politics and the American Political System* (Lanham, MD: Rowman & Littlefield, 2002), 196.
12. Cobb, *Native Activism in Cold War America,* 54.
13. American Indian Chicago Conference and University of Chicago, *Declaration of Indian Purpose: The Voice of the American Indian* (Chicago: University of Chicago, 1961), 3.
14. National Indian Youth Council, *Articles of Incorporation,* 1962, NIYC Records, 1:1.
15. For more on Clyde Warrior's foregrounding of cultural heritage as a tool for resistance, see Paul McKenzie-Jones, "'We Are among the Poor, the Powerless, the Inexperienced and the Inarticulate': Clyde Warrior's Campaign for a Greater Indian America," *American Indian Quarterly* 34, no. 2 (Spring 2010): 224–57. Like Warrior, John Trudell's poetry and speeches regularly underscored the significance of the past to present movements.
16. James G. LeGrand, *Indian Metropolis: Indians in Chicago, 1945-75* (Urbana: University of Illinois Press, 2002), 221; Tony Machukay, "The Tribal-Urban Conflict," c. 1973, 1, NIYC records, 3:1.
17. Machukay, "The Tribal-Urban Conflict," NIYC records, 1.
18. For more on the role of grassroots education in American Indian movement-building, see John J. Laukaitis, *Community Self-Determination: American Indian Education in Chicago, 1952–2006* (Albany: State University of New York Press, 2015).
19. For more on the connections between early- and mid-twentieth-century Native American activists and NIYC's political agenda and practices, see Bradley G. Shreve, *Red Power Rising: The National Indian Youth Council and the Origins of Native Activism* (Norman: University of Oklahoma, 2011).
20. Clyde Ellis, "The Sound of the Drum Will Revive Them and Make Them Happy," in *Powwow,* ed. Clyde Ellis, Luke Eric Lassiter, and Gary H. Dunham (Lincoln: University of Nebraska Press, 2005), 11.
21. For more on tourism and spectatorship in powwow culture, see Philip Deloria, *Playing Indian* (New Haven: Yale University Press, 1998), 128–53. See also, Louis S. Warren,

Buffalo Bill's America: William Cody and the Wild West Show (New York: Alfred A. Knopf, 2005); Linda Scarangella McNenly, *Native Performers in Wild West Shows: From Buffalo Bill to Euro Disney* (Norman: University of Oklahoma Press, 2012).
22. The role of spectatorship and performance in the construction of Indianness has become an important area of scholarship. See, for example, Deloria, *Playing Indian*; Shari M. Huhndorf, *Going Native: Indians in the American Cultural Imagination* (Ithaca: Cornell University Press, 2001).
23. For more on the development of the Ghost Dance, see Louis S. Warren, *God's Red Son: The Ghost Dance Religion and the Making of Modern America* (New York: Basic Books, 2017).
24. Clyde Ellis, *A Dancing People: Powwow Culture on the Southern Plains* (Lawrence: University Press of Kansas, 2003), 14–15.
25. Tisa Joy Wenger, *We Have a Religion: The 1920s Pueblo Indian Dance Controversy and American Religious Freedom* (Chapel Hill: University of North Carolina Press, 2009), 152–54; Ellis, *A Dancing People*, 14.
26. Ellis, *A Dancing People*, 17.
27. Deloria, *Playing Indian*, 135.
28. Articles of Incorporation, Article IV, 2, All Indian Pow Wow Records, 1939–1957, 1:11, Cline Library, Special Collections and Archives Department, Northern Arizona University, Flagstaff, AZ.
29. 1939 program brochure, 2, All Indian Pow Wow Records, 1939–1957, 3:10.
30. Chamber of Commerce brochure, All Indian Pow Wow Records, 1974, 3:7.
31. 1939 program brochure, 2 All Indian Pow Wow Records, 1939–1957, 3:10.
32. Ibid.
33. Ibid.
34. 1939 program brochure, inner back cover, All Indian Pow Wow Records, 1939–1957, 3:10.
35. 1941 program brochure 2, All Indian Pow Wow Records, 1939–1957, 3:10.
36. Ibid.
37. 1958 program brochure 9, All Indian Pow Wow Records, 1939–1957, 3:10.
38. 1950 program brochure, 12, All Indian Pow Wow Records, 1939–1957, 3:10.
39. 1939 program brochure, 2, All Indian Pow Wow Records, 1939–1957, 3:10.
40. 1958 program brochure, front inner cover, All Indian Pow Wow Records, 1939–1957, 3:10.
41. "Powwow Dances Introductions," 1955, 2, 4, 5, 10, All Indian Pow Wow Records, 1939–1957, 1:16.
42. "Powwow Dances Introductions," 1, All Indian Pow Wow Records, 1:16
43. "The Encampment: Instant City," *The Sun*, 1972 Commemorative Guide, section C10, All Indian Pow Wow Records, 1939–1957, 3:3.
44. Ibid.
45. Daniel M. Cobb, *Say We Are Nations: Documents of Politics and Protest in Indigenous America since 1887* (Chapel Hill: University of North Carolina Press, 2015); Joane Nagel, *American Indian Ethnic Renewal: Red Power and the Resurgence of Identity and Culture* (New York: Oxford University Press, 1996).
46. 1975 calendar, Michael Taylor Papers, 7:2, Bailey Library and Archives, Denver Museum of Nature and Science, Denver, CO.
47. Patricia Locke, "Education as War: American Indian Participation in Tribal Education," unpublished white paper, October 1974, 20 Taylor Papers, box 7, folder: "Indian Education Resources Center."
48. Patricia Locke, "An Ideal School System for American Indians—A Theoretical Construct," 4, 7, 8, 12–13, 17–19, Taylor Papers, box 7, folder: "Indian Education Resources Center."

49. Both *Navajo* and *Navaho* are accepted and used spellings. For the sake of consistency, unless a source uses Navaho, I use Navajo. Spellings in archival sources are kept consistent with the creator's choice.
50. American Indian Higher Education Consortium, "Tribal Colleges, an Introduction," 1999, A-1, http://www.aihec.org/who-we-serve/docs/TCU_intro.pdf.
51. Patricia Locke, "Education as War: American Indian Participation in Tribal Education," unpublished white paper, October 1974, Taylor Papers, box 7, folder: "Indian Education Resources Center."
52. For more on the development of tribal colleges, see Paul Boyer, *Capturing Education: Envisioning and Building the First Tribal Colleges* (Pablo, MT: Salish Kootenai College Press, 2015); David H. DeJong, *Promises of the Past: A History of Indian Education in the United States* (Golden, CO: North America Press, 1993).
53. Jack Forbes, "American Tribal Higher Education Proposal," 2, NIYC Records, 6:21.
54. Ibid.
55. Ibid.
56. Ibid.
57. For more on the history of education within the Navajo nation, see Peter Iverson and Monty Roessel, *Diné: A History of the Navajos* (Albuquerque: University of New Mexico Press, 2002); T. L. McCarty and Fred Bia, *A Place to Be Navajo: Rough Rock and the Struggle for Self-Determination in Indigenous Schooling* (Mahwah, NJ: Lawrence Erlbaum Associates, 2002); David E. Wilkins, *The Navajo Political Experience* (Lanham, MD: Rowman & Littlefield, 2003).
58. Steven Crum, "The Idea of an Indian College or University in Twentieth Century America before the Formation of the Navajo Community College in 1968," *Tribal College: A Journal of American Indian Higher Education 1*, no. 1 (Summer 1989): 20–23.
59. Patricia Locke, "An Ideal School System for American Indians—A Theoretical Construct," 8, Taylor Papers, box 7, folder: "Indian Education Resources Center."
60. Ibid., 10.
61. NCC Brochure, 1969, 1, Vertical Files: "Navajo Community College," Cline Library.
62. Ibid.
63. Draft Copy of Accreditation Report, March 9, 1971, 1, Peter Iverson Collection, 13:2, Labriola Center, Arizona State University, Tempe, AZ.
64. Article from *Navaho Diary,* November 4, 1969, Iverson Collection, 16:12.
65. Draft Copy of Accreditation Report, March 9, 1971, 1, Iverson Collection, 13:2.
66. Philosophy section, NCC brochure, 5–6, Vertical Files: "Navajo Community College," Cline Library.
67. Raymond Nakai, Chairman's Speech given at Navajo Community College, October 14, 1968, Raymond Nakai Papers, 6:52, Cline Library.
68. Navajo Studies Brochure, Vertical Files: "Navajo Community College," Cline Library.
69. Ibid.
70. For more on the impact of boarding schools on tribal communities, see Adams, *Education for Extinction*; Lomawaima, Child, and Archuleta, eds. *Away from Home.*
71. "NCC Program Teaches Leadership Skills," *NCC Newsletter,* March 1971, Virginia Brown, Ida Bahl, and Lillian Watson Collection, Cline Library.
72. Press release from the Department of the Interior, Office of the Secretary, April 12, 1972, Sam Steiger Collection, 3:39, Cline Library.
73. *NCC Newsletter,* July 1972, Steiger Collection, 3:39.
74. Navajo Community College, Special President's Newsletter in Honor of the Bicentennial, July 1976, Vertical Files: "Navajo Community College," Cline Library.
75. "Navajos Fill 4 More NCC Posts," *NCC Newsletter,* September 1971, 4, Brown, Bahl, and Watson Collection, 3:235.
76. "History, Culture Instructor Teaches from Navajo Heritage Background," *NCC Newsletter,* February 1971, 5, Brown, Bahl, and Watson Collection, 3:235.

77. For more on the repatriation of cultural resources, see Devon A. Mihesuah, *Repatriation Reader: Who Owns American Indian Remains?* (Lincoln: University of Nebraska Press, 2000); Kathleen S. Fine-Dare, *Grave Injustice: The American Indian Repatriation Movement and NAGPRA* (Lincoln: University of Nebraska Press, 2002).
78. "Eastern Museums Contribute Artifacts to Culture Center," *NCC Newsletter*, July-August 1971, 5, Brown, Bahl, and Watson Collection, 3.235.
79. "Chairman Invites Corporate Reps to Meet on NCC Culture Center," *NCC Newsletter*, July-August 1972, 3. Brown, Bahl, and Watson Collection, 3.236.
80. For more on the collection, repatriation, and interpretation of American Indian history in national and community-controlled museums, see Amy Lonetree, *Decolonizing Museums: Representing Native America in National and Tribal Museums* (Chapel Hill: University of North Carolina Press, 2012).
81. "Grant Will Aid Navajo Studies," *NCC Newsletter*, June 1971, 3, Brown, Bahl, and Watson Collection, 3:2:5.
82. Memo from "A Student" to the Visitors of the NCC Dedication, n.d., Vertical Files: "Navajo Community College," Cline Library.
83. Peter A. Janssen, "Navajo's CC's Unfulfilled Promise," *Change Magazine*, November 1975, 52-53.
84. Ibid.
85. Chief Joseph, as quoted in the Longest Walk Manifesto, January 14, 1879, 2, Robert Robideau American Indian Movement Papers, 21:6, University of New Mexico Center for Southwest Research
86. For more on the cultural and political formation and impact of the American Indian Movement, see George Pierre Castile, *To Show Heart: Native American Self-Determination and Federal Indian Policy, 1960–1975* (Tucson: University of Arizona Press, 1998); Davis, *Survival School*; Hoxie, *This Indian Country*; and Paul Chaat Smith and Robert Allen Warrior, *Like a Hurricane: The Indian Movement from Alcatraz to Wounded Knee* (New York: New Press, 1996).
87. The Alcatraz occupation was organized by another Red Power group, Indians of All Tribes. Although AIM's role in the occupation consisted only of participation, the event inspired AIM leaders to work on a national level.
88. Richard Oakes, as quoted in Smith and Warrior, *Like a Hurricane*, 24.
89. For more on the Alcatraz occupation, see Cobb, *Native Activism in Cold War America*; Adam Fortunate Eagle and Tim Findley, *Heart of the Rock: The Indian Invasion of Alcatraz* (Norman: University of Oklahoma Press, 2002); Troy R. Johnson, *The American Indian Occupation of Alcatraz Island: Red Power and Self-Determination* (Lincoln: University of Nebraska Press, 2008).
90. "The Alcatraz Proclamation," University of North Dakota collections, http://arts-sciences.und.edu/Native-media-center/_files/docs/1950-1970/1969alcatrazproclamation.pdf.
91. Ibid.
92. Ibid.
93. Ibid.
94. American Indian Community History Center Records, 1:1, The Bancroft Library, University of California, Berkeley, Berkeley, CA.
95. "Community History Project," American Indian Community History Center Records, 1:29.
96. For more on collective memory and space, see Michel de Certeau and Steven Rendall, *The Practice of Everyday Life* (Berkeley: University of California Press, 1984); Dolores Hayden, *The Power of Place: Urban Landscapes as Public History* (Cambridge, MA: MIT Press, 1995); Pierre Nora, *Rethinking France: Les Lieux De Mémoire* (Chicago: University of Chicago Press, 2001).
97. "The Alcatraz Proclamation," University of North Dakota collections, http://arts-sciences.und.edu/Native-media-center/_files/docs/1950-1970/1969alcatrazproclamation.pdf.

98. Ibid.
99. AIM Fact Sheet, Finzel American Indian Movement Papers, 1:2.
100. AIM Bicentennial Commission Press Release, July 3, 1975, Finzel American Indian Movement Papers, 1:2.
101. "July 4, 1975: Picnics, Protests, and Politics," *[Washington, PA] Observer Reporter*, July 5, 1975, 5.
102. AIM Bicentennial Commission Press Release, July 3, 1975, Finzel American Indian Movement Papers, 1:2.
103. Trail of Broken Treaties 20-Point Position Paper, http://www.framingredpower.org/archive/other/frp.tbt.19721027.xml.
104. "Indian Protest Sought End of Paternalism," *Washington Post*, November 9, 1972, C1
105. Trail of Broken Treaties 20-Point Position Paper, http://www.framingredpower.org/archive/other/frp.tbt.19721027.xml.
106. The conditions under which such corruption flourished can be linked to the establishment of tribal chiefs through the passage of the Indian Reorganization Act of 1934.
107. "Why the Repossession of Wounded Knee?", 3, Finzel American Indian Movement Papers, 1:7.
108. Ibid., 5.
109. Ibid., 6.
110. Ibid., 8.
111. Carol Talbert Sullivan, "The Resurgence of Ethnicity among American Indians: Some Comments on the Occupation of Wounded Knee," *Ethnicity in the Americas* (The Hague: Mouton and Co., [1976]), 378.
112. Vine Deloria, *God Is Red* (New York: Dell, 1983), 258.

Conclusion

1. Fred Wilson and Mark A. Graham, "An Interview with Artist Fred Wilson," *The Journal of Museum Education* 32, no. 3 (Fall 2007): 211–19.
2. Andrea Burns argues that the separatist political goals of the Black Power movement and the compromises struck by Black Power activists were not at odds with one another, but rather demonstrate the pragmatic approach of museum leadership in institutionalizing Black Power values. See Andrea Burns, *From Storefront to Monument: Tracing the Public History of the Black Museum Movement* (Amherst: University of Massachusetts Press, 2013), 157.
3. For more on battles over curricular standards, see Ronald W. Evans, *The Social Studies Wars: What Should We Teach the Children?* (New York: Teachers College Press, 2004); Gary B. Nash, Charlotte A. Crabtree, and Ross E. Dunn, *History on Trial: Culture Wars and the Teaching of the Past* (New York: A. A. Knopf, 1997); Jonathan Zimmerman, *Whose America?: Culture Wars in the Public Schools* (Cambridge: Harvard University Press, 2002).
4. "Politically Correct Museums," *Economist*, January 16, 1993, 85.
5. Philip Ravenhill, review of *Mining the Museum, African Arts* 26, no. 3 (July 1993): 72–73. For more scholarly analysis of the exhibit, see Fred Wilson, *Fred Wilson: A Critical Reader*, ed. Doro Globus (London: Ridinghouse, 2011); Amalia Mesa-Bains, "Mining the Museum: An Installation Confronting History," in *Reinventing the Museum: The Evolving Conversation on the Paradigm Shift*, ed. Gail Anderson, 2nd ed. (Lanham, MD: AltaMira Press, 2012).
6. Ira Berlin, Lisa Corrin, Leslie King-Hammond, and Fred Wilson, *Mining the Museum: An Installation by Fred Wilson* (Baltimore: The Contemporary in Cooperation with the New Press, New York, 1994), 164.

7. "Visiting Black History Treasures in the Nation's Capital," *Ebony*, June 1988, 78.
8. Jo Blatti, review of *Field to Factory: Afro-American Migration, 1915–1940*, *Oral History Review* 16, no. 1 (Spring 1988): 194-98.
9. "A Show on Women in 1800s," *New York Times*, August 6, 1982, C10.
10. For more on the emergence and evolution of women's history exhibits, see Barbara Melosh and Christina Simmons, "Exhibiting Women's History," in *Presenting the Past: Essays on History and the Public*, ed. Susan Porter Benson, et al. (Philadelphia: Temple University Press, 1986).
11. Jill Austin, Jennifer Brier, Jessica Herczeg-Konecny, and Anne Parsons, "When the Erotic Becomes Illicit: Struggles over Displaying Queer History at a Mainstream Museum," *Radical History Review* 113 (Spring 2012), 187. For more on recent developments in LGBT public history research and interpretation, see Susan Ferentinos, *Interpreting LGBT History at Museums and Historic Sites* (Lanham MD: Rowman & Littlefield, 2015).
12. Mike Wallace, *Mickey Mouse History and Other Essays on American Memory* (Philadelphia: Temple University, 1996), 120.
13. For more on these initiatives, see William S Walker, *A Living Exhibition: The Smithsonian and the Transformation of the Universal Museum* (Amherst: University of Massachusetts, 2013).
14. The Arab American National Museum in Dearborn, Michigan, and the Japanese American National Museum in Los Angeles are good examples of this, as they both carry Smithsonian affiliation but lack the symbolic inclusion of full-fledged Smithsonian institutions.
15. The success of the National Museum of the American Indian is perhaps attributable to the formal relationship between indigenous nations and the federal government, as the blatant colonialism of museums' possession of human remains provided such an obvious target for reform. In addition, the deeply institutionalized nature of American Indian/federal government policy provided a clear target for activism.
16. Fath Davis Ruffins, "Culture Wars Won and Lost, Part II: The National African-American Museum Project," *Radical History Review* 70 (Summer 1998): 78–101.
17. Holland Cotter, "Review: The Smithsonian African American Museum Is Here at Last," *New York Times*, September 15, 2016.
18. Paul A. Shackel, *Myth, Memory and the Making of the American Landscape* (Gainesville: University of Florida, 2001), 47–62.
19. "A Black Group Assails Statue of Suffragists," *New York Times*, March 9, 1997, 28.
20. "National Women's History Museum Makes Little Progress After 16 Years," *Huffington Post*, April 8, 2012, http://www.huffingtonpost.com/2012/04/08/national-womens-history-museum_n_1408662.html.
21. Sonya Michel, "The National Women's History Museum Apparently Doesn't Much Care for Women's Historians," *The New Republic*, April 4, 2014, https://newrepublic.com/article/117259/national-womens-history-museum-apparently-doesnt-much-care-w.
22. Erin Blakemore, "Why a Congressional Commission Wants a National Women's History Museum," *Smithsonian Online*, November 18, 2016, http://www.smithsonianmag.com/smart-news/why-congressional-commission-wants-national-womens-history-museum-180961156/.
23. Michel, "The National Women's History Museum Apparently Doesn't Much Care for Women's Historians."
24. Richard Rabinowitz, *Curating America: Journeys through Storyscapes of the American Past* (Chapel Hill: University of North Carolina, 2015), 298. Likewise, James Green urged academic historians to take up the mantle of public intellectualism, bringing social movement history more into the public sphere. See James Green, *Taking History to Heart: The Power of the Past in Building Social Movements* (Amherst: University of Massachusetts, 2000).

25. Ivan Karp and Stephen D. Levine, eds., *Exhibiting Cultures: The Poetics and Politics of Museum Display* (Washington, DC: Smithsonian Institution, 1991); Ivan Karp, Christine M. Kreamer, and Stephen D. Levine, eds., *Museums and Communities: The Politics of Public Culture* (Washington, DC: Smithsonian Institution, 1992).
26. Karp and Levine, *Exhibiting Cultures*, 2.
27. American Association of Museums, *Excellence and Equity: Education and the Public Dimension of Museums* (Washington, DC: The Association, 1992).
28. Duncan Cameron, "The Museum, a Temple or the Forum," *Curator: The Museum Journal* 14, no. 1 (March 1971): 11–24. See also, Bill Adair, Benjamin Filene, and Laura Koloski, *Letting Go?: Sharing Historical Authority in a User-Generated World* (Philadelphia: Pew Center for Arts & Heritage, 2011).
29. Richard Handler and Eric Gable, *The New History in an Old Museum: Creating the Past at Colonial Williamsburg* (Durham, NC: Duke University Press, 1997), 67.
30. Michael Frisch, *A Shared Authority: Essays on the Craft and Meaning of Oral and Public History* (Albany: State University of New York Press, 1990). For further conversation about the use of shared authority in the digital era, see Adair, Filene, and Koloski, *Letting Go*.
31. Michael Lind, "Reinventing the Museum," *National Affairs* 109 (Fall 1992): 31.
32. Ray Olsen, review of *See, I Told You So*, by Rush Limbaugh, *Booklist*, December 1, 1993, 658.
33. Bryan J. Wolf, "How the West Was Hung, or When I Hear the Word 'Culture' I Take Out My Checkbook," *American Quarterly* 44, no. 3 (September 1992): 418–38.
34. Edward T. Linenthal and Tom Englehardt, *History Wars: The Enola Gay and Other Battles for the American Past* (New York: Metropolitan, 1996); Wallace, *Mickey Mouse History*, 269–309.
35. Lynne Cheney, "The End of History," *Wall Street Journal*, October 20, 1994, A22.
36. "Donor Pulls Smithsonian Gift," *Chicago Tribune*, February 5, 2002.
37. Timothy Luke, *Museum Politics: Power Plays at the Exhibition* (Minneapolis: University of Minnesota, 2002), xv.
38. For more on the role of narrative in social movements, especially on how narrative is productive of identity and meaning, see Joseph E. Davis, *Stories of Change: Narrative and Social Movements* (Albany: State University of New York Press, 2002).
39. For more on the benefits and limitations of identity politics in social movements, see Aidan McGarry and James M. Jasper, *The Identity Dilemma: Social Movements and Collective Identity* (Philadelphia: Temple University Press, 2015).
40. Russell Rickford, *We Are an African People: Independent Education, Black Power, and the Radical Imagination* (New York: Oxford University Press, 2016), 28.
41. Although I disagree with Joseph Rhea's assertion that what he calls the "race pride movement" is a separate social formation from other aspects of the Black Freedom movement, his exposition of race-based heritage efforts as a politically discursive act further demonstrates the power of the past for oppositional movements. Joseph Tilden Rhea, *Race Pride and the American Identity* (Cambridge: Harvard University Press, 1997).

Index

abolition, 12, 30–31, 34, 62, 57, 83, 159
academic history. *See under* history
Addams, Jane, 89, 160
Adickes, Sandra, 29, 33
Aduwa, Battle of, 43
Africa, 8, 31, 40, 43, 49, 52, 54, 57, 67, 83; diaspora from, 13, 24, 34, 44, 54, 64; origins in, 40, 44, 60, 69. *See also* Afrocentrism; history: African; Pan-Africanism
African American Civil Rights movement. *See* Civil Rights movement
African Americans. *See* Black Power movement; Civil Rights movement; federal government: relationship to African Americans; history: African American; race; racism; separatism: black; stereotypes: of African Americans
African American studies programs. *See* colleges and universities: black studies programs
Afrocentrism, 40–45, 50–53, 60, 62, 168–69; in education, 3, 46, 53, 55, 57–58
agriculture, 10, 20, 27, 33, 77, 147
AIM (American Indian Movement). *See* American Indian Movement
Alabama, 15, 52
Alcatraz, occupation of, 150–51, 155
Ali, John, 47
Allen, Richard B., 43
American Historical Association, 73, 109, 125

American Indian Movement (AIM), 3, 129–32, 140, 149–56, 162, 170. *See also* Red Power movement
Amistad uprising, 30
Anderson, Candie. *See* Carawan, Candie
Anthony, Susan B., 75, 78, 162
Apache, 139
archival practice, 2–3, 5, 7, 103–4, 110, 113–18. *See also* history: public; methodology
archives and libraries, 2, 18, 20, 29, 82, 87–88, 111, 152, 160, 173; African American collections, 13, 21–22; community-based, 3, 72, 103–5, 109, 113–16, 127, 172; lack of sources in, 7, 73, 81, 110, 114; LGBT collections, 101, 103–5, 107, 105–18, 125–27, 172 (*see also* Lesbian Herstory Archives); women's history collections, 72–73, 76–80, 90, 95–96, 99, 104, 172 (*see also* Women's Herstory Library; World Center for Women's Archives). *See also* sources, historical
Arizona, 125, 131, 135–36, 141
Arkansas, 143
art, visual, 9, 71, 76, 78, 113, 120, 167, 172; installations, 3, 157–59 (see also *Dinner Party, The*; *Mining the Museum*); sculpture, 163
Asia, 42, 44, 49, 52, 60, 64, 67, 77, 83, 154, 166
Asian Americans, 63, 166
Astell, Mary, 88
Atlanta, Georgia, 22

atomic bomb, 166
Attucks, Crispus, 25
authority, historical, 4–7, 9, 37, 39, 53, 67, 71, 79, 99, 103–4, 109, 116–17, 130, 142, 145, 150, 159, 165, 168, 172
autonomy, cultural, 3, 6, 8, 108; African American, 23, 27, 40–42, 68–69; Native American, 130, 132–33, 140–44, 146, 148, 150, 152–53, 155–56, 162

Bad Heart Bull, Wesley, 153
Baker, Ella, 29
Baldwin, James, 62
Banai, Eddie Benton, 149
Banks, Dennis, 149
Banneker, Benjamin, 25
Baraka, Amiri, 58
Barnard College, 73
Beard, Mary Ritter, 73
Bellecourt, Clyde, 149
Berkshire Conference of Women Historians, 73, 114
Berkshire Conference on the History of Women, 94, 98, 125–26
Bérubé, Allan, 109, 111–12, 121–22
BIA (Bureau of Indian Affairs). *See* Bureau of Indian Affairs
bisexual inclusion, 124
Black Bear, Tillie, 93
Black History Month, 65, 94. *See also* Negro History Week
Black Panther, 60–61, 63, 67
Black Panther Party (BPP), 9, 37, 42, 58–69, 169, 173; liberation schools, 9, 42, 59, 62–69, 172
Black Power movement, 2–3, 8–9, 23, 39–69, 76, 169, 172; academic history and, 48, 58, 62; comparison to Civil Rights movement, 2–3, 12, 27, 31, 34–37, 39–40, 59; comparison to Gay Liberation movement, 2–3, 101, 104, 116, 127; comparison to Red Power movement, 2–3, 130, 134, 145, 154–55; comparison to Women's Liberation movement, 2–3, 71–72, 76, 85, 95–97, 99; conferences, 40, 56; critique of HBCUs, 55; critique of mainstream institutions, 2–3, 41, 45, 48, 50, 52, 55, 65; educational initiatives (*see* Black Panther Party: liberation schools; curriculum: Black Power; University of Islam); integration with mainstream institutions, 57–58, 62; legacy, 158–59, 164–65, 167–68; organizations, 41, 51, 53–55, 57–58, 63–64; origins, 23, 41, 60; periodicals, 41, 48, 58–60, 68 (see also *Black Panther*; *Muhammad Speaks*); writings, 50, 55, 61, 63–64. *See also* Black Panther Party; Malcolm X Liberation University; National of Islam
boarding schools. *See* Indian boarding schools
Boggs, Grace Lee, 93
books, history, 3, 18, 30–31, 78, 88, 92, 97, 103, 117, 121. See also *Gay American History*
Boston, Massachusetts, 50, 105, 113, 118
Boston Marriage, 121
Brown, Elaine, 65
Brown, John, 21, 31, 159
Brown, Louise Fargo, 73
Brown, Robert, 56
Buddhism, 49
Bureau of Indian Affairs (BIA), 6, 9, 131–32, 135, 140–41, 143, 146, 148, 150–53, 155
Busch, Judy, 79

California, 59, 61, 67, 77, 79, 91, 94, 107, 141. *See also* Oakland, California; San Francisco, California
California State University at Fresno, 80, 86
Camp, Carter, 153
Canada, 109, 115, 118
Carawan, Candie, 19, 21
Carawan, Guy, 19–22
Carmichael, Stokely, 40, 59, 64, 68
Carver, George Washington, 34
Castillo, Lupe, 93
Cavallaro, Sahli, 105–6
Cheyenne, 139
Chicago, Illinois, 30, 43, 47, 50, 61, 74, 109, 112, 122, 133
Chicago, Judy, 3, 72, 80–87, 98, 170. See also *Dinner Party, The*
Chicago Eight, 60–61
Chicanos. *See* Latinx
Chief Joseph, 149
China, 64, 67
Christianity, 14, 19–21, 43–44, 49, 60, 83, 158
Cincinnati, Ohio, 118
citizenship, 5–6, 11, 15, 17, 26–27, 35, 37, 39–40, 50, 168, 171. *See also* education: civics; voter registration

Index

citizenship schools, 8, 11–12, 14–28, 32, 37, 40, 169; curriculum, 17–18, 21, 24–28, 37
civics. *See* citizenship; education: civics; voter registration
Civil Rights movement, 2, 8, 11–37, 169, 171; academic history and, 13, 31–32; comparison to Black Power movement, 2–3, 12, 27, 31, 34–37, 39–40, 59; comparison to Gay Liberation movement, 2–3, 12, 104, 116, 127; comparison to Red Power movement, 2–3, 150; comparison to Women's Liberation movement, 2–3, 12, 71–72, 95–97, 99; conferences, 20, 22, 29; critique of mainstream institutions, 2, 12, 23, 27–28, 31; educational initiatives (*see* curriculum: Civil Rights movement); legacy, 158–59, 164–65, 167–68; organizations, 13, 16, 22–23, 26, 29 (*see also* Highlander Folk School; Southern Christian Leadership Conference; Student Nonviolent Coordinating Committee); periodicals, 23; writings, 23, 30–31. *See also* citizenship schools; freedom schools
Civil War, 62, 150
Clark, Septima, 2, 15–18, 21, 23–24, 27, 29, 36–37
class (economic), 22, 31, 48, 55, 59–61, 64, 66, 69, 72, 79, 83, 92–93, 96, 98, 106, 116. *See also* economics; poverty
Cobb, Charlie, 29
Cochiti, 139
Cohen, Jocelyn, 1, 3, 86–91, 97–98, 107
Cold War, 14, 47, 138, 166
collections. *See* archives and libraries
colleges and universities: black studies programs, 54, 58, 61–62, 145; general discussion, 2–3, 12–13, 31, 55, 124–25; specific institutions, 56, 73, 76, 106, 141–42 (*see also* California State University at Fresno; Duke University; Navajo Community College; Radcliffe College; Sarah Lawrence College; Smith College); women's studies programs, 73, 92, 145. *See also* HBCUs; Malcolm X Liberation University; tribal colleges
colonialism. *See* imperialism
Common Sense (Paine), 34
communism, 15, 35, 47, 49, 59–61, 69, 74, 76, 138, 169. *See also* economics
conferences, 3, 73, 164. *See also under* individual movements

Congress, U.S., 6, 31, 33, 94, 131, 153, 161–63
consciousness raising, 72, 74–75, 90, 105, 107–8, 172
Constitution, U.S., 18, 30–31, 163
Crow Dog, Leonard, 154
Crew, Spencer, 159–60
Cuba, 64, 67
cultural autonomy. *See* autonomy, cultural
culture wars, 9, 37, 157–58, 160–61, 165–67
curriculum, 2–3, 9, 158; Black Panther Party liberation schools, 63–67; Black Power, 3, 9, 39–41, 46–49, 53, 56–59, 61–62, 64–67, 168, 173; citizenship schools, 17–18, 21, 24–28, 37; Civil Rights, 2, 8, 12, 17–18, 21, 24–34, 168; freedom schools, 29–34, 37; mainstream, criticism of, 48, 50, 61, 150; Malcolm X Liberation University, 53–59, 64, 169; Red Power, 141–43; standards, 67, 158, 166; University of Islam, 45–49; Women's Liberation, 9, 92–95. *See also* education
Custer, George, 150

dance traditions, 3, 20, 129, 135–36, 138–40, 147, 155, 170
Danzig, Alexis, 119
Daughters of Bilitis, 102, 108, 120
Davidson, Basil, 62
Davis, Madeline, 111, 117
D'Emilio, John, 3, 104, 111–12, 115, 123–124
Democratic National Convention (1968), 60–61
desegregation, school, 15, 17
Detroit, Michigan, 43, 46
Didrikson Zaharias, Mildred "Babe," 84
Diné College. *See* Navajo Community College
Dinner Party, The, 72, 80–86, 90, 96–98, 170–72. *See also* Chicago, Judy
Douglass, Frederick, 31, 65
Duberman, Martin, 2, 32–34, 62, 123–24
Du Bois, W. E. B., 12–13, 35, 42, 51, 62
Duke University, 41, 53–56

Echols, Alice, 75
economics, 11–12, 16, 23–24, 27, 29, 31, 36, 45, 47, 55–57, 59, 60, 67–69, 129, 135, 149, 156, 169. *See also* class; communism; poverty
Edel, Deb, 3, 105–6, 113, 115, 119
Edelman, Marian Wright, 27

education: adult, 3, 14–28, 39, 61–62, 65, 68, 172–73 (*see also* citizenship schools); Afrocentrism in, 3, 46, 53, 55, 57–58; civics, 18, 25, 27 (*see also* citizenship; voter registration); criticism of mainstream, 23, 27–28, 31, 41, 45, 48, 50, 52, 55–56, 64, 142–43, 150; institutions, general, 2–3, 16, 150, 168; institutions, postsecondary (*see* colleges and universities; HBCUs; Malcom X Liberation University; tribal colleges); institutions, precollegiate, 3, 28, 46, 141, 94, 143 (*see also* Black Panther Party: liberation schools; freedom schools; Indian boarding schools; University of Islam); programs, 11, 151, 156 (*see also* citizenship schools; freedom schools; Malcolm X Liberation University; Summer Institute for Women's History); youth, 16, 39, 62, 94, 141–42, 172–73 (*see also* Black Panther Party: liberation schools; freedom schools; University of Islam). *See also* curriculum
Edwards, Faye, 56
Ellis Island, occupation of, 150, 155
emancipation, 13, 21, 62
Enola Gay, 166
Epstein, Rob, 121
Ethiopia, 43, 67
Eurocentrism, 6, 22, 45, 50, 82–83, 143
Europe, 31, 34–35, 43, 52–53, 60, 67, 76–77, 79, 83, 120, 138

Fard, Wallace, 43–44, 46
federal government, 66, 94, 160–67; relationship to African Americans, 14–15, 24, 26, 31; relationship to LGBT folk, 6, 114; relationship to Native American tribes, 3, 6, 9, 131–35, 137, 140–41, 145–46, 148–56, 161–62, 170
Feminine Mystique, The (Friedan), 74
feminism. *See* lesbian-feminism; Women's Liberation movement
fiction. *See* literature
film, 3, 17, 61, 76, 78, 103, 111, 119, 121
Flagstaff powwow. *See* powwows
Fort Lawton, occupation of, 150, 155
Franklin, John Hope, 48, 62
freedom schools, 11–12, 28–35, 37, 40, 50, 172; curriculum, 29–34, 37
Freedom Summer, 8, 20, 26, 29, 32, 34
Friedan, Betty, 74, 93
Friedman, Jeffrey, 121

Frisch, Michael, 165
Fuller, Howard, 3, 54–59, 64

Gage, Matilda Joslyn, 75
Gammon Theological Seminary, 22
Garber, Eric, 121–22
Garnet, Henry, 61
Garrett, Jim, 56
Garrison, William Lloyd, 31
Garvey, Marcus, 41–42
Gay Academic Union (GAU), 105, 109, 115, 123–25, 173
Gay American History, 112–13, 122, 126
Gay Liberation movement, 2–3, 9, 101–27, 169–72; academic history and, 3, 73, 101, 103–5, 109, 113–14, 122–27; comparison to Black Power movement, 2–3, 101, 104, 116, 127; comparison to Civil Rights movement, 2–3, 12, 104, 116, 127; comparison to Red Power movement, 3, 101, 156; comparison to Women's Liberation movement, 3, 99, 101, 104, 116, 127; conferences, 103, 118, 122–26; critique of mainstream institutions, 2, 114–15; integration with mainstream institutions, 101, 103–4, 109, 114–16, 127; legacy, 158–59, 164–65, 168; organizations, 104–5, 109–10, 112–13, 115, 117, 122 (*see also* Gay Academic Union; Lesbian/Gay Researchers Network); periodicals, 103, 105, 112–13, 115, 119–20, 125; writings, 113. *See also* archives and libraries: LGBT collections; Lesbian Herstory Archives; slide shows; sources, historical
gender, 46, 69, 71, 75–76, 78, 85, 90, 108, 124, 144, 155, 158, 160, 163, 172
Gentileschi, Artemisia, 83
Georgia, 22, 106
Gerber, Henry, 112
Germany, 34–35, 60, 120, 138
Gilman, Charlotte Perkins, 78
goddesses, 83, 85, 120, 122
Great Migration, 62, 159–60
Greenwood, Tom, 133
Grimke, Angelina, 78
Grimke, Sarah, 78
Guest, Lucia, 34
Guide to Negro History, 30–31

Haiti, 30
Hamilton, Charles, 64
Hampton, Mabel, 171

Hannibal of Carthage, 43
Harlem. *See* New York City
Harper's Ferry, 159
Hatshepsut, 83
HBCUs (Historically Black Colleges and Universities). *See* Historically Black Colleges and Universities
Helaine Victoria Press, 1, 72, 86–91, 96–99, 107, 170
Heterodoxy Club, 121
Highlander Folk School, 8, 14–23, 30, 32, 35, 40, 169
Highlander Research and Education Center. *See* Highlander Folk School
Hilliard, David, 63
Hinduism, 83
Historically Black Colleges and Universities (HBCUs), 12, 41, 54–55
history: academic history, 3–7, 163–66 (*see also names of individuals and under individual movements*); African, 30–31, 34, 40–41, 43, 45, 50–52, 56, 59–60, 62, 69, 120, 169; African American, 11–37, 39–69, 83, 89, 92–93, 157–63, 171; Asian American, 67, 93, 161; Latinx, 67, 89, 93, 161; LGBT, 93, 101–27, 160, 164, 171; Native American, 60, 67, 83, 93, 129–56, 159, 161–62; public (established field of professional practice), 2, 4–5, 8–9, 97, 157–67; transnational 6, 39–41, 43, 52, 54, 57, 64, 72, 76, 80, 83, 118, 120; women's, 1, 46–47, 66, 71–99, 110–11, 113, 125–26, 160–64, 171
Holmes, Henry, 112
Hopi, 139
Horton, Myles, 2, 14, 16–19, 23, 29
Horton, Zilphia, 17–19
Howell, Donna, 63
Huggins, Ericka, 3, 63–65
Huggins, John, 64
Hughes, Langston, 65
Hutchinson, Anne, 83
Hyacinthe, Jo, 108
Hypatia, 83

Idaho, 149
Illinois, 47. *See also* Chicago, Illinois
illiteracy. *See* literacy
imperialism, 6–7, 54, 56, 60, 67–68, 132
incarceration, 45, 50–51, 61–62, 117, 150, 153, 173
Indiana, 87, 89

Indian boarding schools, 3, 131–32, 143, 145–46, 156
integration: with mainstream institutions, 147, 157–61, 165, 168 (*see also under individual movements*); racial, 14–15, 26, 68, 112–13
International Women's Day, 76, 94
intersectionality, 72, 82, 92–93, 95, 98, 171
In White America (Duberman), 32, 34
Irwin, Inez Haynes, 73
Islam, 8, 42–46, 48–49, 53. *See also* Nation of Islam
Isolde, Ann, 81

Japan, 166
Jay, Karla, 123
Jenkins, Esau, 2, 15–17, 20–21, 36
Jim Crow, 15, 33, 37, 173
Johns Island, South Carolina, 16–18, 20. *See also* Sea Islands, South Carolina
Johnson, Zilphia Mae. *See* Horton, Zilphia
Jones, Barbara, 30
Jonestown, 55
Judaism, 34–35, 43–44, 60
Julius Caesar, 67

Kansas, 61
Katz, Jonathan Ned, 3, 102, 111–13, 115, 122–24, 126–27
Kennedy, Liz, 117
Kessler-Harris, Alice, 92–93
Kidwell, Clara Sue, 93
King, Martin Luther, Jr., 24, 36, 40
Kuda, Marie, 122
Ku Klux Klan, 33, 159

labor movement, 12, 14, 19, 66, 87, 89
Lakota, 135, 152
language. *See* terminology
languages, Native American, 132, 141, 145–46, 148
Latin America, 30, 64, 67, 77, 83, 120, 139
Latinx, 1, 63, 67, 78, 154, 158
Laura X, 3, 76–79, 95–96
leadership models, 11–13, 15, 18, 26–28, 35–36, 54, 56, 69, 91, 124, 131, 133, 144, 146, 151, 154
leadership training, 14–17, 27, 30, 42, 142, 173. *See also* citizenship schools
Lerner, Gerda, 3, 92–93
lesbian-feminism, 96, 105–9. *See also* separatism: lesbian

Lesbian/Gay Researchers Network, 109, 113, 125
Lesbian Herstory Archives (LHA), 105–7, 113, 116–17, 119, 123–24, 171
Lesbian History Exploration, 107–11
lesbians, 79, 88, 93, 96, 102, 104–9, 119–21, 124–26. *See also* Gay Liberation movement; lesbian-feminism; Lesbian Herstory Archives; separatism: lesbian
LGBT folk. *See* archives and libraries: LGBT collections; federal government: relationship to LGBT folk; Gay Liberation movement; history: LGBT; lesbians; separatism: LGBT
LGBT movement. *See* Gay Liberation movement
liberation schools. *See under* Black Panther Party
libraries. *See* archives and libraries
literacy, 12, 15–18, 24–25, 30, 37, 62, 145, 173
literature, 3, 56, 62, 79, 88, 89, 118, 120, 122
Little, Malcolm. *See* Malcolm X
Locke, Patricia, 143
Lomax, Alan, 22
Loomis, Louise Ropes, 73
Louisiana, 23
lynching, 33, 47
Lynd, Staughton, 2, 29–30, 32

MacGregor, Molly Murphy, 94–95
Machukay, Tony, 134
Mack, Benjamin, 27
magazines, movement. *See* periodicals, movement; *under individual movements*
Malcolm X, 2–3, 40, 48–53, 58–59, 66, 154
Malcolm X Liberation University (MXLU), 41–42, 53–60, 64, 68–69, 169, 173; curriculum, 53–59, 64, 169
Massachusetts, 50, 105, 113, 118
McDonald, Jim (Kwame), 56
McDowell, Mary, 89
McNickel, D'Arcy, 133
Meacham, Joan, 163
Means, Russell, 152
memory practices, explicit discussion of, 2–4, 6, 8, 11, 18, 20, 34, 37, 39–43, 53, 59, 67–69, 71–72, 75, 79, 85, 89, 95–99, 101–4, 110, 113, 126, 155–56, 157–58, 161, 171
Menelik, King, 43
methodology, 7–8, 72, 95, 103, 109–12, 117, 122, 160, 165
Mexican Americans. *See* Latinx
Michelson, Avra, 117

Michigan, 43, 46
Milk, Harvey, 118
Mining the Museum, 157–59, 166
Minnesota, 132, 149
Mississippi, 22, 28–31, 33–34
Mitchell, George, 149
Mitchell, Mike, 147
Monahan, Jim, 115–16
Montana, 141
Monter, William, 84
Mott, Lucretia, 162
Mount Rushmore, 152
Muhammad, Clara, 49
Muhammad, Elijah, 3, 40–41, 43–47, 49–52, 59
Muhammad, Wallace D., 49
Muhammad Speaks, 47–48, 50–51
multiculturalism, 64, 92–93, 97, 136, 158–62, 164–65
museums, 9, 95–97, 104, 147–48, 150–51, 157–67. *See also* history: public
music, 12, 18–24, 27, 30, 37, 79, 93, 120, 173

NAGPRA (Native American Graves Protection and Repatriation Act). *See* Native American Graves Protection and Repatriation Act
Nakai, Raymond, 145
National Endowment for the Arts (NEA), 167
National Endowment for the Humanities (NEH), 160, 166–67
National Indian Youth Council (NIYC), 130, 133–34, 142
National Women's History Week, 91, 94–96
National Women's History Month, 91, 94
Nation of Islam (NOI), 8, 37, 40–53, 59–60, 62, 68–69, 85, 169, 173; renaming, 50. See also *Muhammad Speaks*; University of Islam
Native American Graves Protection and Repatriation Act (NAGPRA), 162, 165. *See also* repatriation of human remains and artifacts
Native Americans. *See* federal government: relationship to Native American tribes; Indian boarding schools; languages, Native American; Pan-Indianism; powwows; Red Power movement; relocation, Native American; spirituality, Native American; stereotypes: of Native Americans; tribal colleges

Index

Native American spirituality. *See* spirituality, Native American
Navajo, 129, 141, 143–49
Navajo Community College (NCC), 141, 143–49
Nebraska, 141
Negro History Week, 13, 35, 52. *See also* Black History Month
Nestle, Joan, 3, 105–6, 116, 118–19, 123
New Jersey, 40
newspapers, movement. *See* periodicals, movement; *under individual movements*
Newton, Huey, 3, 65
New York (state), 77–78, 91, 117. *See also* New York City
New York City, 13, 29, 63, 74–75, 89, 105–6, 118, 150, 155
New York Public Library, 13, 29, 160
Nez Perce, 149
nonviolence, 26, 28–30, 34, 36, 68. *See also* Student Nonviolent Coordinating Committee
North Carolina, 41, 53–59, 118
North Dakota, 141

Oakland, California, 59, 63–65, 151
Oakland Community School. *See* Black Panther Party: liberation schools
Oglala, 141, 153–54
Ohio, 118
O'Keefe, Georgia, 73, 83
Olduvai Gorge, 65
Oline, Pamela, 105–6
oral history, 79, 114, 116–18, 148, 151, 160, 165. *See also* history: public
oral tradition, 111–12, 125
orange juice boycott, 113
Oregon, 149
organizations: African American, 97; funding, 22, 57, 63, 92, 94, 148; Native American, 130; professional, 13, 58, 73, 109, 125, 164. *See also under individual movements*
original man, 44, 49
Oxenberg, Jan, 108

Paha Sapa, 152
Paine, Thomas, 34
Pan-Africanism, 39–41, 50, 53–54, 57–59, 64, 69, 168
Pan-Indianism, 3, 129–36, 140–42, 145, 149–52, 154, 156, 168, 172
pan-tribalism. *See* Pan-Indianism

Parks, Rosa 16, 65
Paul, Alice, 73
Pawley, T. D., 56
Pease, Otis, 32
periodicals, movement, 173. *See also under individual movements*
Pine Ridge reservation, 153–55
place, reclamation of, 3, 131, 149–55, 162, 168, 170, 173
Plath, Sylvia, 78
plays. *See* theater
poetry, 93, 102, 113, 120
policy, public, 9, 130–33, 135, 141, 146, 148, 152–57, 152
Poole, Elijah. *See* Muhammad, Elijah
Poor, Harold, 125
Poore, Nancy, 1, 86–91, 97–98, 107
postcards, 1, 3, 72, 86–91, 96–98, 171–73
Potter, Claire, 113
poverty, 13–14, 36, 45, 56–57, 59, 57, 129, 145–46, 148–49, 152, 156, 169. *See also* class; economics
powwows, 9, 129–30, 134–40, 156, 162, 170, 172. *See also* dance traditions
prison. *See* incarceration
psychiatry, 102, 105, 113, 117
public history. *See* history: public
public policy. *See* policy, public

race, 12, 32, 40, 43–44, 47–50, 54, 56, 68, 134–40, 145, 157–59, 163–64, 169, 171; pride, 22, 27, 28, 40–41, 43–45, 53, 58–59, 68–69; uplift, 11–12, 15–16, 21, 24, 26, 33, 35–37, 39–40, 42, 48, 51–52, 55, 58, 68–69, 158; women's liberation and, 72, 76, 82–83, 92–93, 96–98, 116, 171
racism, 13, 29–30, 41–42, 44–45, 56, 60, 68, 96, 159–60, 169
Radcliffe College, 73, 95, 114
Rahman, Majeedah, 63
Reconstruction, 8, 12, 24, 26–27, 30–31, 33, 37, 62, 66–67
Red Power movement, 2–3, 9, 129–56, 170, 172; comparison to Black Power movement, 2–3, 130, 134, 145, 154–55; comparison to the Civil Rights movement, 2–3, 130; comparison to Gay Liberation movement, 3, 101, 156; comparison to Women's Liberation movement, 3, 145, 156; conferences, 133; critique of mainstream institutions, 2, 150; curriculum, 141–48; integration with mainstream institutions, 147;

Red Power movement *(cont.)*
  legacy, 158–59, 161–62, 164–65, 168;
  organizations, 130, 132–33, 151 *(see also* National Indian Youth Council);
  origins, 130, 132–33; writings, 133, 149–50, 153. *See also* American Indian Movement; place, reclamation of; powwows; tribal colleges
religion, 21, 24, 49, 56, 60, 78, 83, 85, 95, 120, 153. *See also* Buddhism; Christianity; goddesses; Hinduism; Islam; Judaism; spirituality, Native American
relocation, Native American, 131–33, 137, 145–46, 151, 172
repatriation of human remains and artifacts, 147–48, 162, 165
Revolutionary War, 25, 30, 34, 66–67, 83
rhetoric as memory practice, 9, 39, 56, 59–61, 67–68, 75, 101
riots. *See* urban unrest
Roberts, J. R., 113
Robinson, Bernice, 15, 17–18, 24, 36
Rockefeller, John D., 66–67
Roosevelt, Eleanor, 73
Rupp, Leila, 114
Russo, Vito, 121

Sacagawea, 83
San Francisco, California, 63, 109, 112, 117, 120, 122, 150–51, 155
Sappho, 102
Sarachild, Kathie, 74–76
Sarah Lawrence College, 91–92
Schapiro, Miriam, 87
Schomburg, Arthur, 13–14
school desegregation. *See* desegregation, school
schools. *See* Black Panther Party: liberation schools; citizenship schools; colleges and universities; education; freedom schools; HBCUs; tribal colleges
Schwarz, Judith, 111, 122
Schwimmer, Rosika, 73
Sea Islands, South Carolina, 16–18, 20–22
Seale, Bobby, 60–61, 64
Seattle, Washington, 150, 155
Sellers, Cleveland, 56
Seneca Falls Convention for Women's Rights (1848), 77
separatism, 4, 158, 162; black, 39–44, 50, 53–54, 56–58, 68–69, 172–73; lesbian, 101, 103–4, 106–9, 121 *(see also* lesbian-feminism); LGBT, 103–4, 114–16; Native American, 142–44, 147, 151, 158, 162; women's, 72, 75, 77, 81, 85, 96, 104
Shabazz, Betty, 57
Shoshone, 83
Sioux, 93, 135, 141, 152–55
slavery, 12, 30, 34, 51, 154; agency under, 31, 33, 61; connections to the present, 12, 20–21, 24–26, 34, 37, 64; interpretation of, 8, 24–27, 31, 33–34, 39, 42, 45, 52, 59, 60, 62, 66–67, 69, 159; legacy of, 42, 69; names given under, 50; Nazi Germany, comparison to, 34–35, 60; origins, 52, 60; resistance and revolts, 7–8, 12, 29, 30–31, 61, 159, 169; shift away from, in historical interpretation, 14, 39–45, 49–50, 52, 69
slave trade, 13, 30–31, 34, 51–52, 56, 60, 62
slide shows, 3, 9, 103, 105, 107, 111–12, 114, 118–22, 151, 172–73
Smith, Barbara, 96–97
Smith, Beverly, 96–97
Smith College, 73, 95
Smithsonian Institution, 92, 159–62, 164, 166, 167
socialism, 15, 42, 124, 170–71
sources, historical, 3, 7–8, 30, 72–73, 77, 82, 87, 101, 106, 109–18, 148, 152, 172–73
South Carolina, 16, 18, 20, 22, 27, 33. *See also* Johns Island, South Carolina; Sea Islands, South Carolina
South Dakota, 141, 150, 152–55
Southern Christian Leadership Conference (SCLC), 2, 8, 23–28, 40, 169, 173
Soviet Union, 47, 76, 138
spirituality, Native American, 3, 120, 129–30, 132–33, 135, 138, 141–44, 150, 152–55
Sprague, Gregory, 3, 109, 111–12, 121–22, 125
Stampp, Kenneth, 62
Stanley, Julie, 105–6
Stanton, Elizabeth Cady, 75, 162
Staser, Karen, 163
St. Bridget, 83
Steakley, James, 121
stereotypes, 172; of African Americans, 62, 172; of Native Americans, 135, 137–40, 156–172
Stevens, Thaddeus, 31
Stonewall Uprising, 101, 103, 119, 160
Student Nonviolent Coordinating Committee (SNCC), 8, 20, 28–30, 35, 37, 40, 56, 69
suffrage, women's, 5, 75, 78, 89, 92, 113, 163
Summer Institute on Women's History, 72, 91–97, 170, 173

Sumner, Charles, 31
Swerdlow, Amy, 92–93

talented tenth, 12–13, 35
Tennessee, 14–15, 23
terminology, 40, 79, 107, 114
theater, 3, 32–34, 66, 120, 172
Thoreau, Henry David, 31, 34
Trail of Tears, 150
Travis, Brenda, 28
treaties, 150, 152–53, 156
tribal colleges, 3, 9, 131, 140–49, 156, 170, 172–73
Trotula of Salerno, 83
Truth, Sojourner, 25, 83, 163
Tubman, Harriet, 25, 31, 67
Turner, Nat, 31

unions, trade, 14, 19, 66–67
universal womanhood, 72, 74, 76, 83, 97
universities. *See* colleges and universities
University of Islam, 43, 46–49. *See also* Nation of Islam
urban unrest, 36, 59
U.S.S.R. *See* Soviet Union

Vesey, Denmark, 31
vice districts, 79, 112–13
Vietnam War, 60
voter registration, 11, 15–16, 18, 24–29, 31, 173. *See also* citizenship; education: civics

Walker, David, 61
Warrior, Clyde, 133
Washington (state), 150, 155
Washington, Booker T., 34, 42–43, 62
Washington, DC, 150, 152, 155
Washington, George, 66
Wellesley College, 73
Wells, H. G., 51
West, Don, 14
westward expansion, 159, 166
Whitman, Walt, 118
Whitney, Eli, 33, 77
Wickliff, James, 112
Wilde, Oscar, 118
Wild West shows, 135
Williams, Frank, 56
Williams, Walter, 125
Willie X, 48
Wilson, Fred, 157–60
Wollstonecraft, Mary, 78, 83

women. *See* archives and libraries: women's history collections; gender; history: women's; lesbians; separatism: women's; Women's Liberation movement
Women's Herstory Library. *See* Women's History Research Center
Women's History Month, 91, 94
Women's History Research Center (WHRC), 72, 77–80, 90, 96
Women's History Week, 91, 94–95
Women's Liberation movement, 2–3, 9, 71–99, 107–9, 160, 169–71; academic history and, 3, 72–73, 76, 82, 88, 91–99, 163–64 (*see also* Summer Institute on Women's History); comparison to Black Power movement, 2–3, 71–72, 76, 85, 95–97, 99; comparison to Civil Rights movement, 2–3, 12, 71–72, 95–97, 99; comparison to Gay Liberation movement, 3, 99, 101, 104, 116, 127; comparison to Red Power movement, 3, 145, 156; conferences, 74, 94, 98, 107, 114, 125–26 (*see also* Summer Institute on Women's History); critique of mainstream institutions, 2, 81; integration with mainstream institutions, 71, 80, 91; legacy, 158–60, 164–65, 167–68; organizations, 74–75, 92, 94, 96–99 (*see also* Lesbian Herstory Archives [LHA]; World Center for Women Archives); periodicals, 78, 82, 96, 102, 119; race and, 72, 76, 82–83, 92–93, 96–98, 116, 171; writings, 74, 76. See also *Dinner Party, The*; Helaine Victoria Press; Women's History Research Center
women's studies programs. *See under* colleges and universities
Woodson, Carter, 13–14, 42, 51
Woodward, C. Vann, 62
Woolf, Virginia, 83
World Center for Women's Archives, 73, 95, 153
World War II, 121, 138, 166
Wounded Knee, 135, 150, 153–55

X, Laura. *See* Laura X
X, Malcolm. *See* Malcolm X
X, Willie. *See* Willie X

Yacub, 44–45, 49, 85
Yellow Thunder, Raymond, 153
Young, Bea, 30

Zodeidah, 46

www.ingramcontent.com/pod-product-compliance
Lightning Source LLC
Chambersburg PA
CBHW020654230426
43665CB00008B/434